Writings of a Re

# Writings of a Rebel Colonel

*The Civil War Diary and Letters
of Samuel Walkup,
48th North Carolina Infantry*

SAMUEL WALKUP

*Edited by* Kemp Burpeau

McFarland & Company, Inc., Publishers
*Jefferson, North Carolina*

LIBRARY OF CONGRESS CATALOGUING-IN-PUBLICATION DATA

Names: Walkup, S. H. (Samuel Hoey), 1818–1876. | Burpeau,
Kemp Pendleton, editor.
Title: Writings of a rebel colonel : the Civil war diary and letters of Samuel Walkup,
48th North Carolina Infantry / Samuel Walkup ; edited by Kemp Burpeau.
Other titles: Civil war diary and letters of Samuel Walkup,
48th North Carolina Infantry
Description: Jefferson, North Carolina : McFarland & Company, Inc., Publishers,
2021 | Includes bibliographical references and index.
Identifiers: LCCN 2021047414 | ISBN 9781476686691 (paperback : acid free paper) ∞
ISBN 9781476644486 (ebook)
Subjects: LCSH: Walkup, S. H. (Samuel Hoey), 1818–1876—Diaries. |
Confederate States of America. Army. North Carolina Infantry Regiment, 48th. |
Confederate States of America. Army—Officers—Biography. | United States—
History—Civil War, 1861–1865—Personal narratives, Confederate. |
North Carolina—History—Civil War, 1861–1865—Personal narratives. |
United States—History—Civil War, 1861–1865—Campaigns. | Soldiers—
North Carolina—Correspondence. | Union County (N.C.)—Biography. |
BISAC: HISTORY / Military / United States | HISTORY / United States /
Civil War Period (1850–1877)
Classification: LCC E573.5 48th.W35 2021 | DDC 973.7/456092 [B]—dc23/
eng/20211001
LC record available at https://lccn.loc.gov/2021047414

BRITISH LIBRARY CATALOGUING DATA ARE AVAILABLE

ISBN (print) 978-1-4766-8669-1
ISBN (ebook) 978-1-4766-4448-6

Front cover image: detail from a print of Samuel Walkup and
officers of the 48th North Carolina (William Clark,
*History of the Several Regiments and Battalions*, 1901)

Printed in the United States of America

*McFarland & Company, Inc., Publishers*
*Box 611, Jefferson, North Carolina 28640*
*www.mcfarlandpub.com*

For my mother and father, sister and brother,
with love and respect

# Contents

# Preface

The study of the Civil War and Southern history has profoundly changed with horrific modern events. In 2014 a white supremacist murdered nine parishioners at the Mother Emanuel African Methodist Episcopal Church in Charleston. South Carolina. In 2017 a neo-fascist rammed his car into counter-protesters at a Confederate monument demonstration in Charlottesville, Virginia, killing one and injuring others. The 2020 killing of African American George Floyd by white police in Minnesota highlighted the ongoing legacy of systemic racism and disparate treatment. Such unspeakably reprehensible acts raise questions about how contemporary historians should view the nineteenth-century Confederacy and those civilians and military who supported it. The racism and slavery undergirding the Confederacy came to the forefront. African American trauma has transcended generations without healing. Monuments, public buildings and streets dedicated to slave owners, insurrectionists, and Klansmen have been reconsidered in response to invigorated demands to rename or re-interpret prior public recognition and endorsement of such dark elements. Confederate nostalgic history and the fallacious Lost Cause narrative must be rejected as inconsistent with the need to fully and accurately consider the African American experience. Some have questioned why further reflective studies of Confederate leaders are even needed.

The Samuel Hoey Walkup writings are an insightful, sometimes conflicted narrative of a lawyer, planter and politician in the Army of Northern Virginia.[1] Even more compelling are the untold hidden stories of his enslaved household: Tom Clutts, Hall Walkup and wife Mary, Margaret Walkup and her children Eliza, Harriett, Fanny, Sarah, Wilson and Jenny, Matilda "Tilly" Walkup, Jinny Walkup, Betty Walkup, Charlie Walkup, and Stephen Walkup and wife Luvina. Their struggles to maintain dignity, endure and resist amidst the profound degradation of involuntary servitude and white supremacy are both commendable and instructive.

1

# Preface

Samuel Walkup was a devout Christian and dedicated family man, solicitous of the well-being of his wife, children and enslaved laborers. He was a Master of Arts literary enthusiast with a fondness for the lyrical, paradoxically especially enjoying Abolitionist poetry. He embraced travel as both a recreation and educational endeavor, preferring travel to the Northern states over Southern locales. As a committed Whig nationalist, he opposed secession until hostilities were well underway. He then became a die-hard Confederate from the Seven Days battles through Appomattox, epitomizing Ulysses Grant's characterization of soldiers who fought valiantly and suffered for "one of the worst (causes) for which a people ever fought, and one for which there was the least excuse."[2]

A compelling central question is why did Walkup embrace such a morally reprehensible institution as slavery? He did treat the enslaved, both domestic and field workers, with a relatively benign management. He provided adequate housing and subsistence. He did not employ corporal punishment and never used racial expletives. Yet he bought, leased and sold other persons, expropriating their labor and subjecting them to a dehumanizing condition.

Walkup must not be viewed in a vacuum. A composite biography is necessary, addressing owners and those owned, interspersed and comingled in a complex relationship of mutual cooperation, resistance, congeniality and oppression. A voice must be afforded these enslaved individuals. Not generally having the benefit of literacy, they are revealed only through Walkup's self-serving accounts and limited public records.[3] Nevertheless, their efforts to affirm human dignity are manifest through strategies varying from cooperation to obstruction. Minnie Parmela Reece Price must also be considered both as Walkup's wife and as a spirited, artistically gifted, college-educated young woman facing her own social and legal constraints, subordination and discrimination. This is a cautionary account of misguided benevolence and good intentions supporting profound oppression. The interaction with Samuel and Minnie and the enslaved household and their family—Tom, Hall, Mary, Margaret, Eliza, Harriett, Fanny, Sarah, Wilson, Jenny, Tilly, Jinny, Betty, Charlie, Stephen and Luvina—is essential to better understand each individual.

# Biography

Samuel Hoey Walkup's military, religious, ethnic and agrarian ancestry had a profound influence on his sense of place, civic duty, Providential faith, and acceptance of Southern society, including slavery. He was a descendent of Scotch-Irish Presbyterians who left the north of Ireland by the mid–1700s to settle at Waxhaw Creek along the frontier borders of the provincial Carolinas. During the Revolution his father Robert served with other Walkups in a light horse company of North Carolina militia under Col. William R. Davie. The Battle of Walkup's Mill was fought directly on family land where British regulars under Col. Banastre Tarleton, supported by Loyalist militia, burned the home place. Devotion to God, country and family shaped the Walkups.

The family's American progenitor was Samuel "The Immigrant" Walkup (also Wauchope or Wahab), born 1698 in Scotland. Along with other lowland Scots he participated in the plantation resettlement of north Ireland and there married Nancy Ayne Alexander of Carrick-Fergus. Their son, James Alexander Walkup, was born November 15, 1724 near Belfast. With devastating droughts in Ulster and governmental encouragement to relocate to America, the family first was in the Valley of Virginia, but left to acquire cheaper land in North Carolina. James constructed the family residence and grist mill on several hundred acres along Waxhaw Creek. Their farming was initially subsistence, raising corn, wheat, oats, poultry and hogs. Hard work and enslaved labor brought Samuel's grandfather and father increasing prosperity. Robert particularly benefited by enslaved cotton production on the Waxhaw's rich river bottom soil. He was a "pious, devout, exemplary, consistent and benevolent Christian" but in common with "all the Walkups" "...too fond of ardent spirits ... this destroyer of the happiness of man."[1] Samuel Hoey Walkup was born January 22, 1818, on that family plantation.[2]

The Walkups were dedicated Presbyterians. They accepted the Calvinist theology of a paternal God acting through time and space to bring about the divine purpose. Providence determined both individual salvation and national destiny. Humanity was sinful and transgressing, to be rewarded or punished by the perfect divine judge.[3] Generations of Walkups, not conforming to the Anglican Church, sought their salvation and sanctification through services, teachings and ecclesiastical discipline at the modest, plain clapboard Old Waxhaw Presbyterian Church in Lancaster, South Carolina, and the similar Trizah Sessions House in North Carolina. Samuel maintained a life-long conviction that God had a unique plan for him, having been divinely elected.[4] Although personally a devout lifelong Presbyterian, he was "very liberal and broad in his religious views," being more ecumenical than his ancestors.[5]

Traditions of military service, community obligation and personal and communal rights were legacies of the Walkup Scotch-Irish pioneer and Revolutionary legacies. Grandfather James embraced the British-American Whig conceptions of personal liberty and opposition to perceived royal oppression, and served as a Patriot captain along with his son Robert, a private.[6] Samuel profoundly admired his Patriot ancestors, particularly their support of the Mecklenburg Declaration of Independence, and undertook research on the life of Andrew Jackson, another child of the Waxhaws. Despite Jackson's Democratic political affiliation, Walkup found Old Hickory a most commendable role model of the stalwart warrior, dedicated family man, committed Christian and civic statesman.[7]

As a youth Samuel lived on the principal family Waxhaw plantation with his older brothers. Father Robert and Samuel's uncle Joseph had inherited the more than 300 acres, dwelling house and outbuilding, with Robert to take the portion encompassing the buildings. Robert was also bequeathed the enslaved laborer Prince and, jointly with Uncle Joseph, the pregnant laborer Dinah, whose child, if born alive, to be held in trust for another Walkup kinsman.[8] By Samuel's time the plantations had been re-consolidated under Robert as a 1200 acre parcel, three miles in length and averaging from one-half to two miles in breadth. Cotton was farmed for commodity sale, with corn, wheat, oats, garden vegetables, pork and poultry raised for home consumption. The farming was performed by ten to twelve enslaved "feald hands" along with several "small" youths that Robert oversaw with Samuel's older brother William.[9] Production was subject to the weather and markets and Robert had to constantly strive to "make a nuf to do us."[10] While only five years old, Samuel experienced the trauma of a house fire that took the lives of his four brothers. Samuel himself was saved by an enslaved youth sleeping in the same room.[11] This heroic intervention perhaps helped foster a

William Walkup, Samuel's brother, owned the Greek Revival house, the most substantial in Union County, constructed in the late antebellum era or at least prior to 1869 on the 1,200 acre family cotton and grain farm. The land was owned by Walkups since colonial times and was the site of the Revolutionary Battle of Walkup Mill. Samuel Walkup's primary occupation was as a practicing lawyer, but he did hold people in slavery performing domestic tasks in the town of Monroe as well as working his brother's fields and those of other Union County planters through lease. Enslaved and freedmen built the William Walkup house, a testament to their artistry and craftsmanship (courtesy Patricia Poland, Monroe, North Carolina).

more sympathetic relationship with African Americans than was typical of most cotton planters.

Walkup studied grammar and college preparation at the highly regarded Ebenezer Academy, in Rock Hill, South Carolina.[12] He took courses in Greek, Latin, classical literature, history, geography, English composition and mathematics. He commenced college at the University of North Carolina in 1837. By mutual assent, brother William chose to manage farming operations, with the expectation of inheriting the family plantation, and Samuel elected to attend preparatory school and university at his father's expense.[13]

At Chapel Hill Walkup studied advanced mathematics, Greek, Latin, French, physical sciences, philosophy, logic, rhetoric and Bible, with legal topics undertaken in the senior year. Textbooks were the primary means of instruction, supplemented by occasional oral or written lectures. He performed recitations and submitted compositions for grading.[14] One Walkup essay was captioned, "Is it likely that poetry will ever flourish in America?" and another "Should literary distinction be awarded colleges as incentives to exertion?"[15] As a member of the Dialectic Society (the "Di"), he honed extempore speaking, debating and parliamentary skills essential for an aspiring antebellum lawyer and politician.[16] He also read widely beyond assigned texts, emphasizing English and ancient classics and poetry. Senior year he studied Constitutional, international and municipal law taught by President David L. Swain. Under that tutelage he critically and thoroughly examined substantive law using William Blackstone's *Commentaries on the Laws of England* and James Kent's *Commentaries on American Law*. He also participated in moot court practicums simulating trial and appellate advocacy.[17]

Given Walkup's appreciation of the educational opportunities afforded him, it is unlikely that he engaged in excessively raucous parties and demonstrations as those associated with the "Fresh Treat" and "Ugly Club."[18] No University records document any specific sanctions for Walkup and his graduating class was noted for generally good behavior and scholarship. Like most students, he did fail to earn commendations and he was not free from demerit during his college enrollment. He graduated in 1841 without distinction in the lower third of his class, but he had read broadly, networked and politicked extensively, enhanced his public speaking presence, and fostered a lifetime enthusiasm for law, music and literature.[19]

After graduation with a B.A. degree Walkup briefly taught grammar school in Charlotte.[20] He then took a hiatus, touring Florida with possible relocation or a new career in mind.[21] Unlike most of his contemporaries who solely read law under the supervision of a practicing attorney, he had chosen a formal university curriculum. To supplement that more abstract academic learning, he completed an apprenticeship under William Julius Alexander, a practitioner in the Mecklenburg, Union and Anson circuit and himself a Chapel Hill graduate.[22] With Alexander's guidance Walkup briefed cases, drafted documents and shadowed and observed his mentor in the courtroom. He had exposure to such practice aides as *Stephen on Pleading, Greenleaf on Evidence, Chitty on Contracts, William on Executors, Crises' Digest of Real property and North Carolina General Statutes* and *Session Laws.*[23] With this extensive theoretical and applied experience, Walkup had little difficulty passing the bar, then consisting only of a brief oral examination by the bench to ascertain general legal knowledge and moral rectitude. In 1843 he secured the typical initial license to practice in the lower county trial courts, with licensure to superior courts and state supreme court awarded a year later.[24] In 1844 he was awarded an honorary M.A. degree consistent the University of North Carolina practice of customarily awarding that recognition to graduates evidencing professional distinction.[25]

Completing law school and securing bar admission did not ensure that Walkup's practice would be prosperous, and he had to supplement his income through farming cotton, corn and hogs.[26] He had to spend considerably to open his law office and acquire necessary law books. In addition to his texts from Chapel Hill, he needed reports setting forth North Carolina appellate cases, legal digests summarizing case and statutory law, topical legal treatises, and form book drafting guides. Perhaps rather than purchase, he might when possible have borrowed books from other local attorneys like mentor William Alexander. Moreover, as a young attorney he had to make a name for himself, competing with veteran practitioners in the Union, Mecklenburg and Anson county circuit.[27]

Much of Walkup's practice was performed in his Monroe office, a detached one- or two-room wood structure at his residence situated near the Union County Courthouse.[28] He drafted deeds, pleadings, trial and appellate briefs, contracts, trusts and wills.[29] Like most rural attorneys, most of his civil work involved real estate with some commercial transactions and debt collection, serving planters, factors, merchants and banks.[30] He actively sought railroad corporate clients, promoting start-up ventures.[31] He expanded his criminal and municipal law workload after 1848 upon securing appointment as Solicitor of the Court of Common Pleas.[32] As Solicitor, he acted in behalf of the State as county prosecutor. The position also entailed examination and legal oversight of the Union County Register of Deeds and Clerk of Superior Court. Upon election to the General Assembly in 1859, he was able to use that public exposure to further retain and build his client base.[33]

Walkup participated in the county militia and benevolent organizations like the Masons as a public service, to grow his practice, enhance personal reputation and gain political stature. During the Mexican-American War, he attended musters and was elected 2nd Lieutenant, 69th Regiment, but did not see service outside the county. He rose rapidly in rank in that primarily fraternal organization, serving during much of the 1850s as a brigadier general of the Eleventh Regiment. Militia musters and court session days, with musical accompaniment by the Waxhaw Band, were opportunities for the aspiring lawyer politician to see and be seen by potential voters and clients. As with his militia affiliation, Walkup also availed himself of the individual and community service opportunities afforded by the local Masonic Lodge.[34]

Walkup's politics were shaped by family and community. For generations the Walkups were committed Whigs, from the party's genesis in the 1830s through its 1860 demise. His extended family were passionate supporters of Henry Clay, with Samuel's younger brother named for their political hero. Walkup found the North Carolina Whigs appealing, with emphasis on preservation and expansion of slavery, state aid for commercial diversification, industrial development and infrastructure, education, public health, and group care and correctional facilities. As a Southern agriculturalist, he was less interested in the national Whig platform of a strong national bank and protective tariffs for Northern industry, but was not openly hostile to that agenda, seeing advantages in using Federal funds for "smart" improvements. He found the Whig emphasis on rule of law, property rights and Constitutionalism a solid basis for economic opportunity. Walkup's political orientation and aptitude as a rising star in the party was recognized at least by 1844 with his designation as Secretary to the Whig State District Convention and his leadership in the Clay Club.[35]

Despite being a devoted Whig, Walkup was never an unquestioning party ideologue. Early in his professional career he supported the Mexican-American War despite national Whig party general opposition to involvement in that conflict. As an officer at a Mecklenburg County militia muster he concurred with the sentiment that although war was "one of the greatest evils and that should be the very last resort in the civilized age, yet the honor of the county, and the rights trampled upon, or her soil invaded, it is the duty of every patriot to stand forth...."[36]

After more than fifteen years fundraising and campaigning for State and Federal Whig candidates, in 1858 Walkup won his own election to the North Carolina Senate, representing Union County in a district safely within Whig control, defeating Democrat Joseph Medley. The party finally rewarded him for all political speaking at barbeques, town halls, court and market days, historic civic anniversaries, college graduations and church socials. Despite Whig endorsement, Walkup emphasized he was his own man, an independent not beholden to convention endorsement. He ran on a platform supporting

Commencing with the Mexican War until the Civil War, Walkup served in Union County as a militia officer. He is pictured uniformed as a general, circa 1850s, with a waist scarf made by wife Minnie, a skilled seamstress and adept homemaker. Walkup saw his militia participation as promoting public service and political aspirations, an opportunity for social engagement, military preparedness and a means of building his attorney client base (courtesy Virginia Adams, Galveston, Texas).

sale of surplus public land to enhance revenue and opposing undue public expenditure unless adequately funded by Federal revenue sharing "disbursements."[37] As a junior Senator he was not eligible for the most powerful committee appointments. Given his interest and experience, he was assigned the Education and Literacy Fund. He kept a low profile during the term, without major floor speeches. He addressed issues important to his local constituency such memorials, commemorations and acknowledgments, and technical concerns relating to magistrates, taxation, voter qualification and militia. He introduced a resolution to loan $12,000.00 to the Carolina Female Academy in Ansonville, North Carolina, an institution in his district where he on occasion delivered the annual graduation address.[38]

In 1859 Walkup ran for United States Congress against three-term incumbent Francis Burton Craige, a popular extreme States Rights Democrat. Walkup campaigned as "the man who never yet voted against the interests of the South—who goes for the Union, the whole Union and nothing but the Union." Craige was portrayed as a Democrat Secessionist "rotten and corrupt to the core," who had opposed President Andrew Jackson's efforts to put down disunion.[39] Walkup also contended Craige was a self-serving politician feathering his own nest by accepting a Congressional pay raise.[40] On his part, Craige supporters called Walkup "the opponent of the democratic party in every respect.... First a whig, then a know-nothing, he has left nothing untried...."[41] Making a special effort to turn out his base, the Walkup campaign called "gallant old-line Whigs" to "arise, awake ... and Walk-up" to the polls.[42] Although he fielded the most competitive challenge faced by Craige, the Democrat won with over a fourteen-point margin.[43]

Having directly addressed national issues in his unsuccessful Congressional bid, Walkup took an increasingly active role in conventions of the Constitutional Union Party. At the state convention in Raleigh, he was present with other prominent Whigs, serving both as a delegate and on the select committee for party business. He shared views expressed by keynote speakers reminiscing the role party idol Henry Clay played in the 1833 Nullification Crisis, the 1820 Missouri Compromise and the Compromise of 1850, and voicing the need to again demonstrate "enough salt in North Carolina to save the county" from "the maladministration of the Democratic party with all the difficulties and dangers which overhang our nation."[44] At the national convention in Baltimore Walkup was a delegate along with 1852 Whig vice presidential candidate Governor William Alexander Graham. Walkup supported candidates John Bell and Edward Everett on the national ticket. The party platform of Constitution, Union, rule of law, national security, public liberty and property rights was fully consistent with Walkup's Whig orientation.[45]

Running as an incumbent for his state Senate seat in 1860, Walkup emphasized his record stressing "honesty, equity and Justice." He promoted fairly assessed taxes prudently spent. He sought to render "equal justice to all classes, and let the burdens fall equally upon all in proportion to their ability to pay." He declared, "It is the happy privilege of every citizen to claim equal rights and the duty of each patriot to share equally the burdens of Government."[46] Upon reelection, Walkup was much more active addressing issues of statewide and national import.[47] In addition to routine matters, the controversial, contentious Senate term dealt with impending disunion and civil conflict. Along with other old Whig Unionists constituting an Opposition Party, he consistently and persistently argued for prudence and dialogue in the face of State's Rights Democrats advocating secession. He opposed a boycott of Northern products and unsuccessfully sought to erect a United States flag on State Capitol grounds. He criticized the unauthorized and illegal seizure of Federal Ft. Caswell, Brunswick County, North Carolina, by secessionist paramilitaries. He stridently opposed Governor John Ellis's message that promoted secession and military collaboration with other slave states, voting unsuccessfully not to publish or distribute that gubernatorial address. Walkup ardently maintained that disunion and affiliation with a confederacy would not best protect property rights, including slave chattel. At every opportunity he opposed calling a state convention for secession, indicating he would only support a limited discussion of the state's role in an ongoing Federal union. He passionately addressed the Convention Bill, setting forth legal and pragmatic arguments against secession. Citing John Marshall, Andrew Jackson and Daniel Webster, Walkup emphasized Federal supremacy. Neither the President, Congress or Court had done any "palpably unconstitutional" ... "dangerous infraction of our rights" and in fact had upheld slave property rights through the *Dred Scott* decision and the Fugitive Slave Law. He maintained the states could not legally unilaterally leave the union. Lincoln's election was not grounds for secession in any event, and the Federal government had the right to collect public revenue and defend its forts, arsenals and other public property against either vigilante mobs or state militia. Even though possessing these legal entitlements, he hoped the national government would refrain from exercising such powers and instead, in prudence and forbearance, engage in "magnanimous" dialogue with the Southern states. His fondest desire was to preserve Union "in its purity and entirety, and after that moment of excitement and passion shall have pass away the North and South could again hail each other as friends and as equals, and shall together in unity, as brothers enjoying securely all their political rights."[48] Walkup would consistently oppose disunion until actual hostilities ensued with the Confederate attack on Ft. Sumter and Lincoln's call for mandatory state participation in repressing rebellion.

Walkup first met Margaret Parmelia "Minnie" Reece Price at the 1854 annual commencement of the Carolina Female College.[49] He had been invited by the college trustees to deliver an address on morality, civic engagement and Christian stewardship.[50] He was a 36-year-old attorney, militia officer, County Solicitor and Whig politician in Union and Anson counties. She was a 17-year-old attractive, personable student at an institution known for educating "preachers' daughters" in Latin, classical literature and ancient history.[51]

Walkup and Price shared mutual interests and a strong personal attraction. They had a common Scotch-Irish ancestry and residence in the same general locale. Like Walkup, Price was a descendent of Scotch-Irish Presbyterian immigrants who arrived at Steele Creek, Mecklenburg County, North Carolina, by the mid–1750s. The family progenitor, John Price, built the "Rock House" around 1770 on 1250 acres abutting Price Creek on the north side of the Catawba River. The Prices were active Patriots during the Revolution, serving in the militia and fabricating swords. Like Walkup, Price was devoted in attendance at Presbyterian services, prayer meetings and church. Both loved literature, particularly poetry, and were musically adept, he in flute, she in piano. Given her youth, a courtship did not commence until after 1858. At that time Walkup was an established attorney, County Solicitor, State Senator and militia general. Price's parents had predeceased her and she was living with her uncle Robert Wallace McDowell and Aunt Eluira, a cultured upper middle class family distinguished for "true Southern hospitality."[52] Walkup had previously been dating a rich redhead to whom he "had almost sold" himself. He became reacquainted with Minnie at the parlor of a mutual friend and several agricultural fairs and public events, at one of which Minnie expressed her interest by "buying" him at a charity fundraiser.[53] He took note of her "angelic grace" ... "agreeable form and loveliness."[54]

After a short engagement, Walkup and Price were married October 4, 1860, by Mecklenburg County Presbyterian Pastor Jethro Rumple. Samuel considered the nuptial a profound blessing and undoubtedly a consolation, having lost his 1859 race for a Congressional set to Francis Benton Craige, a States' Rights Democrat. The newlyweds honeymooned north to Washington, Philadelphia, New York City, Saratoga and Canada, including romantic Niagara Falls. While visiting the District of Columbia, the Walkups were invited to a White House reception where Minnie played piano at President James Buchanan's invitation.[55] The couple returned to Monroe to begin married life with their enslaved in a rented Italianate style white wood frame residence as a "family white and black."[56]

In this upper middle class Victorian household Minnie was multifaceted, undertaking self and family cultural improvement and structuring social activities by reading literature and periodicals, corresponding, conducting and attending concerts, and planning domestic, community and church events. She was an "exemplary housewife" enjoying interior and exterior design and landscaping.[57] She

Although a frugal home administrator, Minnie fabricated and appreciated quality clothing and enjoyed entertaining. She and Samuel were particularly compatible, sharing a Scotch-Irish ancestry, religious devotion, and a love of poetry, music and travel. Samuel deferred to Minnie in running the household, and appreciated that she was college educated. Throughout the Civil War, with Samuel serving at the front, she managed their Monroe home, family finances, and child care, education and religious instruction of their daughters (courtesy Virginia Adams, Galveston, Texas).

took a personal interest in tailoring for her husband, fashioning an elaborate officer's silk sash for his militia uniform.[58] She actively participated with her husband as an equal in religious observation and moral

13

education. Samuel exercised what he envisioned as a loving paternalism toward a wife he considered his intellectual equal. Nevertheless, he did not advocate a role for Minnie or other women in industry or politics. He encouraged her work in religious and social agendas, but did not want to "metamorphose her into a beast of burden, to transact the toilsome drudgery of life...." He elaborated, "She rules supreme around the family and social circle and should rather distinguish herself as a faithful wife, a tender mother, or an amiable friend, than as a furious partizan."[59] Minnie appears to have conformed such that much of her work entailed functional and fiscal domestic management, especially direction and oversight of the enslaved house laborers Stephen and Matilda.

Walkup was an upper middle class Protestant lawyer, politician and slave owner of his time. He was not a bold social reformer. Social engineering was an unnatural deviation giving rise to "liberty unrestrained and unchristianized" degenerating "into the wildest license and Radicalism."[60] He believed in a providential American exceptionalism. United States constitutionalism and rule of law preserved what he viewed as an essential linkage of property rights with civil liberty. For him the fundamental role of government was as an instrumentality of a virtuous, educated citizenry supporting God-given rights. He envisioned America as having an obligation to fulfill its manifest destiny, declaring, "A constant stream of emigration is every day rolling from the old States to more fertile regions, to enlighten and refine the rustic manners of the rude pioneers. Westward the course of empire takes it way...."[61] He evidenced a Victorian assurance in the inevitability and "rapid progress" of social improvement through science.[62] He wholeheartedly endorsed domestic morality and paternalistic missionary outreach. To maintain Divine blessings he asserted Biblical values must be promoted. He asserted that African American colonization of Liberia and missionary activities were a "solemn duty" to ensure "self preservation" as a nation.[63] He uncritically maintained that slavery in the United States constituted a beneficial environment for the moral and intellectual education of the enslaved, stating, "No Missionary efforts could have so effectually evangelized and civilized so great a number of Africans, so speedily among us in the South...."[64]

The lives of the African Americans at the Walkup Monroe home and Union County farm must be extrapolated solely from public records and owner commentary. No writings authored by Tom Clutts (Klutz), Hall Walkup and wife Mary, Margaret Walkup and her children Eliza, Harriett, Fanny, Sarah, Wilson and Jenny, Matilda "Tilly" Walkup, Julia

"Jinny" Walkup, Betty Walkup, Charlie Walkup, and Stephen Walkup and wife Luvina are known, and they were thought to be unable to read or write.[65] Unfortunately the enslaved are viewed through Walkup's patriarchal, self-serving perspective. Like all owners, he exercised his absolute unilateral discretion to direct how and where the enslaved lived, worked, ate and dressed. In response the enslaved strove to maintain self-expression and personal dignity through craft and artistry and religious and family affirmation. The enslaved also utilized complex, alternating subtle and overt strategies of cooperation and confrontation in dealing with Samuel, Minnie and William. At the time of his marriage, Walkup owned Stephen, born 1829, and Matilda, born 1849.[66] He inherited Stephen as a bequest from father Robert.[67] Prior to her marriage Minnie owned Hall and Mary and perhaps some of the other enslaved. Whether Minnie inherited the enslaved or received them as a wedding gift from her family is uncertain. She may well have been afforded the opportunity to select individuals to take to her new home. Since she had no prenuptial or marriage contract, under the law of coverture her husband exercised control of the enslaved.[68] Ownership and control of enslaved domestics contributed to her "lady-hood" status as an economic and socially privileged woman in the upper twenty-five percent of Southern citizenry.[69] Tom Clutts, born 1815, was a Mulatto enslaved laborer/farm worker, possibly owned by a third party (perhaps Walkup's brother William) and employed under contract to Samuel. He cohabitated with Lelia Clutts, but it is uncertain whether his Mulatto wife was slave or free, and whether she resided in the Walkup household.[70] In addition to the more frequent diary discussions of Matilda, Stephen, Tom and Hall, Samuel Walkup mentioned other enslaved. He described Sally as "worth a high price" and Margaret "as good a hand as any." He referenced giving his daughter and wife the slave children Harriet, Sue and Sarah, and noted Jenny and Charles.[71] The enslaved did domestic chores at the Monroe house and also worked on the Walkup farms, plowing and seeding corn and cotton in the spring, repairing fencing, carting compost to the fields, making cotton harvest baskets and picking crops in late summer. Like most small planters the Walkups did not employ an overseer. Samuel Walkup, his wife and/or brother William personally managed the enslaved, whether in Union County or the battle front. With Samuel away in Virginia Minnie assumed a more central role in directing the enslaved. William was available to impose discipline on the enslaved should Minnie be reluctant to do so. Tom and, at various times, Hall Walkup and Stephen Walkup worked as Walkup's "camp servants" from 1862 into 1864. As such these enslaved provided a vital link between the front lines and home, being able to travel back and forth alone communicating and implementing Walkup's instructions. Within the severe constraints of an evil institution, camp servants earned privileges and a leadership role in both the black and white community. While the motivation of the enslaved remains a point of conjecture, in the Walkup situation a real fraternity seemed to have existed between master and enslaved, to the extent such relation was possible. Whether such camaraderie was truly founded on mutual concern and affection, or rather pragmatic self-interest and survival, remains uncertain. Samuel Walkup on numerous occasions wrote home about his enslaved, and, unlike many owners, seemed genuinely solicitous for their health apart from their well-being solely as chattel. On their part, when at the war front Tom, Hall and Stephen inquired about the health of the white Walkups back in Monroe.[72] Samuel Walkup allowed these camp servants to earn their own money performing tasks for other soldiers and intervened when troops of the regiment cheated his slaves. His practice was not to use racial epithets in discussing Blacks. He did not record any incidents of truancy or runaways. Why those enslaved by Walkup did not try to escape is uncertain. There is no indication they knew about the Emancipation Proclamation. Perhaps no viable opportunity was afforded, the work environment might have been less horrific than servitude under malicious owners, or the enslaved resorted to other forms of resistance and self-affirmation. Nevertheless, Walkup deemed Hall and Stephen his chattel property to be leased out, sold and bequeathed, and benefited from their non-volitional labor.[73] Matilda Walkup, sometimes called Tilly, was an enslaved nursemaid caring for Samuel's infant daughter Lelia Eugene, born July 21, 1861. She was that one female, 11 years old, described in the 1860 Union County Slave Census. Tilly was in poor health and progressively deteriorated through 1861. At the frontlines in Virginia, Walkup wrote home solicitous of her "feeble" condition, asking Minnie to administer cod liver and iron supplements. Tilly died July 5, 1862.[74] Minnie developed a close relationship of mutual dependency with Tilly. Walkup remarked to Minnie that Tilly was "so attentive to our beloved child and takes so much interest in her that I would be glad if she could have good health. She would be of great service to you if well."[75] Hall Walkup, an enslaved farm laborer, was born 1836. Around January 1865 Hall commenced cohabitation with Mary, born 1835, and they legally solemnized their marriage when permitted by law in 1866.[76] Eliza, born 1853, was

The enslaved men, women and children worked beyond sunup to sundown at the house in the county seat of Monroe or on the William Walkup plantation in Waxhaw. In town these laborers cultivated the vegetable garden, maintained the house and premises, drove the buggy, ran errands, carted firewood, tended fireplaces and stoves, cooked, and provided childcare and nursing for Samuel, Minnie and their daughters. On the Walkup family plantation and at other sites, the enslaved undertook all aspects of cotton, grain and hog production, processing and market logistics, and building and equipment maintenance. During the Civil War Samuel at various times had Hall Walkup, Stephen Walkup or Thomas Clutts accompany him as "camp servants," in which capacity they traveled between Union County and the Virginia frontlines, acting as Walkup's trusted agents, carrying supplies and communications to Minnie, William Walkup and various Monroe clerks, merchants and planters. Although Samuel Walkup deemed these unfree laborers "family" and provided them customary food, housing, clothing and religious instruction, he did not reflect on his inhumanity evidenced in buying, selling and leasing African Americans and expropriating their work (*Harper's Weekly*, May 12, 1866, Library of Congress).

Margaret's daughter and was an enslaved domestic having a close work relationship with Minnie.

Walkup embraced and exemplified the antebellum social and ideological ideology of his planter community and supported the Confederate slaveocracy after Civil War hostilities commenced. Tragically, such an extremely well-educated professional and civic leader of devout religious and ethical belief was unable to transcend his environment.

Walkup clearly epitomized the moral dilemma and ambivalence faced by the well-meaning, devoutly Christian slave owner. Paradoxically he demonstrated deep familiarity with Abolitionist literature and cited such work with apparent endorsement and no disclaimer or criticism. Like Thomas Jefferson in regards to slavery, his behavior did not rise to his aspirational morality. Walkup profited both as an individual slave owner and as a facilitator of involuntary servitude. In his capacity as a lawyer, he prepared bills of sale to convey enslaved as property, chattel mortgages in which enslaved were collateral, and estate and partition settlements whereby enslaved families and friends were separated and transferred to different owners.[77] That conflicted "good" enslavers like Walkup were able to reconcile owning persons as legal property, expropriating the fruits of their labor and depriving them of liberty, is the most profound indictment of the antebellum South and a measure of the tenacious, insidious and corrupting nature of involuntary servitude. Walkup and the vast majority of pre-war whites, North and South, did not act to free slaves. Because Walkup apparently did not separate families, beat, overwork, breed, or seek sexual favors from his enslaved, he embraced the gravely erroneous but dominant Southern white narrative of slavery as a paternal institution.[78] He envisioned himself one of those "kind masters" to "obedient and Trusty servants."[79] He was unable to volitionally renounce the systemic malignancy constituting America's original sin.

Finishing his State senate term in 1862, with peace initiatives exhausted and fierce fighting underway, Walkup raised a Union County company and was designated captain.[80] Using his poetic skills, he wrote lyrics for a rousing, patriotic anthem for his Company F.[81] At the April 11, 1862, formal organization of the 48th Regiment at Camp Mangum, Raleigh, he was elected lieutenant colonel.[82] After rather perfunctory training, the regiment was dispatched to Tidewater Virginia as a component of Robert Ransom's brigade. Walkup's frequent correspondence back home to Minnie related that her "Soldier Husband" quickly adapted to camp routine, securing his own provisions as an officer, organizing distribution of uniforms and accouterments, supervising drill, attending religious services and visiting fellow officers and camp guests. Even early in the war, he was noting logistical impediments impacting the availability and pricing of salt, sugar and coffee, and even butter and eggs.[83]

As an officer Walkup did not exemplify the stereotypical antebellum cavalier. He did not behave like a spoiled, privileged Southern

Early in the war Walkup remarked on the usually stellar qualities of his subordinate officers. These men, primarily farmers, merchants, clerks, teachers and students, had voluntarily joined motivated by patriotism and community cohesion. Names shown in numerical order: 1. Samuel H. Walkup, Colonel; 2. William Hogan Jones, Major; 3. W. H. H. Lawhon, Captain; 4. John R. Winchester, Adjutant and First Lieutenant; 5. John A. Thompson, First Lieutenant. As a lawyer, politician and militia officer, Walkup personally knew most of the Union County contingent (William Clark, *History of the Several Regiments and Battalions*, 1901).

aristocrat. Instead he was shaped by his Calvinist ancestry and middle class work ethic. He did not engage in profligate and indulgent activities or squander money. He did not give way to uncontrolled impulses or resort to violent expression. He did not promote himself over community interests. He readily accepted necessary discipline and organization. Recognizing the Confederacy had little margin for error, he sought to implement structure to shape a regimental culture promoting battle readiness and maximizing restricted resources.

Walkup experienced fighting after mid–July with the Seven Days Battles. The regiment was assigned to Ransom's Brigade of Benjamin Huger's Division. Walkup's first engagement was an artillery attack on Federal gunboats operating below City Point on the James River. The 48th came under responding naval artillery fire and fell back "in order and disorder, but mostly disorder" without casualty.[84] At French's Farm the regiment advanced on an open field against superior numbers sheltered by fencing and trees, and not adequately supported, fell back. General Ransom confronted Walkup as to why soldiers in the regiment had taken to cover and the regimental flag bearer had refused to advance. Walkup then led an advance overtaking the enemy position but incurring significant 48th Regiment officer and soldier casualties.[85]

Reassigned to John G. Walker's Brigade of Thomas Jackson's Second Corps, the regiment advanced into Maryland. The initial objective was to damage the Chesapeake and Ohio Canal and to participate with Jackson in the capture of Harper's Ferry. Walkup was concerned with Confederate staggering in the face of a numerically superior forces and questioned the competency and ability of General Walker, a "timid, cautious man" without "energy, vigor and sagacity."[86] As Lee's scattered forces concentrated at Sharpsburg, the regiment was rushed forward to the Dunkard Church to address a critical breach in Jackson's line that threatened the security of the entire Confederate army. Facing "a terrible fire of artillery and musketry," Walkup had to draw his pistol and threaten to shoot his soldiers who refused to advance. The Federals were driven back but the regiment lost about half its men killed or wounded.[87] Retreating back into Virginia, Walkup noted great fatigue though "marching and hunger and loss of sleep."[88] In light of inadequate supplies on the Maryland campaign, Walkup wrote Governor Vance chiding him for the failure of the state to appropriately provision the regiment with necessary food, medicines, cooking utensils, clothing, shoes and blankets. He petitioned the Governor to address the regiment's "destitute condition" and relieve "some of the severe trials of a soldiers life."[89]

At Fredericksburg the regiment initially occupied "the most exposed and dangerous position" on Marye's Heights and Willis' Hill, and had no entrenching tools to throw up a breastworks. Posted beside the Washington Battery "in full view of the enemy," from 1:00 p.m. to darkness the regiment "remained exposed to a most destructive fire from shot, shell and small arms...."[90] Exposed to fire from thousands of Federals in a railroad cut, the open fields beyond and houses in the town, the regiment sustained casualties disproportionate to other Confederate units. Walkup himself was wounded in the right hip but remained in action. He indicated a small number of his soldiers acted cowardly and feigned debilitating wounds, for which they were subsequently censured by public parade. Walkup vehemently denied a "false and slanderous" rumor circulated by Gen. Ransom that the regiment broke and ran.[91]

Walkup placed emphasis on being both adequately attired and equipped to perform his duties as regimental colonel. His diary entries and correspondence made frequent reference to acquiring cloth for uniform tailoring and securing other clothing and shoes, together with necessary side-arms and military accouterments, paid for by his officer allotment or personal funds. He was even more concerned with the needs of his regiment and made frequent inquiries about clothing, arms and provisions to both Confederate and North Carolina quartermasters and officials (*Confederate Veteran*, Columbia, Tennessee).

Walkup went home on leave in January 1863 so he did not travel with

21

the regiment to its posting at Pocotaligo Station, South Carolina. In May he reunited with the regiment at Kinston, North Carolina. At the request of the ailing Col. Robert Clinton Hill, Walkup assumed commanded of the regiment at the Gum Swamp engagement. Regiments in Gen. Ransom's brigade broke and ran in "the most disgraceful affair of the war" and had to be saved by Walkup's regiment charging "half thigh deep in mud."[92]

Walkup did not fight at Chancellorsville or Gettysburg. His regiment did not invade Pennsylvania and was held back to protect Richmond and the vital South Anna bridge on the Richmond and Fredericksburg Railroad. Through the fog of war and disinformation, Walkup initially believed Gettysburg was a Confederate victory. He elatedly related, "Gen. Lee has completely defeated Gen. Meade at Gettysburg, Pa. and taken from him 40,000 prisoners, and is pursuing him towards Baltimore city, Md. and has Washington city within his grasp." Walkup anticipated his regiment being dispatched north to follow up on the purported advances, and planned to purchase "cheap" commodities in occupied Federal cities.[93] By July 10 he had learned the enormity of the Confederate defeat, and lamented Lee would "scarcely be able to re-cross the Potomac without fearful loss, if not destruction of his whole army." Federals were "like a pack of wolves elated with victory, enraged by invasion, prompted by hate with national pride and rush upon him with double or terrible force for his annihilation and nothing but the favor of God, great generalship and hard fighting can retrieve him and his army."[94]

After Gettysburg, the regiment was reassigned to Major Gen. Henry Heth's division of Lt. Gen. A.P. Hill's Corps. Walkup took summer leave, but was present at Bristoe Station October 14, 1863. There Walkup's regiment was "shamefully sacrificed" by A.P. Hill's impetuous attack on the rear guard of the Army of the Potomac without reconnaissance and adequate support.[95] With only the brigades of Cooke and Kirkland battling two Federal army corps supported by artillery, enfilading fire and protected by a rail cut, the regiment "suffered the heaviest loss of any battle we had yet been in...."[96] Walkup lamented that Gen. Hill "kills 1000 by carelessness...."[97]

Walkup communicated frequently with Minnie about his family and the enslaved Monroe household. Especially during the winter of 1863–1864 with his regiment assigned to picket duty along the Rapidan and encamped at Orange Court House, he had free time to reflect and reminisce. He chided, "Soldiers have an insatiable craving at all times to hear from home and receive letters from their loved ones there." He acknowledged Minnie's work in operating the household, conceding "... you are managing better than I could if at home." Nevertheless, he gave Minnie specific instructions regarding Hall and Stephen. Hall was to be supplied with new shoes, clothing, blankets and cap, and either hired out "to whoever gives the most" or retained to work brother William's plantation. Stephen was not to be hired out as he might be needed as a personal camp servant as "There is an order not to use white men as cooks or ostlers, and we cannot get Negroes, only from home." Walkup also contemplated using Tom Clutts as his field servant, in which instance Stephen could be hired out or assigned to work any newly acquired acreage.[98] Shortly thereafter Walkup informed Minnie that he had hired out Stephen to a Union County planter friend for 400 pounds of pork. Brother William was tasked with hiring a camp servant. The enslaved laborer was to be "an active boy" whose owner would be paid two or three hundred dollars or "an old sound Negro woman 45 to 50 years of age who could cook and work" and earn some wages she would be permitted to retain.[99] He sent home a derogatory, demeaning parody of "a philosophical darky" discussing the war and patriotism. Walkup unthinkingly deemed that writing humorous and fitting for his wife and young children.[100] Even as Confederate defeat became increasing more probable, Walkup continued to actively manage the enslaved with Minnie, seeking to have "'our 'Jinny' hired out in return for provision of her food, clothing and housing or instead paying someone $50.00 to keep her and child."[101]

The year 1864 commenced with Walkup complaining about his treatment as a candidate for full colonelcy. Lieutenant colonels like Walkup were routinely required to appear before a merit examination board comprised of generals and colonels to ascertain competency in tactics and regulations. He viewed the requirement as a personal affront and contemplated resigning "rather than silently submit to the indignity of going for examination before a board organized expressly to reject for incompetency and rid the army...."[102] One of the hearing officers advised a "sullen" Walkup to summon witnesses as concerns relating to his "want of discipline would have to be met."[103] At the hearing a captain characterized Walkup as undoubtedly gallant and able to rally soldiers during crisis, but "only tolerant on drill and discipline" and frequently issuing mistaken orders causing confusion. Walkup exemplified his superior lawyer skill, presenting favorable testimony and even correcting the presiding hearing officer on technical points. With satisfaction Walkup noted he passed "a very credible examination."[104] He stated he had no doubt of being appointed full colonel of the 48th, but nevertheless still contemplated resignation because of the "insult" to his "self-respect" and failure of his regiment to receive deserved recognition.[105]

Walkup's elation in successfully passing board examination was short lived. Perhaps distracted in preparing for his hearing, or himself not timely notified, Walkup neglected to inform a soldier in the regiment of a court martial death sentence for desertion as required by regulation. Walkup deemed the soldier's sentence unjust and tried unsuccessfully to have the verdict set aside on a technicality. The condemned private went to his execution "unprepared and much concerned." Walkup was then charged by Gen. A.P. Hill for gross neglect of duty.[106] For over a week he was under arrest, relegated to camp before release to resume duties.[107]

Walkup noted the increasingly precarious state of the Confederacy. Desertions were multiplying despite such punitive sanctions such as solitary confinement, reduction in rank, forfeiture of pay, hard labor and execution. Enslaved camp laborers were escaping across the front lines.[108] He noted both a personal and unit need for clothing, stating, "I am getting too ragged for a North Carolina Field Officer" and that his regiment only received "a very slight and insignificant surplus" after other regiments in the brigade had first dibs.[109] Even though a colonel, he yearned for home and cessation of hostilities, but acknowledged, "...we are in a dilemma, where we must risk everything or lose all. We must fight through or be degraded and disgraced. We must fight for self-preservation, for existence. If death or mutilation nearly as bad comes, we are worsted. But if we escape both and find our families safe and secure our independence the prize will not be too great for the prize we seek."[110]

Despite deteriorating prospects for victory Walkup's army life continued with its usual monotonous routine. He visited fellow officers at the front, shared in supper messes, worshiped in camp revivals and wrote home to family, friends and business associates.[111] He paid a "free Negro" in the camp a significant amount of money to fashion a knife.[112] He undertook his first effort to drill company officers, but made "a miserable failure, quite in confusion.... I would almost as soon fight a battle."[113] He invited his old Whig colleague Governor Zebulon Vance to visit camp and make a campaign reelection speech to the regiment. Vance made "a tolerably good speech" but with "too little seriousness and too much buffoonery" for an assemblage that included Generals Ewell, Early, Stuart, Gordon, Rhodes and Ramseur. Vance requested Walkup say "amen" whenever he concurred with the sentiment expressed.[114] A chivalrous equestrian tournament reflective of Sir Walter Scott's medieval pageantry was held with local women in attendance.[115] When a heavy snow fell, the regiment, as a component of Cooke's Brigade, engaged other Confederates in lively, vigorous "great sport" snowball fights, performed with intricate tactical maneuvering, capturing flags and soldiers and bruising heads.[116] That same day by confirmation order of Gen. A.P. Hill a court martial sentence of death was conducted before the assembled soldiers.[117]

On the Monroe home front Minnie experienced her own profound challenges as she was thrust into unaccustomed expanded responsibilities. Socialized in attitudes of upper class white female "weakness," she was able to transcend such constraints as she rose to the financial, physical and emotional challenges of maintaining a home amidst wartime ravages and deprivations. With Samuel away fighting and brother-in-law William increasingly involved with militia and home guard duties, Minnie took on an enhanced role in managing the enslaved household and on occasion even those enslaved working on the Walkup cotton plantations. She apparently maintained at least an adequate work relationship with the enslaved and did not voice fear of racial violence as did some home front white women. Instead, she increasingly relied on the labor, competency and companionship of the enslaved.[118]

Spring and summer 1864 witnessed almost continuous fighting in Virginia as Gen. Ulysses Grant pursued maximum engagement and attrition. At the Wilderness the 48th was in the thick of fighting as Heth's Division opposed more than 25,000 Federals in tangled forest undergrowth. Walkup was placed in temporary command of Cooke's Brigade and personally directed by Robert E. Lee to concentrate forces and "hold that point at all hazards." The regiment had stacked arms to eat rations and was commencing to dig breastworks with bayonets when assaulted. Entirely surrounded by the enemy, the field was "stubbornly contested" until Longstreet's corps advanced. Lee inspected the lines and was cheered.[119] Walkup criticized the Third Corps' failure to more timely engage, stating his superior A.P. Hill "was guilty of ... folly" and "criminal negligence."[120] In the race to the strategic crossroads at Spotsylvania Court House Walkup again was "fighting very hot." He privately denounced "Drunken General Early," who had assumed temporary command of A.P. Hill's Corps, for ordering, despite protest by brigade commanders, a "fool's errant" assault against Federal batteries.[121] As Grant relentlessly pressed eastward, the regiment faced heavy

artillery and musketry fire while constructing and manning breastworks. Walkup regularly anticipated night attacks so the regiment
remained in front trenches, lights out, with arms ready behind advance
warning pickets.[122] He noted discomforts of water, mud, dysentery and
seed ticks.[123] As Gen. Grant moved southward, the regiment forced
marched to the North Anna River and Turkey bend. Walkup noted "Lee
is outsmarted by Grant and let him get the start of him to Richmond."[124]
Walkup also critiqued A.P. Hill as "proud, haughty, old maidish son, and
selfish-looking misanthrope and loves to be a tyrant and vexish, snaps
and snarls at everything and everybody."[125] With ongoing enemy assault
imminent, Walkup pressed the regiment's building of extensive field
earthworks with limited tools, stating, "I dig my own hole for safety, and
it is much needed." In the ensuing battle of Cold Harbor, the Federals
launched a massive general assault on the entire six-mile Confederate
front. He related, "Our regiment sustained the brunt of that day's fight
... without water and food all day, 13 or 14 hours, greatly fatigued, our
flag shot in four or five places and colors over 200."[126]

Grant's continued movement south crossing the James River
toward Petersburg set the stage for the last nine months of the war. As
Confederate forces followed and engaged the enemy, Walkup observed,
"Their sharpshooters are skillful and terrible and make us cautious and
vigilant."[127] On June 15, 1864, under artillery shelling and fire from infantry snipers and dismounted cavalry, he incurred a "glazing" shoulder
wound "which cut a hole."[128] The injury did not take him out of action.
He noted the enemy's superior firepower with their cavalry using Burnside and Spencer breech loading carbines and Colt revolving rifles.[129]
With the regiment in line of march behind troops led by Gen. George
Pickett, Walkup remarked on "Pickett's much whuffed division," stating,
"Old Lee makes himself an undignified paternal fussy-puff for his petted and spoiled darlings."[130] In addition to his painful wound, Walkup
suffered other complications, such as bloody bowels.[131] Concerns with
his own health and regimental duties were compounded with the
need to address citizen complaints about unauthorized military foraging. He sympathized with those subject to such "depredations" and set
guards over private property but was unable to locate and apprehend
the thieves.[132] Near summer's end he received sick leave and returned to
Monroe.[133] Back home, he wrote Governor Vance about overly aggressive Home Guard seeking deserters in Union County. Walkup stated
there were few deserters there, and such white men present but subject to draft were essential to save the growing and maturing crops,

The 48th North Carolina was deemed among the most reliable "shock troops" of the Army of Northern Virginia, participating in most of Lee's major battles. At Antietam and during the Overland Campaign, the regiment was particularly distinguished in potentially saving Lee from catastrophe. The regiment routinely suffered heavy casualties, depleting its roster. Walkup appreciated the role of the flags and their standard bearers in motivating troops and sustaining the prestige and dignitas of the regiment. Given the increased probability that the color bearer might be killed, wounded or captured, Walkup deemed only the most upstanding capable and worthy of the honor (North Carolina State Archives and History, Raleigh, North Carolina).

particularly sorghum molasses and fodder. He emphasized that his county "has very few slaves" to do the necessary agriculture.[134]

By the start of 1865 Walkup was back with his regiment in winter quarters at the Petersburg outer defenses on Hatcher's Run. Between drilling and daily inspection of pickets, he read novels and ate modest messes with fellow officers.[135] Minnie sent him butter and other relatives and friends in Monroe shipped opossum, pound cake, sausage, dried beef and molasses.[136] Walkup was concerned with the rapidly deteriorating conditions both in Union County and Virginia. Gen. William Tecumseh Sherman was marching though Piedmont North Carolina, destroying crops, provisions and infrastructure.[137] Concerned about his family facing regular Federal troops and stragglers and Confederate deserters, he worried when he did not hear from Minnie for nearly a month, stating, "The Yankees were there between them and our forces. I can only look heavenward for comfort."[138] When he did receive word, he learned his brother-in-law was murdered by Union marauders who sought to ascertain the location of secreted-away gold.[139] With desertions increasing exponentially throughout the Army of Northern Virginia and in his own regiment, Walkup tried to raise morale. He addressed his soldiers with a patriotic exhortation, a military band serenade, and special whiskey rations. The speech was well received and he noted with satisfaction, "They carried me corn shucking style to my tent on their shoulders ... in fine glee."[140] Nevertheless, desertion continued unabated and he observed with concern, "Our men are deserting, half of them or more go to the Yankees and those who go home will, I greatly fear, be very troublesome there. They are just the sort of men to commit cruel and wanton outrages and insult the unprotected. I feel very much inclined to resign and come home to protect my family."[141]

Walkup fully appreciated the desperate circumstances, acknowledging that only a concerted, total self-sacrificing military and civilian commitment could avert impending defeat. He noted, with a "told you so" realism, "Our cause looks gloomy in the extreme. Those men who thought the securing of our independence so easy a matter, who precipitated the South in so disastrous a war, who owe their greatness to their country's ruin, are or have reaped those bitter fruit...."[142] He contemplated a last-ditch effort: "I am willing to fight desperately to the end, if the people will rise up and do what they can. But if they lie down and submit without a struggle ours would be a useless sacrifice. It would be useless for a few to struggle with over-whelming odds and under all imaginable disadvantages."[143]

The end came quickly for the regiment and the Army of Northern Virginia. The regiment was held in reserve but witnessed Lee's last significant offensive at Fort Stedman. That bold night assault employing subterfuge and select shock troops was a desperate effort to capture earthworks and a rail head and break and roll back the Federal line. The attack was initially successful with Gen. John Gordon taking three-quarters of a mile of the enemy's front and several forts with a minimal loss. Under shell and mortar fire, Walkup "saw our forces in the Yankee fort recoiling and the Yankees retaking possession" with Confederates incurring significant killed, wounded and captured. He anticipated Lee's defenses would soon be broken as "'Our force is very weak.'

... It is true we have entrenchments before us, but we generally have to fight outside of them as we are too few to man them against a strong assault." He instructed Minnie not to send clothing or food or anything else as "we will be killed or captured.... Lee will have to evacuate Richmond or be captured before April close and perhaps in ten days.... There is no reasonable prospect for good news."[144] Confederate lines broke at Five Forks and the following day the regiment was driven from its works as Federals swept the entire front. Walkup and his remnant regiment retreated as part of Lee's general evacuation and was further depleted by persistent Federal pursuit. As a component of the rear guard, the regiment attempted to protect the wagon train, but was unable to do so and retreated in disorder before a surrounding large force of Federal infantry.[145] "Every man was left to take care of himself."[146] At Appomattox Walkup received his parole and surrendered his regiment, so reduced in number, to about one hundred, as not to even constitute an ordinary company.[147]

Walking home from Appomattox, Walkup was physically and financially exhausted. Still recovering from injuries incurred at Fredericksburg and the Wilderness, he had to mentally readjust to civilian life. His wartime investments in nine additional slaves and Confederate bonds were disastrous. He lamented, "I owned very little real or personal property except in slaves." He had to rebuild his law practice, salvage existing clients and attempt to solicit new business in an economy devastated by the war in general and more specifically Sherman's deprivations. He bemoaned, "My profession (law) is utterly worthless in the present unsettled politics and conditions of the country." He contacted his former commander Brigadier General John Rogers Cooke to request a recommendation for employment with the National Express Company and wrote its president General Joseph E. Johnston asking for an appointment.[148] He obtained, at least on a provisional basis, his former position of County Solicitor.[149] In that capacity his prosecution of criminal defendants was monitored by the Freedmen's Bureau assistant sub-assistant commissioner, Complaint and Prosecution branches, for compliance with the Civil Rights Act of 1866. During the initial months back home Walkup's first priority was to feed his family. He worked a garden and hog pens himself with his wife and hired freedmen when available and affordable. The formerly enslaved laborers Hall and Mary, who were then able to legally marry, remained in Monroe and along with former enslaved Elizabeth Walkup and Eliza Walkup, worked for Samuel, Minnie and their young daughters. Minnie was thereby able to maintain her "lady-hood" social status as a woman having domestic help. The other African Americans who had worked at either the town residence or the Walkup family plantations appear to have left Monroe after emancipation.[150]

With his legal practice struggling and farming no longer a viable supplement to income, Walkup sought to revive his political career after a four-year hiatus. He ran against James Ramsey and William Sloan for the Sixth Congressional District. He navigated a potential political land mine by declining to endorse either Jonathan Worth[151] or William Holden,[152] the contenders for governor. Walkup allowed supporters to portray him as "a Confederate Savior" and he critiqued Ramsey as never having learned "to love the Confederacy."[153] Despite Walkup's earlier identification with slaveocracy, he had repudiated involuntary servitude. Although both his contenders expressly opposed African American suffrage, Walkup was silent on that contentious issue. A major issue was whether the prevailing candidate would be permitted by the Republican dominated Congress to take the mandatory "iron clad" loyalty test oath and be seated. Walkup asserted he could establish present fidelity to satisfaction of Congress. He campaigned as having "signalized his devotion to the Union by resisting every attempt at its disruption, but when she (North Carolina) once had ... severed her connection with the old Government, acted bravely and honorably in her defenses."[154] He was "a devoted Union man" who "bravely and boldly proclaimed his anti-secessionist sentiments" and "'all that man could do to save he country he did' ... but he could not stand quietly by , and see his section run over, without sharing the fate of his friends...." When he did enlist in the Confederate army in 1862, he acted with his "whole soul, and many a bloody battle-field attest his gallantry and devotion."[155] He had taken the Appomattox parole and oath of allegiance and amnesty and was "as loyal a citizen as lives in the United States, and as firm supporter of President Johnson's reconstruction...."[156]

Walkup won election by a razor thin margin of 58 votes.[157] He went to Washington December 1865 but the House of Representatives Clerk refused to accept his credentials in common with most other Southern elects to both houses who could not take the Iron Clad Oath.[158] Initially undeterred, Walkup and the North Carolina delegation sought Johnson administration support and dialogue with Republican leadership. He was staying at the exclusive Willard Hotel with the North Carolinian delegation, but ultimately had to go back to Monroe when his money and prospects were exhausted.[159] Months later, he still lamented,

"If I could only get my seat in Congress that would make up much of the losses ... but that door seems effectually shut up against me. I have no hopes there."[160] He stated he would never hold an office incompatible with "manhood and self-respect."[161]

Walkup was elected as a delegate to the State Convention of 1865 that was tasked with reorganizing North Carolina government for readmission to the Union. He was the last delegate to arrive, present certificate, qualify and be seated. The Convention embraced the theme "Going Home" and abolished slavery, repealed secession and repudiated war debts incurred in furtherance of rebellion. Like most of the delegates Walkup supported the agenda necessary to secure state readmission. He did not oppose suffrage for freedmen.[162] He grudgingly but pragmatically accepted the inevitability of a new post-war federalism imposed by Washington with state status further subordinate to national governance.

With his Congressional aspirations dashed, Walkup increasingly eschewed politics and avoided public controversies. He deemed himself a Conservative Democrat, but not an advocate of the repressive "Black Codes" denying freedmen fundamental liberties.[163] He did not endorse nor participate in Ku Klux Klan and "rifle club" vigilantism, but he did not specifically denounce such reprehensible violence.[164] Although he did not oppose the Fourteenth and Fifteenth Amendments, he only guardedly accepted Governor William Holden's civil rights initiatives. While he did not seek election as a delegate to the State Constitutional Convention of 1868, he made no objection to the ensuing law that most Democrats disparaged.[165] Regarding Radical Republicanism, he publicly reflected, "We are therefore more interested in trying to get bread to keep from starving, than in reconstruction or political matters. I presume our people will, all who can, register and vote for Sherman's bill, and acquiescence for peace and Union, whether they like the plan or not."[166] Like Robert E. Lee, Walkup did not publicly oppose Congressional Reconstruction, but in private he denounced that agenda. Corresponding to a former Confederate superior, he complained, "My only hope is the magnanimity of the people of the North or the fears of the radicals from abroad. We have more sympathy from those we met in battle, than from such old grumbling, unprincipled, broken down political hacks as Stevens, Wilson, Sumner."[167] Having been denied the participation in the political process his Congressional seat would have afforded, in frustration he later declared, "It looks like it is more difficult to make peace and get reconstructed than it was to carry on the war. I think if the

Texans, Arkansians, Louisianans, Mississippians, Georgians and North Carolinians were once more in line of battle with Lee and Johnston we could get terms much better and be thoroughly reconstructed in a very few days and the Yankees much more accommodating."[168]

Despite diligent efforts to re-establish his law business, Walkup still struggled financially. He contemplated relocating to Texas or "some new country" to practice law, farm or teach. He lamented lawyering paid "poorly" in Monroe. He observed, "The law has sunk as a (the most) reputable profession, because everybody can be admitted to the bar here now-and magistrates, sheriffs, constables, etc. are crowding the profession, therefore it becomes degraded."[169] Walkup himself tried his hand at trade, combining his own funds with monies raised with friends to purchase mules, horses and tobacco locally for resale in Georgia. The venture was an unmitigated failure in a market "very greatly depressed" where "it is difficult to sell anything." He suffered significant losses by "this unfortunate speculation" and regretted "...my dearest ones had to suffer with me...."[170] He did obtain modest income with appointments as a director for the Wilmington, Charlotte and Rutherford Railroad and the Peoples Bank of Monroe.[171] Needing more adequate, consistent income, he ran for and won election as Union County Clerk of Court in 1874.[172] In that capacity he maintained court pleadings, dockets and other judicial records, received filing fees and fines paid into the court, approved guardianships and served as judge of probate and estate administration. As Clerk he had to forego private legal practice in his county.[173] His tenure as probate judge was especially demanding and subject to prolong litigation given the heightened complexity of estate administration with Reconstruction's repudiation of insurrection contracts and debts and the worthlessness of Confederate bonds and currency.[174]

In the last decade of his life Walkup reminisced about his war experiences and reviewed and edited his Civil War diary. He associated with local veterans who served under his command, who later organized a "Camp Walkup" chapter.[175] He acquired and critically read history and biography written from a Confederate perspective, including the works of Edward Pollard and John Esten Cooke. Walkup apparently accepted some tenets of the Lost Cause narrative as a means of coping with both his personal financial challenges and collective Southern defeat. Reading sympathetic biographies of Robert E. Lee and Stonewall Jackson, Walkup perceived his own wartime service emulated such portrayals of manly courage, Christian virtue and devotion to superiors and subordinates. He viewed himself as one of those "patriots fighting for their altars and their firesides."[176] However, he did not idolize Lee as an unparalleled military mind and instead deemed Grant a superior tactician and strategist. Moreover, unlike Jubal Early and other prominent Lost Cause authors and many former Confederates, he did not try to minimize the role of slavery as the cause of the war. With slavery abolished, Walkup did not sentimentalize or defend chattel servitude or advocate for white supremacy and African American subordination.[177]

With his health declining, Walkup devoted time not working as Clerk of Court to community endeavors. Having previously attended the small Tirzah Church in Waxhaw, Walkup and Minnie worked as "leading spirits" with other congregants in 1873 to establish the First Presbyterian Church of Monroe. They were among five other charter members who generously provided large sums to purchase for reuse the Methodist Episcopal Church, a one room building at the corner of Windsor and Church Streets. Walkup had been active with the Sabbath School founded by his sister Sarah Walkup Belk Simpson that predated First Presbyterian. At his new church Walkup was one of the first two Elders and taught and served as Superintendent in the Sabbath School.[178] Minnie was quite active as President of the Ladies' Aid Society and seldom absent. The Walkups often advanced the minister's salary and other collections. They maintained an "upper room" or "prophet's chamber" at the family residence, reserved for ministers.[179]

Walkup continued his service with secondary and collegiate education, utilizing his antebellum experience as a commencement speaker and state senator assigned the education committee. He leveraged his legislative knowledge and networks to secure a private act of the General Assembly establishing Monroe High School and designating him an incorporator.[180] Walkup was elected as a trustee of Davidson College from the Mecklenburg Presbytery and served as President of the Board.[181] As an attorney he had handled property acquisitions by the highly regarded liberal arts college as it restructured facilities, faculty and the student body after the challenging years of the Civil War.[182] In his capacity as trustee, he participated in award of degrees, faculty selection, budget approval and general institutional governance.[183] Walkup was undoubtedly honored to also secure a Board of Education trustee appointment for his alma mater, the University of North Carolina. He likely obtained the position in recognition of his recent service on the Conservative district executive committee.[184] The university had closed in 1871, caught up in political controversy with a Conservative

Democratic legislature battling Governor William Holden's biracial civil rights initiatives. Reopened in 1875 with Conservative Party governance, university administrators observed, "We shall have the hearty cooperation of the trustees and but little interference from them."[185] Due to his deteriorating health, Walkup did not attend the trustees' organizational meeting and did not actively participate in administration.[186]

Walkup's health drastically deteriorated throughout 1876 as he faced work and financial pressures. He related, "I am closely confined to my office and have very little time to spare. Money is scares and times pressing."[187] Walkup anticipated his impending demise, stating, "I have lived a longer life than any of our family.... Let us be ready for the change when it comes and make sure of our Eternal Life—and not spend Eternity in regretting our delay and folly."[188] He sought reinvigoration by visiting mineral springs to bathe in and drink the medicinal waters and through mountain excursions. Sick for about three months, he was confined to bed for six weeks. Thomas Win-

After the Civil War Minnie struggled to raise and educate their five daughters. Family financial prospects were considerably diminished. In a devastated post-war economy Samuel sought to reestablish his law practice and recoup losses in Confederate bonds. Husband and wife remained active in their community, promoting education and church engagement. As Samuel's health progressively declined, due in large part to his wartime injuries and exposures, Minnie and their daughters served as his caregivers (John Hugh McDowell, *The McDowells, Erwins, Irvins and Connections*, 1918).

34

chester Becket, his local physician, attended him for seventeen consecutive days in October, and consulted with two other specialists. Walkup failed to rally and died from chronic diarrhea and other morbidities incurred during the war. General D.H. Hill, his friend since the war, described the passing as "a noble man" entering "the portals of immortality." Walkup's last words were, "I feel no pain. I have no fear."[189] He was eulogized as "a good man, and one in whom everybody had confidence" and "one of the best citizens of Union County," whose death left "a void hard to fill."[190] He was 59 years old and was survived by wife Minnie and their five daughters. His life was insured for $5000.00, so the family was "comfortably provided for."[191] The funeral was conducted by the Presbyterian pastor in the new Methodist Episcopal Church, the largest public facility in Monroe. All business in town ceased for the service. The procession to the grave conducted with Masonic honors was the most attended gathering in town history.[192]

Minnie died peacefully three years later, aged 43, and was buried with Walkup at Suncrest Cemetery. In a declining, frail state for almost a year, she had been daily attended by daughter Lelia Eugenia who left Peace Institute in Raleigh shortly before senior graduation. At the deathbed, distraught Lelia asked Minnie where to go for advice after her passing, and received the whispered reply, "Go to God." With both parents having died, the "light of the home had gone out" and the residence was closed and the children went to live with their uncle William Walkup.[193]

The black and white Walkups and Cluttses/Kluttses maintained cordial post-war relations. Some Walkup surnamed freedmen not members of the Samuel Walkup household did emigrate to Liberia to escape white vigilantism.[194] However, those formerly enslaved by Samuel Walkup remained in Union, Anson and Mecklenburg counties upon emancipation. Into the 1870s the freedman teenagers Elizabeth and Eliza Walkup lived in the Samuel Walkup Monroe residence and worked for Samuel and Minnie as hired domestic servants.[195] When Elizabeth married Charles Achus in 1874 Samuel and Minnie attended the wedding and served as legal witnesses.[196] Julia "Jenny" Walkup secured employment in Union County with a white property owner, John Andsey, but had to seek help from the Freedmen's Bureau in securing annual wages due for 1866.[197] Hall Walkup and wife Mary were able to accumulate personal property and farmed in nearby Caswell, Mecklenburg County, apparently without children. Hall remarried Dora Pegram in 1882.[198] Stephen remained in Union County in Sandy Ridge township, a freedman community of Walkups, Houstons, Iveys, Winchesters,

Millers Deeses and Cuthbertsons known for empowerment through education and cooperative economic, social and religious engagement. Stephen apparently fathered three families, one with Riney Walkup, one with Dina Winchester (Walkup) and one with Luvina Walkup. After cohabitating for about twenty-five years Stephen and housekeeper Riney were able to legally marry in 1866.[199] Their three children, Margaret, Lee and Stephen, Jr., helped out on the family farm. Stephen had been hired out by Samuel Walkup in 1863 to John H. Winchester and on that plantation met enslaved laborer Dina Winchester. Starting in 1866 Stephen and Dina had four children together: William, Mary, Emma and Lillie. That Winchester/Walkup family resided next door to the Riney Walkup family. By 1880 Stephen had remarried. His wife Luvina was about his same age and maintained the family home with his grandson Stephen Buck, a farmer born enslaved in 1862, and granddaughter Elizer Buck, born 1872 and in school. Both Stephen Walkup and Luvina had learned to read and write.[200] Stephen "Steve" Walkup, Jr., sharecropped cotton on the Ross Plantation in the Marvin community of Union County for several decades, and provided domestic services such as cutting firewood, gardening and buggy driving for the Maggie and Sallie Ross sisters. He also worked in Sandy Ridge for the Frank Ernest general store, gristmill, lumberyard and molasses refinery, and the Frank Crane store hauling produce for market in Charlotte. Steve was a founding member of the Marvin AME Zion Church.[201] Thomas Clutts/Kluttz was employed providing transportation services for the Freedmen's Bureau's Salisbury District Office reuniting African American families that had been sold apart or disbursed by war. He then moved to nearby Wadesboro, Anson County, to work as a barber, upholsterer and laborer. He was the first African American barber proprietor and municipal magistrate in that county.[202] He adeptly used politics to advance his business interests through alliance with the white Democratic establishment.[203] He was deemed "well known and very respectable" and "esteemed by whites and blacks alike."[204] Thomas married Delia, a Mulatto laborer fifteen years his junior whose father was from North Carolina and mother from Virginia. Their teenage son William lived at home and worked as a laborer while attending school. In her mid-nineties in 1880, Thomas's mother-in-law Mary Bates from his prior marriage lived with the family.[205] Thomas died in 1890. As surviving head of household, Delia worked as a laundress operating out of the family residence. She lived with daughter Ruth who learned to read and write and was employed in the family business.[206] Grandson namesake William Thomas "Tom"

Those enslaved by Samuel Walkup developed expertise in cultivating the cash crop cotton and home economics, skills that were to be later employed during Reconstruction into the twentieth century. As freedmen they industriously grew cotton to sustain and educate their families and to purchase land, surmounting racial oppression and the economic subjugation of sharecropping. While some freedmen previously held in bondage by Samuel Walkup's extended family chose to relocate to Liberia to escape vigilante violence, segregation and discrimination, African Americans from his household remained in Union, Anson and Mecklenburg counties. These freedmen farmed, performed domestic service for Samuel Walkup or served with the Freedmen's Bureau. Descendants went to college at Tuskegee, served as magistrates and entrepreneurs, and undertook early civil rights activism (*Harper's Weekly*, May 12, 1866, Library of Congress).

Kluttz, Jr., born 1892, attended Tuskegee Institute for high school/collegiate training during Booker T. Washington's presidency, studying in the Agriculture Department under George Washington Carver and participating in the Military Department Band.[207] Tom left Tuskegee to apply his skills as a dairy farmer in the Birmingham, Alabama, area before returning to Anson County where he continued to demonstrate a lifelong enthusiasm as a nationally recognized poultry breeder.[208] In Wadesboro in the 1920s he founded the "Famous Kluttz Family Band" that regularly played in the city's annual Emancipation Day parade. He was a successful businessman serving the African American community as a realtor, bondsman and mortician. He performed numerous civil duties as chair of the board of trustees of Keeslers Chapel A.M.E. Zion Church, city school committeeman, head of the local chapter of the Elks and Knights of Pytheans, and chair of the area Red Cross Black Division during the Second World War.[209] Tom was a zealous advocate for African American business interests and civil rights. He diligently promoted racially equitable distribution of governmental services, particularly public improvement and municipal infrastructure for his community.[210] Black and white Walkups and other descendants of the household still live in Union, Anson and Mecklenburg counties.

# Walkup's Civil War Journal and Correspondence

*April 1862–April 1865*

## April 1, 1862

Our company "Waxhaws No. 2," left Monroe, North Carolina, for Charlotte and Raleigh, North Carolina, with about 50 men.[1] Captains Wiant,[2] Walden[3] and Alexander[4] left about the same time. We lay over in Charlotte Tuesday night until Wednesday night for want of transportation.

Lyrics by Walkup, sung to "The Camels Are Coming:"

From the birthplace of Jackson, Hurrah, Hurrah;
We come from the red hills of Old Waxhaw;
From the country where freedom first brightened to law,
Where each bush struck a foeman with terror and awe.

Our sires fought bravely at Walkup's old mill;
They drove back the foeman, at Hanging Rock hill;
At Charlotte, at Cowpens, and glorious Eutaw,
Where the Brittons fell thickest, was at Old Waxhaw.

Her descendants are Guilford, and Kings Mountain boys,
Moores Creek, Alamance, and Old Waxhaw,
And glorious old Mecklenburg, who never will yield,
While her liberties threatened, by foes in the field.

Our State was the first to come into the bond;
The last to desert those who intended her wrong;
Though last in forbearance, she's first in the fight,
And thrice glorious Bethel, is proof of her might.

Once more for our freedom, our swords we will draw;
We'll yield to no power but justice and law;

And woe to the tyrant who falls in the paw,
Of the liberty loving, from old Waxhaw.

No banner shall wave in advance of this flag;
No true son of Waxhaw, behind it will lag;
No band be more glorious, more worthy of applause,
Than the band and the banner, of the Old Waxhaws.

Then accept ye this flag, with the smiles of the girls,
Whose hearts will go with you where ever you are,
And when dangers thicken, remember with joys,
Of returning in triumph, to the Old Waxhaws.[5]

## April 2, 1862

Got off the cars and reached Raleigh on the 3rd. Took up quarters at Camp Mangum[6] without tents for two nights, 3rd and 4th, on 5th got tents[7] and formed regiment No. 48th: Capt. F. L. Wiant, Union County, Co. A; Capt. A. A. Hill,[8] Davidson County, Co. B; Capt. A. M. Walker,[9] Co. C, Iredell County; Capt. B.R. Huske,[10] Co. D, Moore County ; Capt. J.W. Walden, Co. E, Union County; Capt. Samuel. H. Walkup,[11] Co. F, Union County; Capt. W. H. Jones,[12] Co. G, Chatham County; Capt. E. C. Alexander, Co. I, Union County; Capt. Jesse Atwood,[13] Co. K, Forsythe County.

## April 9, 1862

Elected field officers for 48th Regiment North Carolina Troops. Col. R. C. Hill[14] of Iredell County of army, Capt. Samuel H. Walkup of Union County unanimously [elected] Lt. Col., Capt. Benjamin H. Huske of Fayetteville [elected Major].

## April 11, 1862

Hugh Wilson[15] elected Captain of Co. F unanimously [having initially declined], and then reelected 3rd Lieutenant and promoted to Captain and other lieutenants declining any promotion in his favor. 1st Lt. T. J. Clegg[16] of Moore County promoted Captain [Co. F].

## April 15, 1862

I left camp and visited Vance's Regiment at Kinston, saw brother H. C. Walkup[17] and returned home to buy a horse.[18] Our camp was moved to railroad about same time.

## APRIL 18–20, 1862

Bought horse of Ledbetter for $200.00, got clothes in Charlotte, paid off bills in full from sale of house and lot to Wilkinson for $2300.00 and sent Minnie to pay all.[19]

## APRIL 23, 1862

Got to camp and left again Saturday 28th for Steele Creek Church, where I met my wife, and had Lelia baptized by Dr. S. Phan.

## MAY 1, 1862

Camp removed to Goldsboro,[20] horse injured, got to camp at Fair Grounds, where we remained and drilled until June 1st.[21] Was sick at Camp Mangum and Goldsboro of diarrhea a week.

## MAY 23, 1862

❖ Letter from Walkup at Goldsboro, North Carolina, to wife Minnie:

My Dearest Minnie:

I wrote to you a few days since, but now have a chance by William Moser to write to you again today. We will leave this place for Weldon, North Carolina on tomorrow or next day and I write to you in order that you may direct to me at Weldon unless we go to Garysburg about four or five miles beyond Weldon.

I am still unwell with dysentery, and have discharges of pure blood, mixed with some mucus and some loose natural discharge. I have no pain and feel pretty well but rather weak. Robinson, Winchester and others have had the same and it did not hurt them, so that I think there is no danger and only a little inconvenience in running out frequently attending the case.[22] If I had another flannel shirt with a strip of flannel over the stomach and bowels to put on when I pull off the other, I don't think I should have dysentery at all. I will buy a piece of flannel and have it sewn onto my other shorts. I had another pair of drawers made, but would be glad if you would send me the other coarse pair I left at home, unless I lost them on the way. If you know of anyone coming to Weldon, I should be glad if you would get Mr. John Shoots to buy me some six or twelve dozen eggs and pack them up in saw dust in a box and some 5 to 25 lbs. butter and send to me at Weldon by some means or other. I suppose the butter can be had for $.20 to $.30 per pound or $.35, and the eggs for $.15 to $.20 per dozen and we can readily dispose of the surplus at any price it costs us.

We will get a sack of java coffee at $1.00 per pound and keep about 25 lbs. I may send you ten lbs. if I can fix it before Mr. Moser leaves.

I would be glad if you would buy enough of colored stuff either light woolen or calico small striped or checked to make me two shirts to wear without coat, to be plaited around the front part of the body like Turner's or Dr. Lorme's, or Dr. Chears.[23] Don't make the sleeves so long as the two you last made.

I have not yet received a line from you since I left, although I heard about you as Henry Houston and Marion Helms passed you as they came on last Tuesday, on your return from Charlotte and told me you looked quite well and I have written to you four times. Tom[24] is well and doing well, although not at all pleased with camp life. He attends on me very well since I have been unwell, got two chickens and cooked well for me and made a soup. My horse also does very well.

We had a severe rain and hail storm on yesterday. Hail large nearly as partridge eggs and strong wind. Our tents all leaked some, but mine is large and has fly cover and I kept myself and clothing dry. The health of our regiment as usual. Captains Wiant, Wilson and their lieutenants all well. Wiant has recovered his health but not strong. Sgt. Robert Strong has a cough and so have I but not bad. Sgt. Grey has jaundice, but is up.

You will direct your letters etc. to me at Weldon as we have left Goldsboro. You need not think of visiting us at all at Weldon as you can have no accommodations there. Tom is anxious to hear from his wife and know whether the clothes he sent home by James Nesbit came to hand.

My darling love in conclusion let me tell you not to be uneasy about me, as I feel quite well. Give my respects to Miss Lizzie, Miss Lelia and let me hear from you soon.

Your ever loving and affectionate "Soldier Husband"[25]

## May 25, 1862

❖ Letter from Walkup at Goldsboro, North Carolina, to wife Minnie:

My lovely Rose of Sharon:

You will doubtless be surprised to learn that we are still at Goldsboro. We expect to leave for Weldon on tomorrow, but may not get off for two or three days for the want of transportation.

I write more on account of your satisfaction than because I have any news to communicate.

I received your very kind letter on the day I wrote by William Moser; was grateful to learn that you were all well but poor Tilly.[26] I sympathize with you in her feeble health. She seems so meek, patient and forlorn as if she had no friends and is so attentive to our beloved child and takes so much interest in her that I would be glad she could have good health. She would be of great service to you if well. Let her take the cod fish liver oil, but more especially the tincture of iron to give her strength and tone and she will improve.

But "Lelia who is our darling pride; Lelia, bright Lelia Gay who dances lightly by your side all the livelong day." Bless the little bundle of happiness. She has "one tooth." I am rejoiced to hear it and that she got through so well too. I think it better for her bowls to be affected than her brain. Give her some of the diarrhea mixture in the pantry and there is a variety of them to check the bowels. I hope yet to see her with a real full set of teeth and then she can say Dada, Papa and Mamma to perfection.

I am sorry our removal will cut off a contemplated visit. Perhaps Weldon may offer some advantages for a short trip. I will let you know when I get there. You will direct to me letters or any bundle to Weldon, North Carolina as Lt. Col. 48th North Carolina Troops.

Tell John Shoote and H. M. Houston and H.G. Wolf to get me some 6 to 12 dozen eggs, and some 5 to 25 lbs. of good butter and box up and forward to me at Weldon. What I don't need I will divide with the others and it will cost the same. You can pay for them and for the box. Send them by express. We have not eaten many of your pickles yet and still have half the catsup on hand.

We had Lt. Anderson and wife to dine with us yesterday. She is the daughter of Hon. James C. Dobbin of Fayetteville, North Carolina, former Secretary of the Navy under President Pierce and a very clever lady. She is boarding at Mr. W.K. Lane's and she enjoyed herself very much. Her husband is a nephew of Major Huske of my mess. We had a pleasant dinner party and I should have been happy to have had you and Lelia to have graced the table with your presence. Tom Clutts did his best under the pressure of the circumstances. We had fried ham, coffee, biscuit and butter. Got some milk. Had a good rice pudding for the second course and for the third course, sent to us by Farmer Lane, cream and strawberries mixed up with loaf sugar. We had enough at our dinner to take a mess at supper. I hope you will visit Brother William[27] and help yourself or visit my good friend D.A. Covington and get a few messes. I don't know what you will do for salt if you get out.

It is almost impossible to get any. I did not get the coffee I thought to have sent you. I may yet send you 10 to 15 pounds if to be had. I would suggest that you get Mr. H.M. Houston to haul you several cords of his cord-wood and get Hall to cut it up and put it under the house to keep dry for firewood.

The weather is quite cold today (Sunday) and we have fires before our tents. I have recovered my health, in fact was not sick, only troubled in my bowels as before stated.

We go this evening to hear Rev. William Johnson, a Presbyterian, preach in Goldsboro. He is from Lexington in this state and is said to be a great preacher.

If the refugees get to Monroe and you take in any boarders, you must charge them high enough to pay all expenses and for the trouble. They should not pay less than $15.00 per month, but I presume you will not be troubled with them. Our friends generally well. Renty Gley is well. I heard from him yesterday.

I would like to spend this evening with you in closer communion then I am doing at present.

My respects to Miss Lizzie.

Your most devoted husband

## MAY 28, 1862

My wife and Mrs. Chears visited us in camp and remained until June 1st when they left for home and us for Virginia.

## JUNE 2, 1862

Monday. Arrived at Petersburg and Dunn's Hill Camp,[28] healthy and good camp ground, just after Battle of Seven Pines. Remained here and drilled until June 24, 1862.

## JUNE 10–13, 1862

Ordered to go on some unknown expedition with three days rations, started with arms, picks and crowbars on Petersburg & Norfolk Railroad. Had much time and lay in the cars, went 40 miles to Blackwater River and tore up the track and burnt and destroyed the bridges and culverts for some eight miles. Has scarce eating until evening of 12th, got good supper and had good old Virginia Cheer for $.25 and got a house floor to sleep on and arrived in camp Sunday morning 13th for breakfast. We did a very foolish thing to destroy so much of the best railroad in the country I ever saw unnecessarily, for the Yankee had done the same thing on the Norfolk side and taken away the iron, so between friend and foe it is hard to tell from whom old Virginia suffered the most.[29]

## JUNE 12, 1862

◈ Letter from Walkup at Petersburg, Virginia (Dunn's Hill Camp), to wife Minnie:

My ever Charming Minnie,

I had begun to feel fretted because I had not heard from you and calculated to get seriously vexed, if you did not write so that your letter could reach me by tomorrow; when yours of the 9th came to hand today, grateful as the cooling waters to the thirsty throat, or refreshing showers to the summer parched field and gave me the news I longed for so much to hear; that you and darling Lelia, two idols planted nearest and forever in the center of my heart, were both safely at home and well in a great measure. I had feared to hear bad news from home, but it was rather from poor Tilly, or perhaps Lelia, than anyone else as they were both sick, especially the former.

I am quite well and feel considerably better since I heard from you and this is one of nature's loveliest evenings, cool, quiet, clear "and twilight grey has in her sober livery all things clad."

The river Appomattox runs between us and Petersburg nearby, by its falls and dams produces a soothing music calming and pleasant to the feelings of the soul. I think of you and Lelia often and all my nearest friends far away, in the noble Old North [State], and all the joys of sweet home with its tender appreciation cluster around me and then I pray that this terrible war may come to a speedy close, and wish again that I had you, or your own dear self any "your" Baby or "our" darling here with me to enjoy such an evening, the solemn music of the murmuring waters with me.

Joys, comforts and happiness are twofold dearer to us when we are deprived of them and we cannot relish them so well until we feel their want. It is the thirsty soul who delights in refreshing and cooling waters. The fever stricken patient who can appreciate health, the tired wayfaring homeless traveler overtaken by night and dangers in a strange land who can estimate the priceless blessings of "Home Sweet Home" with wife, children and friends around him. And although I am surrounded with health, friends, and all this pleasant scenery, I feel an "empty void still aching in my breast." I feel somewhat lonesome, because the two loveliest objects are waiting in the scene. The casket is here, but the jewels that adorn it and give it value are in Monroe. Now that is poetry enough to do for a good while. I will come down to matters of fact and of business.

I have written to you several letters, the last about the 8th or 9th. We are still at Dunn's Hill in camp and don't know when we will leave. The prospects for a fight at Richmond are growing more uncertain and is thought will never come off, though pretty heavy firing is heard every day in that direction. It amounts to nothing as nobody gets hurt. Stonewall Jackson (who married a daughter of Dr. H. Morrison, [and who] is a brother-in-law of Gen. [D. H.] Hill)[30] is the great excitement now and strong reinforcements are being sent to and against him, and it is thought the great fight will take place with him. The Yankees are becoming alarmed at his success and are thought to be withdrawing their forces from Richmond to send against him, whilst our friends are sending strong reinforcements to him. We may possibly be sent there too, but the prospects are not tending much that way and we will likely rest here, or may go back to Goldsboro.

Dr. Chears has not heard from his wife yet. He is quite well. He and I were talking of getting divorces or running off with some other gal or resigning to come home to whip someone or kill a Yankee, or so some rash thing unless we heard from certain individuals in Monroe. But my better nature has prevailed since your letter arrived and I want to feel like fighting anyone who could doubt that I had the most beautiful, kindest and cleverest wife in Christendom, to say nothing of the Baby. Capt. Wiant, Stitt, Turner, De Lorme, Winchester, Thomas, everybody from Monroe are well. Capt. Wilson's health is not good. He says he will resign before a month.

We had a grand review by General Ransom last Monday. I commanded our regiment which did remarkably well. None surpassed it and General Ransom expressed his admiration at the whole performance as surpassing his most sanguine expectations and which would have graced much older [commanders]. We don't like Ransom much. The ladies of Petersburg were out to see us parade; they were numerous, well pleased and beautiful.[31]

Dr. Miller's letter has never reached me yet. I am glad he got the pistols so cheap. I thought $75.00 each would be the cheapest they could be had for. I am glad you got your coffee and have such a fine garden. I say sell the cow (Fowler) and Dump too, if you want. Tell my good friend Shoote to assist you and give him my best respects.[32] Tell him to send ten pounds of butter and six dozens of eggs put up well in a box with sawdust. Send it by express to Petersburg and I will pay him 25 per cent on the whole cost with many thanks. Eggs here bring $.50 to $.75 per dozen, and butter $.75 per pound, chickens $1.25 and $.75 each, mutton $.35 and beef $.30 per pound. I don't know what I wrote to Brother William. Some nonsense I reckon.

I am glad you have true friends who send you what you need, potato slips, etc. and that you have good mess to eat. We live well here too, The strawberry season is yet upon us. I hope Lelia will soon get through cutting teeth and show a row or ivory when I come home to greet her Da-da-da with.

If she and you and William are spared to me I can bear many hard misfortunes in other respects. Tell poor Tilly to cheer up and you do believe me as happy as circumstances will permit. Lt. Stewart is quite well. Respects to Lizzie and Miss Ellen H.

Yours as ever

[Postscript June 13] We hear firing towards Richmond this morning but not heavy. Good bye my meek, patient, tender, loving and tenderly beloved wife and innocent and joyful child.

## June 13, 1862

❖ Letter from Walkup at Petersburg, Virginia (Dunn's Hill Camp), to wife Minnie:

Well, honey darling, I learned that Mr. Simon Moser was going to leave here today for home tomorrow and therefore detained by letter, knowing you would get it sooner by Mr. Moser than if sent today by mail. As I have expended my fancy figures that you say you cannot appreciate, with occasional flashes of poetry in the first part of this general epistle of Sam to Minnie, I will not put anything of the kind on this continuing note.

We had another grand review today by General Ransom: three regiments of infantry, one or two battalions of infantry and several companies (three) of artillery. It was well done but not so good as we had the other day, though on a larger and a more varied scale, having some batteries of artillery and among them Brem's of Charlotte.

The ladies were out in full trim and a fascination,[33] but not one that I saw had half the charm for me that a certain black-eyed, cherry lipped melting beauty in Monroe has. But whose cherubic baby equals almost her lovely mother. But I forgot this looks like poetry and figures which you say you patiently endure but can't appreciate. Some people may not appreciate beautiful and touching things, but I like eggnog, strawberries, sugar and cream, plum-pudding pastry, etc., etc. But high above them all I adore beauty when it is in possession by me in the person of a lovely wife-child—go figure—I know you can't miss the figure now.

I hope you have paid over to Tom's wife the ten dollars he sent. Tom is well and doing very well. We have no news from Richmond of importance. It is reported that McClellan has withdrawn beyond the Chickahominy River.

I hope this will find you and Lelia well and Libby better.

Let me hear from you often. You can't imagine how much good your letters do me. Kiss "our" precious little darling for me her Da-da-da.

Your own dear loving husband

## June 17, 1862

Ordered out again on secret service which turned out to be to get ice from the Epps house on the branch of the James River and in sight of the gunboats, for the North Carolina Hospital at Petersburg. We got the ice, 11 or 12 wagon loads safely. On the next day marched to City Point two miles from our camp, with 48th and Ransom's 49th North Carolina regiments and guns of Brem's Battery[34] to fire upon the gunboats. Capt. F. L. Wiant's and Capt. A.A. Hill's companies were ordered to fire upon the boats 1000 yards distant from the end of the railroad below the bluff which they did under my command, one volley from each company and then retired, without notice from the gunboats. Brem's two small rifled cannon then opened fire upon the gunboats from the bluff and after three or six rounds having struck the Galena[35] and other ironclad boats (there being others and some transports), they returned. Our guns were about 80 or 100 yards from the bank of the bluff. Myself, Col. Hill and Ransom and Lt. Anderson[36] stood on the point of the bluff and observed the effect of the shot until after the enemy began a severe shelling and we directed when the shot was too low, too high or on either side. Some Minie balls began to whistle about us, and we got under cover of the railroad bank. But as the boats began to move towards us, and one shell from the boats stunned and knocked down two of our artillerists, we all retired back to where the other companions were posted behind a ravine near one-half mile from the river and found the shell raining thick there and spreading consternation among the men.[37] Col. Hill in advance of me some time had ordered the men to retire, and they were doing so quite rapidly when I came up. My horse was where they went from and was much excited and alarmed at the sounds and the firing and falling timbers and when I loosed him, both regiments and all the men except Lt. Anderson were 100 yards ahead of me and crossing a high bank raised over the ravine for the railroad, along which we had to pass. The enemy's fire from above and below were concentrated on this point and was very terrifying and dangerous and shell and shot flew thick and fast and crushed down the timbers. We succeeded in passing free of harm, and though scattered and shelled for a mile further, escaped unhurt and got together and lodged securely with but little to eat, or sleep on. We, however, got a very excellent supper and breakfast for $.50 each, and on the next day we arrived back in camp smartly fatigued and glad to have escaped the dangers to which we had been subjected.[38]

## JUNE 24, 1862

Wednesday left Richmond before breakfast, about sun up, and marched to near Seven Pines about five or six miles on the Williamsburg Road, got some breakfast and took the field, a brisk picket firing kept up and occasionally a wounded or dead man brought in.[39] Marched in line from old field on left of road to woods, lay down there and some of our regiment suddenly took sick and fell back to the river. Co. A (Capt. Wiant) sent forward as scouts. Order came to fall back and take position on right of road in front of battery and near edge of woods, where we lay.

Capt. Wiant's company sent out as pickets. A brisk picket firing kept up occasionally and some smart engagements by a Georgia and Louisiana regiment in front of us. Our battery threw some shells over us, two of which exploded in our lines, wounding one of Capt. Wiant's and one of Capt. Moore's[40] (formally Capt. Alexander's) men in the head. A few of enemy's shells thrown [upon] us and a rifle shot or two whizzed by. We were ordered about 12:00 into the battery, and received some heavy shelling, our battery replied, [an] aide came up and complained that the 48th had fallen back and were not supporting Col. Doles of Georgia regiment in our part. Some sharp remarks between him and Col. Hill, Hill offering to advance and attack. About an hour and a half, either by orders from Gen. Wright, or W. Ransom, or otherwise, we were ordered to advance through a field 500 yards to the edge of woods, upon the enemy, which we did. Capt. Wiant's company still being out as pickets were ordered in and were not with us. We, 480 (men and officers) advanced in line of battle, saw some Yankees firing around further corners of fence into woods on our left. At about 150 or 140 yards received first fire from enemy from woods. We fell and returned a round or two. Brown Laney was here shot in finger just in front of me and Dick Bailey's gun on his left shoulder disabled. I ordered Laney to be still and Bailey to take his gun. We rose and advanced at double quick about 100 yards through fire and again were ordered to fall. Our left having crossed a fence came within ten paces of the enemy in the woods, our center and right in field some 10 to 30 paces of fence and woods on our left, and 50 yards from fence in front. Here we fought under a most galling and murderous fire for ten minutes. Capt. Clegg was severely wounded just in front of me, Adjt. Anderson also, on his left, and others, Capt. Michael[41] on my right ten paces and Capt. Walker on my left 15 paces and several men killed and wounded. The regiment began to retreat, there being only some 20 or 50 left.[42] They retreated in two directions, many towards a house and others to a wood cord pile. I tried to halt them in a ditch and thereafter and some difficulty and threats and aid of Gen. Ransom, who came up here and asked me in a very decided tone, "Col. Walkup, what does all this mean?" I replied that the men had retreated here and I was trying to form them again for another advance, but found it was very difficult to do. He told me to shoot them down if they refused and asked where the men were who refused. I told him some were behind that rail and he went to the rail pile pistol in hand threatening to shoot and accused Major Huske, who was there and wounded, of cowardice. Just before Ransom came I had ordered out Correll[43] with the colors, who came out and stated that he was too weak to go further with them. I ordered him to sit down on the edge of the ditch and the other men to form on him and whilst calling upon the men to come forward, Correll again got behind the wood pile and did not come with the colors when called upon and there were no others belonging to the color guard there. I then seized the colors, remarked that I would carry them. A Virginian officer asked me to let him take them, who ought to have been attending to his own battalion and trying to urge them up. I stated I would carry them myself. Lt. H.M. Miller then came and stated that he was acting lieutenant in Co. G and asked permission of me to carry the flag, stating emphatically to the Virginian that no outsider of the regiment should carry the flag. I allowed Miller to do so. Correll here came up and proffered to take the flag. I refused to let him have it, as he did not come when I wanted him to do so and said Miller should carry it. I then asked if no man would fall in line and Spray stepped up and said, "Colonel, I will go for one." Ransom came up somewhere about this time. He then advanced, I in front of the battalion of about 100 men. The others were scattered, some at the battery, some at the house and others at their places. We took our original ground behind the center about 25 yards from the edge of the woods and were doing so, and as Ransom was speaking to urge us to fight for our dead and wounded (about 50 yards in the rear) a volley was fired at us and Gen. Ransom and aide fled. The 12th and 49th Virginia lined the fence on our right, the 4th Georgia has just come up as our lines gave back in to save Capt. A.A. Hill's company from being flanked and drove fierce at the enemy. The 1st Louisiana also came up on their left and 23rd Georgia. The enemy were driven out of the woods leaving many dead and wounded on the field and were followed by the Georgia and Louisiana with great slaughter in crossing a lane. We took up our dead and wounded, 17 killed and 88 wounded, many of whom have since died, amounting to about 30 or 25 among whom I regret to mention Capt. T. J. Clegg, Sgt. James Nesbit[44] and others of our regiment and best and most gallant boys. We did not find out the number of the enemy killed and wounded but suppose it must have been between 400 or 500 killed and wounded chiefly by the Louisiana and Georgia regiments. We took a markers flag, 20th Indiana and learned from one wounded prisoner that they had three regiments in action and that the woods in their rear was full of Yankees, Hooker's Division, and the Northern papers say Gen. McClellan was that day on that part of the lines, and it was a very important point for them and from which they expected to advance and turn our lines and march upon Richmond.

This day was the opening ball which finally resulted in making the Yankee's army famous for taking such scientific back steps and escaping from Gen. Lee to his gunboats [Walkup's subsequent edit]. Our boys generally fought with great coolness and bravery and had the 4th Georgia, 1st Louisiana, 12th and 49th Virginia moved simultaneously with us, we must have driven the enemy with great loss from the field without our regiment losing more than every fifth man. They did not any of them come to our relief until we fought 10 or 15 minutes, which with balls flying as thick as those came from behind fences and trees, firing both in front and flank, was an age, and sufficient to have annihilated our devoted little band of heroes.[45] Our wounded and some of the Yankees were taken to Richmond and our dead were sent there and buried. Lost in killed and wounded from:

Wilson's Co. F—2 killed and died, [mortally] wounded
Walden's Co. E—2 killed and died, [mortally] wounded

Moore's (Alexander's) Co. I—3 killed and died, [mortally] wounded
Wiant's Co. A (not engaged)—none killed, 2 wounded (Colored)
Walker's Co. C—2 killed and wounded of whom died
Clegg's Co. D and H—3 killed, 6 wounded and 3 officers
Jones's Co. G—2 killed and wounded of whom died
Michael's Co. H—0 killed
Atwood's Co. K—3 killed and wounded of whom died

(Capt. Clegg died about July 9; Major H. B. Huske died July 15, both victims of erysipelas.)

## June 26, 1862

After sending off our dead and wounded to Richmond, we lay in the batteries, most of the day, and at night at near sundown heard heavy firing on the upper Chickahominy near Mechanicsville and New Bridge, which kept up till 10:00 p.m. and began at sunrise the next morning.[46] The first of the great battle on our left by Jackson, Longstreet and the Hills. Gen. Branch and his North Carolina led the attack and Campbell was killed.

## June 27, 1862

We advanced as pickets on our old battleground and beyond it and saw many unburied Yankees still there swollen and fly blown. Col. Vance's regiment and Georgia regiment were in advance of us. Col. Vance's 26th were on picket the night after our fight and suffered some from the firing of the enemy, were in fact driven in panic behind our battalion but again advanced.

Heavy firing still continued on our left wing.

## June 28, 1862

Saturday. We marked ten miles to our extreme left, crossing Chickahominy at new bridge build by the Yankees and arrived at their deserted camps.[47] Viewed the bloody battlefield, where friend and foe lay in thick clusters, which showed the dreadful and well fought contest. It was wonderful how anyone escaped. The camps were full of powder and many of our regiments helped themselves liberally to the spoils. The lines must have been from one to two miles wide and three or more in length driving back line after line and taking battery after battery. The generals gaily dressed looked as if they fought with great gallantry. Many wounded were still on the field and the woods and bushes as well as killed and wounded unfolded a tale of danger and horrors, which few live to witness and but few witness and live. It makes one wish with Cowper for a "Lodge in some vast wilderness" so that his ear may not be pained with war and bloodshed by his fellow man.[48]

## JUNE 29, 1862

Sunday. We were ordered to be ready to march at 1:00 a.m. and got off by 4:00 a.m., recrossed the Chickahominy at New Bridge by daylight and arrived near sundown, opposite to Drewry's Bluff, passing the 43rd North Carolina and others.

## JUNE 30, 1862

Monday. Marched to near Allen's Farm on James River, took up line in a wheat field and in evening advanced to Allen's Farm, again formed line of battle between enemy and river, to cut off his anticipated retreat to his boats. A heavy cannonading and musketry heard about a mile or two off between Longstreet, Jackson, the Hills, Magruder and the Yankees. We placed as flankers on the left, advanced and filed left through woods under severe shelling, that frightened the boys terribly. Our lines kept together, some of the regiment in front of our artillery broke and got into confusion. Graham's Petersburg Battery behaved disgracefully, the 43rd North Carolina got into confusion, 45th and 50th North Carolina also. We fell back about a mile and got no supper or breakfast till late, some crackers and meat after.

## JULY 1, 1862

Tuesday. We formed line of battle and after lying some hours fell back and took dinner (crackers and some meat) and again about 4:00 p.m. advanced to Allen's Farm and formed line of battle and advanced through the woods and lay in a swamp, some shells rattling by us. We again advanced a little beyond the place we occupied the evening previous and could plainly hear the firing of cannon, shell or musketry and cannonades and cheers of the parties engaged. The fight continues four or five hours and until 9:00 or 10:00 p.m. We were said to be within 500 or 600 yards of the enemy line in the bend of Turkey Creek and in front of White Oak Swamp.[49] We then fell back one-half a mile and lay under arms without bed clothing, and some without coats and all without supper or anything to eat Wednesday. We were about forming a line of battle to advance when a very heavy rain came up and we were drenched to the skin. It was then ordered that we fall back two miles and take up our position by Gen. Holmes as both he and Wise concluded from certain indications the enemy had received reinforcements as vehicles were heard to go rapidly to the river and slowly (as if loaded) back. We fell back to the woods behind our wheat field and Eli Stewart and Major Crowell visited us and brought some good things to eat, a fire was kindled and preparations made for drying our cloths and spending a comfortable night. I was ordered to visit some of our sick two miles or three miles in rear and about dark met our other regiments marching in the mud toward Drewry's Bluff. Not being able to cross the creek in consequence of the current of men and wagons and artillery until 11:00 p.m. and despairing of finding my regiment at night, I waited at the Hospital until daylight next morning and getting my clothing and accoutrements set off in pursuit and after passing the pontoon bridge over James River found as fatigued and exhausted, sore footed a set of men as ever ought to march.

## July 3, 1862

I caught up with the regiment and tendered my horse which Capt. H. Wilson rode and we arrived at Drewry's Bluff (passing 53rd and 43rd North Carolina) about 8:00 a.m. Here we struck camp and having nothing to eat were hospitably entertained by Col. Hall of the 46th North Carolina Regiment and remained here and heard a Fourth of July oration.

## July 4, 1862

Friday. Lt. Col. Jenkins[50] of the 46th North Carolina Regiment, my brother Col. William W. Walkup came here this day.

## July 5, 1862

Saturday. Stayed in camp and recruited until July 6th.

## July 6–12, 1862

Sunday. We left camp at Drewry's Bluff and were ordered to march through an excessively hot day to Petersburg and Prince George Court House and after heavy and sultry march arrived at Petersburg in evening, at our old camp and found it had been partly plundered and were at daybreak for marching orders, which however were countermanded Monday. Since which time we remained in our old camp recruiting, with many sick and others taking sick from disease until Saturday when we marched over two miles east of Petersburg to Camp Lee Saturday, July 12.

## July 13, 1862

On Sunday heard our first sermon from our chaplain, Rev. William Johnston.[51]

## July 15–16, 1862

Tuesday. C. Austin, Sheriff[52] arrived and brought news from home. My wife still in Charlotte, my nurse Matilda died Saturday. Wednesday, July 16 heard of the death of our gallant and agreeable friend and fellow soldier, Major B. R. Huske.

## July 17, 1862

Thursday. Bad news from home by Minnie's letter about my beautiful nephew Willie Walker Miller.

## July 18, 1862

Friday. By brother William's second letter. The only hope of his parents, the promising Willie W. Walker, died on Monday 14, 1862, two years, two months and four days old. His parents will scarcely bear the loss. The loan is retaken.

## July 24, 1862

Brigade review at Camp Lee by Gen. French, got a letter from brother Henry Clay Walkup telling of his health and S. Henry Walkup's[53] wounds.

## July 26, 1862

Sent in command of a detachment on fatigue party to throw up entrenchments on Friends Farm, and Capt. Dimmock the engineer not coming, we struck up a camp and got wet Saturday might and returned to Camp Lee Sunday for dinner.

## July 28, 1862

Monday. We were ordered again (9 companies), none from 2nd Georgia Battalion, 3rd Arkansas 2 companies, 30th Virginia [and] 2nd, 27th, 46th and 48th North Carolina 2 companies each (A and E of 48th) on fatigue party and legion entrenchments of railroad near New Market race course on Friend's Farm and remained at work until when we were ordered suddenly back to Camp Lee.

## July 30–August 1, 1862

Began our march, our 48th Regiment under my command, Hill sick. 4th Brigade toward City Point and Daniel's Brigade and Ransom's Brigade and about 40 pieces of artillery, mostly rifled cannon including four heavy siege guns—Long Tom and Charlie and two others not yet christened. The two former I believe were taken from the Yankees at the Battle of Manassas. All under command of Gen. D.H. Hill, Cols. Daniel and Manning being present and in command. All marched cautiously and delayed until about two miles from City Point, and there took a southern direction for eight or nine miles opposite McClellan's camp at William Furrs and about one and one-half miles from the river full of gunboats and transports. The last seven miles of which we passed after dark and arrived at our camp fatigued and hungry, about 11:00, and having no bed clothes lay on the cold ground and without fire, for fear of discovery, being wet with perspiration we became cold and very uncomfortable before morning. My horse came with my bed clothes about an hour after we lay down, but the boy who brought him could not find me, and I only found out that he came next morning. We had some boiled ham and loaf bread and made some coffee, and after dinner moved in lines of battle half a mile or more lower and remained with arms stacked before us all night. The whole evening was raining and we were wet and could have no fire or shelter and had only ham and crackers to eat.[54] Many of the men eat their meat raw. We remained until 2:00 a.m. when our artillery under cover of night, having got into position about 600 yards to a mile of the vessels and camp of the Yankees, opened a heavy and we think a devastating fire and cannonade upon them with their light all burning. They replied to some extent and killed one man and wounded four or five of our artillerists. After half an hour firing they ceased and retired and only got off by daylight. At 3:00 a.m., August 1, 1862, we took up arms and remained under arms until 6:00 in the morning when we began our march back to Petersburg, greatly surprised to have escaped a severe shelling from the enemy; some shelling was done after we left our camp. Our march was harassing and annoying on account of delays occasioned by the moving of the artillery port. We got little or nothing to eat, until we arrived in camp about half an hour by sun. We also held our election of Governor, members of the Senate and House of Commons and Sheriff in our and other regiments on 31 of July. Col. R.C. Hill left August 4 for Statesville.

## AUGUST 6, 1862

Saw Brother Henry Clay Walkup who stayed all night with me. Tom Clutts and Hugh Wilson left for home, Tom to stay until 21 or 22 of August and return with mess sheet and provisions for me. Jim Paxton died in hospital 5th of August.

## AUGUST 9, 1862

Ordered to new camp at Avery's where entrenchments were and are being thrown up. Ground, water and shade inferior to present camp.[55]

## AUGUST 13, 1862

New camp called Camp Stonewall, Gen. J.G. Walker in command. W. Smith, Assistant Adjutant General, drew up charges against eleven deserters Co. E , one Co. F. and two Co. G. and detailed Tysor,[56] Lt. Co. G. and Lt. Dowd[57] [Co. D] to pursue deserters.

## AUGUST 16, 1862

Order at 7:00 p.m. dress parade, to be ready with two day's rations to march to Prince George Court House by 8:00 with 40 rounds of ammunition. Got ready after much importuning to those whose wives, fathers, friends and notables had come in and many had fits of misery somewhere, believed to be in the liver or knees. Went to within one mile of Prince George Court House. The poorest apology I ever saw for a country town in my life, three houses constitute the whole town and they hard cases, returned next day to camp in the evening and found box from William Walkup.

## AUGUST 18, 1862

Col. R. C. Hill returned from Statesville, N.C.

## AUGUST 19, 1862

Eli Stewart's box ($17.10) and freight came to hand. Had orders to march, countermanded and new orders given to march.

## AUGUST 20, 1862

Towards Richmond very dusty march, passed Pontoon Bridge and camped two miles from our first battleground of June 25. Very rainy all night and next day 22nd arrived at camp near Randolph's octagonal house.[58]

## August 23–26, 1862

Richardson arrested and released Sunday 24th by me, and Col. Hill rearrests him and talked of arresting me for releasing him on 26th, Tuesday.

## August 27, 1862

Wednesday. We left Richmond and arrived Thursday morning August 28, by railroad to Rapidan River at 2:00 a.m. the 28th, having passed near Hanover Court House the scene of Gen. Branch's flight in full view and came to foot of Blue Ridge about four miles from Orange Court House and fifteen from Gordonsville and in full view of that beautiful scenery equal to the Catskills or Peakskill on the Hudson, except the evidence in full view of the battlefield between Pope and Jackson of about August 10, the battle fought on north of Rapidan River about four or five miles from railroad bridge.

## August 30, 1862

Saturday. Many forces left for the active army. We had about 15,000 or 20,000 men in camp the night before and our wagons arrived with our baggage today, in good time to save suffering, brought our bedding, clothing and cooking utensils and some provisions.

## Aug. 31, 1862

Sunday. We have orders to march in the morning towards Jackson and Lee, near Manassas.

## September 1–2, 1862

Monday we left Rapidan River and got to Culpepper Court House about twelve miles and had a severe rain and got wet, having passed Rapidan River and Cedar Run, the scene of Jackson's fight with Pope. We left Tuesday, Sept. 2 and came to Jefferson City, about the size of Bellaire, South Carolina.

## September 3, 1862

We came by the White Sulphur Springs owned by William Hutchins or Huggins and burnt by the Yankees, in their vandalism. It is a charming place, and will compare favorably as a watering place with Saratoga, New York. We also passed through Warrenton, a beautiful town, nearly as large as Charlotte or Yorktown, where the ladies are said to have been so rejoiced to see Gen. Stonewall Jackson that they greeted his arrival with cheers and carried water in vessels to his men in the streets. The Yankees had left there only last Tuesday before the fight at Manassas. My baggage, a trunk and contents, were left at the house of Mr. Rice W. Payne and Mr. Semmers, by Major Wiant in the smoke or meat house, who kindly offered to keep it securely. The house was the headquarters of Gen. McDowell shortly before.

## September 4, 1862

We passed Buckland, a small village, and got to Gainsville, near the battleground of Manassas. There I visited the classic ground of two former battles. Beauregard and Johnston-Scott and McDowell, July 21, 1861, which resulted in a rout of the latter but not made effective by the former, and the still more extensive battle of August 28 and 29, 1862, between Stonewall Jackson, Lee, Longstreet, Winder, Ewell and A. P. Hill vs. Generals Pope, Banks, Burnsides, McClellan and Halleck utterly wanting the battle. [Some contend] the victory is greatly exaggerated. I visited the battlefield in the evening and rode five miles in circumference. [Some] think it not half as severe or bloody as the Battle of the Chickahominy near Gains Mill and Cold Harbor. They are in error who say that it was so. Here I hope to correct an erroneous impression made from a wrong view of the case. For hearing so much of the fight I begged and obtained leave to revisit the ground and found where Longstreet fought, on the right of the turnpike, and saw the slaughter of red coat Zouaves. I counted from one point as I sat on my horse 56 Zouaves and did not see all that by slight change of position I might have seen. The line was one-fourth mile long, about 100 yards wide and there must have been from 500 to 700 fallen on the hill, then the valley between that and another hill was pretty thickly strewn with red and blue coats and the hill beyond was strewn with blue coats nearly as thick and extended a mile or so in length and breath. 2000 killed is a fair estimate of Longstreet and his cooperators slaughter besides the wounded and [at] the least exceeding 500 killed. I then went on the left of the turnpike and saw Jackson's operations along a railroad cut and banks. It was awful beyond description,[59] dead men and horses lay rolled in indescribable confusion, about the railroad cut and within ten steps of it a whole regiment of Yankees seems to have fallen to their eternal sleep before the cool and well aimed volleys of Jackson's men. Then the next ranks behind bravely fighting behind rocks were piled almost as thick as they could lie for a half mile or more in length and 150 to 200 yards, in some places a quarter of a mile in width. Some three thousand at least or more must have slept their last uncovered sleep here and lay ghastly grinning and bloated in this desolate Aceldama far beyond the Chickahominy or any battle ever fought on the American continent. In the woods I counted on one tree not exceed six inches in diameter 37 balls, 15 or 20 of which would have struck a man and fired from the Yankee side.

Our forces gave back here, for want of ammunition and recovered driving all before them again with great slaughter. The lines altogether must have extended from five miles in length and three in width. The enemy surely lost more than 5000 slain and our loss in killed could not have been more than 1000 or 1500. All ours were buried and very few of the Yankees. Their loss in killed and wounded must have been 25000, ours not more than 5000 and perhaps less.

## September 5, 1862

I passed by Sudley's Mill on Bull Run, through a barren and poor country to Gum Spring where I took dinner and saw the stragglers pass destroying stocks and corn in their range, and met with our forces at Goose Creek, a rich and pleasant stock and grazing country.

## September 6, 1862

Saturday. We passed Leesburg, Virginia, a handsome and respectable town near which place on the river at a bluff, Gen. Evans drove back the Yankees last fall or spring with great slaughter. We camped at night four or five miles north of Leesburg and in sight of the mountain three miles off, where the notorious John Brown was hung for his raid upon Virginia at Harper's Ferry which is about 15 miles above this place. We were near the Potomac and Point of Rocks near where Gen. Evans whipped the Yankees and drove them into the river.

## September 7, 1862

Sunday. Passed the Potomac River near where Gen. Evans whipped the Yankees at Leesburg, very shallow to about knees, or half thigh deep. The infantry stripped off their pants, drawers, shoes and stockings and the sight was comical to see the boys wading like cranes over the rocky ford and cringing as their tender feet struck the rocky bottom. Our Arkansas and Virginia bands played "Dixie" and "Maryland" as we arrived on the shores of the "U.S." We passed the Ohio and Baltimore Canal and crossed and camped near Buckeystown and encamped near Monocacy River where William Wilson took sick and was left, and where my horse lost his fore shoe and I offered in vain $2.00 to get one old shoe put on and finally gave a Negro of the 24th Regiment $2.00 to make and put on a shoe.

## SEPTEMBER 9, 1862

We camped at the bridge, next night at Monocacy River and the next day went four miles to Jackson, Lee, Hills camp on Monocacy River four miles east, but in sight of Frederick, Maryland. We then returned to Buckeystown and thence by a long and fatiguing night march to the aqueduct on the Baltimore and Ohio Canal over Monocacy River and lay around until near daylight but affected nothing.

We lost one captain not of our regiment shot, and two men taken prisoner. Retired, as it would take two days to destroy the aqueduct bridge, and got to sleep around 4:00 a.m.[60]

## SEPTEMBER 10, 1862

Wednesday. We left one sick and barefoot near Jackson's and the Hills' camp four miles east of Frederick.

## SEPTEMBER 11, 1862

Saturday. At 7:00 last night we left Monocacy River, and left Maryland. Ransom's and Walker's Brigades with several batteries of artillery (24 pieces) and all our baggage train and drove off cattle and after travelling with great fatigue all night, hungry and weary from loss of sleep, we recrossed the Potomac River at Point of Rocks ford about four miles higher up than we crossed before. We halted about half a mile before we got to the river, where the railroad and canal crossed and I was so fatigued that I lay down about 3:00 a.m. and slept until the rear guard of Ransom's Brigade waked me up at daylight, when I crossed the river, passing regiments in their shirt tails and among them Capt. J. T. Davis[61] in 49th enjoying the wade pleasantly and in fine humor. We passed Point of Rocks, a village about the size of Lancaster, South Carolina, on the Maryland shore, and camped half a mile from the river in Virginia. I slept on my horse as we traveled along, and many others, in fact the regiment generally, fell to sleep whenever we stopped to rest, which we did often, as armies with wagons, trains and artillery over rough and hilly roads move annoyingly slow and make the marches more tiresome than faster traveling. The truth is we were alarmed at the danger of being cut off and bagged by Yankees. Two large armies triple our number were understood to be surrounding us, and Jackson, Lee, the Hills,

Longstreet, etc. had left for Baltimore, Annapolis, Harrisburg or north-west and we left in a very precarious position and our Gen. Walker is a timid, cautious man, and lacks energy, vigor and sagacity and Ransom has still less. Rockets were seen going up and pickets were hovering around us and rapidly galloping off, so Ransom told Major Wiant. The move may have been prudent and proper, but it strikes me that our march ought to have been directed towards Jackson and our main army. But I suppose Walker was obeying orders and the move was strategic.

## SEPTEMBER 12–14, 1862

Marched through Piedmont Valley, a fertile, picturesque, real scenery, and over the mountains, rather a disaffected Dutch community, houses neat, tidy and farms also stone fences and [stone] houses. Camped near town of Hillsboro, a rock built town and a pleasant country beyond the mountain. We surrounded and entered a narrow valley, moved towards Harper's Ferry, which we reached Saturday the 13th and were greeted with shell upon our arrival. Kept watch on the Harper's Ferry road until daylight, then went to the top of the Loudoun Heights, where we remained all the day, Sunday, Sept. 14th overlooking the splendid scenery here, and the meeting of the Potomac and Shenandoah Rivers from opposite points and then bursting through the Blue Ridge and draining a vast region leaving it very fertile between the two rivers and some 80 miles in extent, a scene which Thomas Jefferson said that a trip across the Atlantic Ocean was worth to behold. We had nothing to eat until in the evening and about one o'clock a severe cannonading was opened from Harper's Ferry upon our lines on Loudoun Heights, and our Jackson and Hills on the northwest between the river and upon McLaws' Division on Maryland Heights on the southeast. Gen. Miles commanded the Yankee's forces.[62] Some musketry was heard late in the evening. Lt. Robinson of French's Battery was killed and Major F. L. Wiant of 48th North Carolina was slightly wounded on the shin bone of the left leg by a fragment of a shell whilst sitting securely, as he thought, behind a block house. We remained all night on the north side of the mountain without clothing or provisions, to watch the road leading up the Shenandoah River and prevent the escape of the Yankees. Next morning heavy cannonading began shortly after daylight, Monday, Sept. 15th from Gen. Jackson on the side of the mountain we occupied and was replied to by the enemy's batteries and ours all joined. Soon our musketry opened and soon the enemy sent up the white flag and surrendered 14,000 men with a loss of only two killed and a dozen wounded on our side and not many more killed and wounded on the enemy's. Some say 300 Yankees killed. Gen. Miles was killed or mortally wounded. We did not visit the battleground but walked to our camp up the river Shenandoah five miles and crossed bare-footed at Colbert's Mill and took tea which was very fine. We helped ourselves without leave in the morning to loaf and butter, honey and milk, peaches, pears, apples and grapes. I offered the widow lady [when she] returned afterwards pay. She refused and said we were welcome.

## SEPTEMBER 16–17, 1862

We left at 2:00 a.m. and marched about 18 or 19 miles to opposite Shepherdstown, crossing by wading, I among the rest. I walked all the way, leaving Major Wiant my horse, as he was wounded. We got something to eat for supper, beef boiled on the coals and left without breakfast before daylight to be drawn up in line of battle about one and one-half miles to our right (the 17th) and remained there until about 10:00 a.m. and were then ordered to our left in great haste where the enemy were hotly pressing Gen. Jackson.[63] After a hurried march of two miles we reached the field of battle and went immediately into action, through a piece of woods facing a terrible fire of artillery and musketry.[64] Several of our men were killed and wounded in the woods and many hesitated and took shelter behind trees and could not be forced forward. When we passed the woods we crossed a fence and under a most galling fire of grape and canister from the artillery and musketry and many of our force could not be rallied beyond the fence. I drew my pistol and threatened to shoot and scolded but with very futile effect. I mounted the fence and moved forward exposed to a terrible fire which swept everything before it and saw our regiment breaking and the whole gave way in confusion and retreat in disorder. I tried to rally them in the woods behind the brow of a hill, but was not aided by our Colonel Commandant, who led the retreat [and was] not listened to by the men. Capt. Richardson,[65] Turner[66] and Witherspoon[67] and part of Walden's Company were disposed to aid me but the Colonel having left, the men followed and left the 2nd or 22nd South Carolina begging us to stand by them. They however had better shelter than we, and many of our men fell here, among whom were the gallant Lt. Witherspoon and Private James Winchester, and we fell back to a rock wall, where I with difficulty retained about 100 men from Turner, Richardson and Walden's[68] Co. E, making the most of the force. After some ten to fifteen minutes our Colonel returned with 20 or 50 men from about 100 yards in our rear and formed with us and the 2nd or 22nd South Carolina (about 50 men) and a Mississippi regiment of equal number. We suffered a galling and terrible shelling here, without damage and after an hour or more were ordered off further to the left, where we got water and took a position in the woods and had the most frightful shelling I ever yet heard.[69] We then, having had nothing to eat all day, took up camp, and roasted some roasting ears and ate and receiving an order from Gen. D.H. Hill went back to find his lines and came where we rallied by the stone wall and slept on the ground without cover all night, very comfortably.[70]

## September 18, 1862

Wednesday. We took up position at the edge of the woods where we had just fought the day before and visited our wounded and dead under a flag of truce. We removed them and buried our dead and picked up some India rubber wrappers and hammock, etc., helping the wounded, friends and foes, to water which they begged for so earnestly. I let the Yankees have their wounded from our side of the picket and talked with some of their officers, who began to discuss the tiresomeness of the war and argue for Union. I replied that, "That was not a subject we could hold discussion, however glad we would be for the war to end." They took good care of our wounded, better than we did of theirs I fear.

## September 19, 1862

Saturday. We left about 11:00 p.m. and with great caution marched all night through mud and by very difficult road, crowded by two or more brigades abreast, striving for the way, and waded the Potomac on our retreat towards Winchester, or south. I walked and let Major Wiant have my horse. I was greatly fatigued. We crossed the river five miles below Shepherdstown about daybreak and one man of the 46th was killed by accident of his gun. The cavalry was left to detail their crossing of the river. The river banks were very steep and slipping and almost every man fell down. They all clung to each other and pulled up by hard labor. Our clothes were wet and we exhausted by marching and hunger and loss of sleep, fell down on the top of the hill and slept an hour and dried by fire and continued to march. The enemy soon came up and after heavy cannonading were replied by our artillery, at right a great number crossed over and were being completely severed by us. After dinner we continued our march to a bridge on the Opequon River near Martinsburg, having crossed the Baltimore and Ohio Railroad and late at night took up camp.

## SEPTEMBER 20, 1862

We about faced and marched back to the turnpike five miles south of Shepherdstown, where after zigzagging without any definite object until evening, we left at the most harassing and inconvenient time imaginable (after dark), when we might have more easily have gone at 3:00 p.m., and repassed by a different route to rear the place from which we had started in the morning and marched the 15 or so miles over a rough and hilly and dark road, so dark in many places that we could not tell whether we were in the road or in the woods. The artillery got lost and most of the troops worried through to about a mile from our former camp at the bridge near Opequon Creek by nearly daylight. This morning Major Wiant suddenly resigned his commission, which was accepted and he left for home by way of Winchester, carrying letters to my wife and William and Dr. Miller from me and my India rubber coat to my wife. Marion A. Helms[71] was also taken in a dying condition to Winchester Hospital with several other wounded.

## SEPTEMBER 21, 1862

Sunday. We remained in camp all day at the bridge over Opequon creek or river two miles from Martinsburg near the northern point of Virginia about 20 miles from Maryland and 30 from Pennsylvania. Col. Hill becomes more complaisant and consults me for the first time on the appointment of officers. William Wilson[72] appointed 2nd Lt., Walker's Co. C and William D. Howard[73] elected 3rd Lt. [Hugh] Wilson's Co. F, Richardson promoted to Captaincy of Co. F. We go in washing and wash, or rinse, our clothing and Capt. Turner, Lt. D. and J. Stitt[74] wash shirts and drawers and look for body lice. The night cold and men have no blankets or bed clothing, all left behind near battlefield.

## SEPTEMBER 22, 1862

Monday. Tom washes my clothing in Opequon River and we remain in camp today.

## SEPTEMBER 23–25, 1862

Received letters from Minnie by William Corr from her and William by R.C. Delong and Miller Walkus.

## SEPTEMBER 28, 1862

Sunday. Still in camp. Left Opequon River Saturday 27th, came in Longstreet's Division, to which we are attached, to four miles from Winchester, a fatiguing march of 20 miles.[75]

## OCTOBER 1, 1862

Wednesday. Still at camp near Winchester. The scene of Jackson's battle with [Nathaniel Banks].

## OCTOBER 4, 1862

Saturday visited Winchester, a nice town of 5000 inhabitants.

## OCTOBER 5, 1862

We changed camp about three-fourths of a mile towards Winchester. Great want of forage. Col. Hill gets a furlough for 40 days and Major Hill is in town attending to his brother.

## OCTOBER 10, 1862

Friday. Officers examined by Board detailed to go to Raleigh for clothing etc. 51 suits received from C.S.A. at $16.00 each.

## OCTOBER 11, 1862

❖ Letter from Walkup at camp near Winchester, Virginia to North Carolina Governor Z. B. Vance:

> Governor Z. B. Vance,
>
> I lay before you for your consideration the destitute condition of our regt. with the hope that you, who have experienced some of the severe trials of a soldier's life, may hasten up the requisite relief.
>
> We have present six hundred and nineteen men rank and file in the 48th Regt. N.C. Troops. There are of that number fifty-one who are completely and absolutely barefooted, and one hundred and ninety-four who are nearly as bad off, as barefooted, and who will be altogether so, in less than one month. There are but two hundred and ninety-seven blankets in the regt. among the 619 men, which is less than one blanket to every two men.
>
> In truth there is one Company (I) having 66 men and only eleven blankets in the whole company. The pants are generally ragged and out at the seats and there are less than three cooking utensils to each company. This sir is the condition of our regt. upon the eve of winter here among the mountains of Va. cut off from all supplies from home and worn down and thinned with incessant marchings, fighting and diseases—can any one wonder that our regiment numbering over 1250 rank and file has more than half its no. absent from camp, and not much over one third (449) of them fit for duty? The country

is filled with stragglers, deserters, and sick men and the hospitals are crowded from these exposures. A spirit of disaffection is rapidly engendering among the soldiers which threatens to show itself in general straggling and desertion, if it does not lead to open mutiny.

Add to this that our surgeons have no medicines and don't even pretend to prescribe for the sick in camp, having no medicines and you have an outline of the sufferings and prospective trials and difficulties under which we labor.

What is said of the 48th N.C. is equally true of other regiments in the service from N.C. and from other states too. But you are aware how the matter stands with N.C. The State agreed to and did receive from the Confederate government the commutation money and assumed to furnish clothing, shoes, blankets, etc. to the soldier.[76] This she has utterly failed to do, or to give the commutation money in lieu thereof. She has received the money and has failed to furnish the clothing for which she has been paid by the Confederate government. Our regiment entered the service 1st of April last. They received generally one suit each except socks, and nearly all received one pair of shoes. Only about one third of them received any blankets and very few of those who furnished their own blankets have been paid any money by way of commutation. We have passed six months in the service and you well know we have received hard service during that time. Our scanty clothing, which we had [obtained] independently of the government of either N.C. or the C.S. has been lost for the want of the means of transportation; and finally all that we had, except what we had on our persons, was lost when we crossed the Potomac after the later battle of Sharpsburg, Sept. 17th. This of course was no fault of N.C. but one of the misfortunes of war. I mention these things to show that our destitution is no fault of the regiment. It was in fact mainly the fault of the misfortune of the C.S. government in not furnishing us with sufficient means of transportation and the casualties incident to war. But what I do insist upon now is that North Carolina who always has maintained a character for the prompt and faithful performance of all her contracts, should now exert herself to her utmost capacity with her patriotic energy and zeal to supply these just and pinching wants of her own citizens and save them from the extreme sufferings now rapidly approaching and already felt in the coming winter. Just think of our ragged and barefoot men with one blanket only and scarcely one to any two men and having no tents, or even flies to shield them from the cold rains and winter blasts in this northern clime, having so few cooking utensils that their constant use cannot supply the demands of the regiment, and having no medical supplies, and having no other rations except of flour and eternal beef. And think of the sick, who constitute nearly two-thirds of our army, in such a condition. And surely, surely with these facts before them, the generous and patriotic State of N.C. will be just and faithful in fulfilling the engagements which she had made to and been paid for by the Confederate States. She will thus alleviate the miseries likely to befall her own sons, and save them and herself from their disgrace that may otherwise obscure their fair fame, and darken her history now proudly standing forth among the brightest of the Southern States or of the nations of the earth.

What we most pressingly need just now is our full supply of blankets, of shoes and of pants and socks. We need very much all our other clothing too. But we are in the greatest need of these indispensable articles and must have them, and have them Now. Otherwise how can the Government blame the soldier for failing to render service, when it fails to fulfill its stipulated and paid for contracts? A contract broken on one side is broken on all sides and void. If N.C. cannot fulfill her contract for clothing, blankets and shoes, she ought to rescind it and refund the money and let the C.S. government do it. Or measures should be immediately taken to give free transportation with security from loss by the way, to such articles as the parents, wives and friends of the suffering soldiers would immediately and joyfully send from home to their relief, and the State should pay over the commutation money to those furnishing the supplies, which indeed they would generously furnish at any sacrifice, without pay, if they were assured the gift would reach the beloved objects of their bounty and not be lost on the way. The State should however promptly pay for it and thus relieve the destitute family of the soldiers for the sacrifice made to him in his necessities and thus doubly bless in both giving and receiving favors.

The soldiers of the 48th N.C. and from all the State will patriotically suffer and bear their hardships and privations as long as those from any other State, or as far as human endurance can tolerate such privations, but it would not be wise to experiment too far in such times and under such circumstances as now surround us upon the extent of their endurance. With Lincoln's proclamation promising freedom to the slaves, what might the suffering, exhausted, ragged, barefooted, and dying non-slaveholders of the South, who are neglected by their government and whose suffering families at home are exposed to so many evils, begin to conclude?[77] Would it not be dangerous to tempt them with too great trials?

Dear Sir, you will please not to consider me obtrusive in this communication to your Excellency. I feel the very earnest and solemn responsibility of my position as commander of this regt. at this critical period and under these trying circumstances and wish to do all I can to remove the evils by seeking a speedy supply of blankets, shoes and clothing and therefore beg your earnest attention to the premises and your zealous and I hope efficient aid to supply our necessities. I send with this paper Lt. R. H. Stitt of Co. A 48th Regiment N.C. in whose care any clothing etc. will be attended to in the promptest manner, and who also can give any further information required of the condition of this regiment. The Quarter Master, Capt. Hayne, is too sick to leave his post.

Hoping to hear a favorable response and receive a speedy supply I remain very respectfully[78]

> Your Excellency's most obedient Servant
> S. H. Walkup Lt. Col. [Commanding]
> 48th Regt. NC Troops

## OCTOBER 13, 1862

Monday. R.H. Still left for Raleigh on business for regiment and McNeely[79] and Alex Godfrey[80] died at hospital 10th or 12th.

## OCTOBER 17, 1862

A slight skirmish upon some of our cavalry yesterday. The enemy said to be advancing from Martinsburg, Shepherdstown and Harpers Ferry or Charlestown in heavy forces upon us. We were aroused 1:30 a.m. and ordered to be ready to move by daylight [on] 17th. We got ready but did not march. I drew pay from Capt. Hayne for from 9th of April to 1st of May and from 1st of June to 1st October at $170.00 per month, [for a total of] $799.00 and sent $500.00 home to my wife by Capt. John W. Walden through Commissary R. R. King,[81] with orders if my wife was not home to pay over the $500.00 to H.M. Houston for her and have Walden's receipt for it. I paid Capt. Turner $10.00 borrowed of him and owe nothing except to F.W. Poer $50.00 my note for borrowed money, and have on hand $300.00. I fear we will get into a heavy fight in a day or two and if so will in trust my friend R.R. King and my trusty boy Tom Clutts to take charge of me and my effects in case of accident. I made my will today and signed one made some days ago and had it witnessed by Dr. Chears and J. R. Winchester, dividing equally my property between my beloved wife and child and giving the household and kitchen furniture to my wife extra with other things therein mentioned.

◆ Letter from Walkup at Winchester, Virginia, camp to wife Minnie:

My very dear beloved and affectionate wife:

Your last letter, which was looked for with suspense, dated 8th October, was received 15th October and was very grateful to my hearing heart. I apprehended that I would hear bad news from home, somehow or other, and your letter dispersed by fears.

I was happy to learn that you and Lelia and William and family and all the rest were well and that you had visited and found them all so kind and clever. The fact is my dear we have great reason to be thankful for so kind, affectionate and self-denying friends and we should be, as we no doubt are, grateful for it and equally kind and attentive to their wants and comforts and let them see how highly we prize and appreciate such disinterested worth and whole generosity.[82]

I wrote by Capt. John Walden, who has resigned, but who has not yet got off, and sent one or two letters by him by mail. I will probably send this by him also if I see him, and if I send it by Capt. Walden and can get my money due me, $799.00, I will enclose $500.00 to you. If I send by mail or don't get the money, I shall enclose nothing.

You see my love, if I could do as you suggest, which would be so grateful to us both, viz., "Resign and come home", I could not make more than one or two hundred dollars in this year. But if I remain in the service, although exposed to considerable danger, I can send you money enough to make you and Lelia comfortable, though at a great sacrifice to us all. Yet many have to sacrifice much more for much less pay. Some lose friends and all get only $11.00 per month and clothing and rations if they miss wounds and death, and my clothing and rations will not cost more than three or four hundred dollars per annum. It may cost still more as things are getting much higher. Bacon brings here $.75 per pound, honey $.50 to $1.00 pound, butter $.75 to $1.25, etc. with other things.

We had orders tonight at 1:30 a.m. to be ready to march at daylight and the whole camp is busy cooking and packing up. I suppose we will move south, but don't yet know to what place we will go. I will write and inform you as soon as we reach the point of our destination.

It is said we were defeated at Corinth, Mississippi by General Rose-
crans who defeated Van Dorn, Price and Lowell.

But reported that Gen. Bragg has defeated Gen. Buell with great
slaughter in Kentucky, and Gen. Stuart has made incursion into
Pennsylvania and taken about 1,000 to 1,500 horses and as much
clothing and shoes as his men could carry and destroyed immense
amounts of U.S. stores, probably two to four millions of public property destroyed and he returned safe to Virginia. He captured many of
the things saying that he pressed them into the service of the U.S. for
Gen. McClellan.

I read all your letters and as I have stated before, the one sent by
William Coon came the day after Capt. Davis left today.

My health is tolerably fair. I am somewhat troubled with my bowels,
dysentery, but doing pretty well. Dr. Chears has no medicine and Dr.
Lindsey will return in a day or two but without medicines. We might
as well have no surgeon as no medicine. In fact it might be questionable whether we would not be better off without either surgeons
or medicines.[83] Tom is well and glad to hear from Lelia and sends
love to her and wishes her to write him a letter soon, so that he can
hear from her. He has no clue to his money, though I believe a fellow
named Eber Griffin[84] got some money. I had him searched with some
others, one of them a Rogers[85] (son of Rushing Rogers) but we only
found them with $16.00 (Griffith) and $10.00 (Rogers) when they
had declared they had none at all or not exceeding a dollar a few days
before. Tom is making some again and has $5.00 or $10.00.[86]

We had a heavy rain last night and felt a fine sense of comfort as we
were shielded from the pattering drops by our fly and Indian rubber
clothes over our bedcovers, but many a poor fellow in camp had to
take it as it fell and stand by the fires, yet they seem cheerful and bear
it bravely.

William Baucom[87] and Britton Belk[88] are right sick in camp. J.S.
Godfrey in hospital and Henry Moser in camp with a cough. It is now
sun-up and we are still here. I may add to this letter perhaps in pencil.
Give my love to all and kiss my delightful Lelia.

Your loving husband in haste

[Postscript] I got my pay $799.00 and send you $500.00 by Capt.
Walden, who is as honest a man as we can meet with who will be sure
to hand it to you, if he gets home safely. It makes a big roll and can't
be put in the letter—all in $5.00, $12.50 40 sheets $500.00. Perhaps

the bills may be changed for larger bills which can be more conveniently carried. It is not worthwhile to let everybody know you have money. It might tempt someone to rob you. If you don't like to keep it by you, you can put it in care of my friend Howard Houston. Ask him to put it in his safe and give you a receipt for the amount. You can draw it as you need it. You could also pay C. Austin for his house rent, or pay anybody that you or I owe, or let Brother Mac have any he may want via. Capt. Walkup, things you can get from the farm.

[Postscript, Oct. 1862] Love, it seems Capt. Walden will never get off. It has been two weeks since he applied for leave to go, and he is still here. I have written about one/two letters to send by him and enclose three and this last note and shall write more by him. I will send by mail in a few days.

I am about well, and we are still in camp here. I will send someone from my regiment to Charlotte to be there the 10th or 20th days of November next to receive any clothing the friends of the 48th Regiment may wish to send and they will go safely—socks, shoes, pants, blankets, quilts, etc. You can send my things the same time—a couple of linen shirts and drawers would be comfortable. You can send them, and if I don't come home, you can make them whether I do or not. Make them long in the sleeves, tail and legs.

Love, then again

## OCTOBER 20, 1862

We are still in camp and did not move. We were reviewed today by Gen. Longstreet and I have seen reviews of militia much better done. I saw but don't know Gen. Longstreet. I saw where he was but did not identify him. We had two more brigades out. Gen. Ransom commanding my regiment was on the left of Walker's Brigade and had to begin the movements quickly. I was scarcely able to do duty from dysentery but got through.

## OCTOBER 23, 1862

Thursday. Walker's and Ransom's Brigades, with Branch's and French's Batteries (Walker's Division) left camp near Winchester and marched 16 miles to Millwood, a fine looking little village near the Shenandoah River and about 15 from Harper's Ferry, where we took up camp. I left my $500.00 with a letter to my wife to be taken to her by Capt. Walden, but after dark he came to the regiment and is still with us.

## OCTOBER 27, 1862

Last night near Upperville, Virginia, was an awful night in camp upon soldiers, without tents and blankets, cold, raining and very high winds, tents blew down and got all wet. We moved camp to a place very windy and cold. Still got back and no prospects of clothing.

## OCTOBER 28, 1862

Tuesday. Sent detail from each company here for twenty days to get shoes, clothing and blankets. Turner (A), Mabry[89] (B), Potts[90] (C), Dowd (D), Plyer[91] (E), Simpson[92] (F), Tysor (G), Smith[93] (H), Howie[94] (I), and Stafford[95] (K), and Beasley[96] to Richmond ten days for knapsacks, got big apples from Mrs. Carter by Tom and sent one by Turner home to Minnie, weight one pound. Move camp in morning.

## OCTOBER 29, 1862

Wednesday. We were waked up at 4:00 a.m. and ordered to be ready to move at a minute's notice as the Yankees were advancing, we got up and moved off. I leading our brigade and after starting remained standing until 9:00 a.m. when we moved three miles to Paris and took up camp and as soon as we struck camp the order came again, stating that the enemy were between there and Upperville at present, less than three miles behind.

## OCTOBER 30, 1862

We were ordered to be up and ready and left at 7:00 a.m. for Middleburg with 27th and 48th and two guns of French's Battery for mill five miles from Middleburg. [Obtained] thirty barrels of flour and two loads of bacon. We got back at night with many complaints and excuses, sore feet, pains innumerable, calluses plenty too.

## OCTOBER 31, 1862

Friday. We are ordered to go back and move at 7:00 and camped on top of mountain.

## NOVEMBER 1, 1862

Very pleasant on top of a mountain in Piedmont valley. Extra Billy Smith's District a fertile, tidy, picturesque and polished society, with fine homes, densely populated, the country one of the finest looking places yet seen. Late camping, men are greatly fatigued. We took our start early, crossed one branch Rappahannock and came near Jeffersonville, about 15 miles from Culpepper Court House. Made about 12 miles, got near Amissville, which we avoided on account of smallpox.

(Got my trunk, cloths and liquor from North Carolina from Warrenton 29th October. Near Paris all night.)

## NOVEMBER 2, 1862

Sunday. We reached Culpepper Court House and there met Longstreet's Division, camped in an old piney field.

## NOVEMBER 3, 1862

Fine weather. Wrote home to William Walkup and Millie and Lt. Beasley, Richmond, Virginia. Stephen Timmons arrived in camp from home all well. The boys yelled at the railroad whistle.

## NOVEMBER 4, 1862

Tuesday. We camped at battlefield of Cedar Run and had our baggage brought from Richmond to Culpepper.

## NOVEMBER 6–8, 1862

It snowed and blew very cold night of 5th and 6th and on our next day, we sent for our baggage in the cold, part got theirs and we were under marching orders, but sent some, over 100, back next day, Saturday, to overlook the baggage and follow. We began our march about 3:00 p.m. and marched over Robertson River, which was waded and very cold, and took up camp about 9:00 p.m. very cold. We left baggage and guns and detailed our guard to stay with it and some flour. They moved up next morning, as did the detail for clothing.

## NOVEMBER 9, 1862

We passed a most splendid river, the mountains covered with snow and interspersed with sunshine, clouds and shades and passed Madison Court House near which at 12:00 we struck camp.

## NOVEMBER 10, 1862

Left Monday [today] for west of town.

❖ Letter from Walkup at Madison Court House to wife Minnie:

My dear wife Minnie:

I wrote to you last from Culpepper Court House since which time we have removed to this place about 16 miles. We left Cedar Run

Mountain Friday evening and marched in the night until about 8:00 crossing and wading Robertson River (I mean the regiment). They said it was very cold. We passed some fine mountain views yesterday. The mountains were covered in snow. The sun gleamed out in spots over the scene, though we were in the shades and clouds and quite cold. The view was spotted like a huge leopard skin, or heaps of iced pound cake with green boughs for dressing. We got to Madison Court House about 12:00 yesterday, Sunday 9th and have remained here quite comfortably dining on sweet and Irish potatoes, cabbage, apple pies, chicken and turkeys in addition to our usual meals. They can be bought on reasonable terms. We had a cold snow and wind last week at the battlefield of Cedar Mountain, and got a good part of our baggage from Richmond there. We have several tents and flys and could have had more, but we cannot carry them. I sent by Sgt. Beasley to Mr. Potter 13 lbs. sugar in Culpepper and we are doing pretty well.

Col. Hill has not yet returned. Capt. J.T. Davis has arrived and says that Samuel Neal is well this morning. He is in our division. Gen. Walker has left and we are under the command of Gen. Ransom and Brig. Gen. Cooke.[97] You will direct to me at Richmond, Ransom's Division, Cooke's Brigade. We don't know which way we will move nor when we may remain around here for a few days and then go toward Richmond. The Yankees are south of us and keeping Stuart's cavalry at bay and driving them back. We may have an attack from them or make one before long. We hear heavy cannonading this morning in that direction about 25 miles off. I don't know when Capt. Turner and company will find us on their return as we all keep moving.

I have no additional news to send you. If you get the newspapers from Richmond you will find them more reliable than the news from camp which is very uncertain and contradictory. Jackson's Corps is about Warrenton. D.H. Hill's about Paris and towards Culpepper Court House and Longstreet's about and below (south of Culpepper Court House). Gen. Siegel is in Jackson's rear about Leesburg, and McClellan and Burnsides may be about there too. I don't know who is between us and Richmond. We have no news from Lt. Gen. Stuart. We heard today by a paroled prisoner of regiment who has returned to this camp that James McKey is dead and he helped to bury him at the hospital in Sharpsburg, Maryland in the 26th September. I think this may be considered true and reliable. The informant is from this regiment and was with McKey. J.J. Costly[98] is dead also of Co. F. Our boys are not suffering as much as they did before we got our baggage as most have got a change of clothing, some got shoes and some got blankets.

I have not heard from you since 17th October at McDowells. I wish to know whether you got the $500.00 I sent to you by Capt. Walden and wish to know whether you wish to keep Hall next year and carry on a small farm at Monroe, if we can rent Chears Farm,[99] and whether you prefer renting Austin's house again or not, and at what price, or whether you will take some other place, suit yourself. But make Austin take less and do a good deal more about fixing up his lot fences. I presume you have sent my things by Capt. Turner before this letter arrives.

I can't promise any time to get home, much as we both desire it. I know I would feel better if I could get home a few days. For I feel right smartly worn down and not altogether well. Yet I can't say I am sick either. My horse still limps a little but not so bad. Tom Clutts is well and doing finely. We still have little or no sickness in camp now. We sent our sick off to Richmond from Culpepper.

My love, you must get Mr. H.M. Houston and John Shoote and G.P. Houston to assist you in anything you need, such a wood, provisions, etc., during the absence of Brother William. They will attend to your wants. You had better make a contract for wood with Mr. Michael Osborn and not get out of wood. I am sorry you did not get flour in time before it got so high, but you must get it as you need it.

I dreamed of you and Lelia last night. Oh how I wish dreams would sometimes prove realities. I saw Lelia smiling, her eyes gleaming with childish glee, walking and looking at me courting notice and climbing up the steps to come to me and you were sitting by me looking well pleased with her childish efforts to reach us. Oh how much more cheerfully could we endure all these deprivations if we knew they would have a speedy termination. But I fear we have a long and bloody time to come on yet before peace will be made and unless Providence in His mercy aids us in some way unforeseen, I yet fear the final results may be disastrous to our Cause. The North fight with endless perseverance and the South are becoming exhausted, demoralized and sick of the continued drain upon her resources. God's Will be done. I hope and believe we will come out victorious.

Stephen Timmons got back from home to camp here last week. He called on you but you had not yet returned to Monroe, and from last accounts you had not reached there the 26th October. I expect to hear from you at all events by the 18th November, when Turner gets back.

Give my love to Brother William and Jane, Jimmy Houston and family, Stephen, Julia, Sally and Able, and my respects to my friends in Monroe. Tell Major Wiant I am happy to hear that he has begun the practice of medicine, accountancy, etc. Dr. Chears wears his overcoat and it does him good service.

Keep my darling babe for us both my own dear Minnie and let us hope that in good time we shall meet again and be happy until then.

Believe me your faithful and affectionate husband

## November 11, 1862

Petitioned for furlough for 25 days on grounds of private business. Witness in capital case, State vs. Richards, and bring supplies for four companies of 48th Regiment.

## November 13, 1862

Thursday. Renewed petition for leave of absence.

## November 16, 1862

Sunday. News of McClellan's disgrace and Burnside's elevation. Had rawhide overshoes made yesterday. Still in camp at Madison Court House. Name of a good red apple Milan. Letters from home and William.

## November 18, 1862

Tuesday. Got returned of my application for a furlough disapproved. Took up march for Orange Court House at 9:00 a.m., thence for Hanover Junction at 1:30 a.m. the 19th. Orange Court House weather moist and warmer. We left Orange Court House and arrived Mt. Church about 17 [miles] towards Fredericksburg. Received letter today from Col. William Walkup stating insurrection among Negroes etc., of his difficulty with Jasper Shannon[100] about John Shannon's[101] falling out before battle of French's Farm, and Hugh Wilson, Captain, statement that John Shannon was in the fight. Now Capt. Wilson is mistaken as Lt. F. Richardson well knows and John Shannon admits he was not in the fight at French's Farm 25th of June 1862. He took suddenly sick that morning just before or at the time we went out to the battleground and did not leave camp and he fell out on the march before we crossed the Chickahominy two days after pretending to be sick with John Miller McDowell,

King and Wolf. Wolf fainted at French's Farm and none of the above rejoined us until after Friday 27th June until we returned to Petersburg about 10thJuly. I make this record for the truth of history and know it to be true. Shannon acted cowardly from the first day after volunteering, tried various ways to get off then and finally came under compulsion to camp when I sent Lt. B. F. Richardson for him with orders to bring him in handcuffed. A correct statement I find upon further inquiry from W.D. Howard is that John Shannon was in the fight on 25th of June at French's Farm. That he was close to him and saw Shannon shooting wildly, nearly straight up and called for him to shoot lower. It was on the 26th June, that next day after the fight, that John Shannon fell out pretending to be sick, when we were again ordered to the breastworks and when we fully expected to have a fight. He left with the baggage and he continued to remain sick on the next day after when we went to our old battleground on picket duty and was not there but remained in camp 27th. There early in the morning of 28th we were sent up and crossed the Chickahominy River ten miles, where heavy firing had been heard, and John Shannon, Miller, Wolf, King and McDowell all took sick and fell out before we reached our breastworks on this side of the river and there staid, until after we returned and passed to Malvern's Hill, Drewry's Bluff and Petersburg where they returned to camp. He, Shannon, was sick and left in Petersburg when we went to Maryland and fought at Sharpsburg and did not return until we reached Opequon near Winchester sometime one or two weeks after the Sharpsburg fight and he has now fallen back again whilst we are on the road to Fredericksburg and expecting a fight Nov. 21, 1862. These facts I know and am confirmed by the testimony of William D. Howard, First Lt. B.F. Richardson, Second Lt. Hugh A. Grey and all the company. It was rather more disgraceful to fall out on the day after the battle which we got into rather unexpectedly, than upon the next two days when we really expected the next [battle] when the heavy firings on the Chickahominy we felt pretty sure we would get into a big fight. Add to this his shuffling to keep from coming to the regiment, his brother Andrey's bad conduct and his brother Jasper's conduct in staying at home and it makes an exceedingly unenviable record for the patriotism and bravery of the Shannon family. So much for that.

## NOVEMBER 21, 1862

Friday. We left Spotsylvania Court House and got to Jinnys or Guinea's Station and turned suddenly to Fredericksburg where we expected to fight.[102] It rained last night and part of the day today, roads very heavy with (troops) and much falling out, particularly by the bare-footed men, about one-fifth of the regiment. One whole company, G, Captain and all fell out except one man and he shoeless. We got to camp late and wagons deep on night.

## NOVEMBER 22, 1862

We moved towards Fredericksburg about seven miles passing McLaw's and Hood's Divisions, somewhere Frank Wyatt and father lived. Talked to a refugee lady of Fredericksburg close by the house. We turned off at that place to camp and saw there Generals Lee, Longstreet. McLaw's headquarters in Wyatt's house, expected battle and bombardment of Fredericksburg.

## NOVEMBER 23, 1862

Sunday. Beautiful day and no battle.

## NOVEMBER 26, 1862

Turner and Robert Howie arrived, Simpson and Plyler the day or so before from home. No supplies from home further than Richmond. Got gloves and scarf from Julia and letter from home.

## NOVEMBER 27, 1862

Inspection by Major Peyton, Adjutant and Inspector General.

## NOVEMBER 28, 1862

Moved camp about one and one-half miles from Fredericksburg.

## NOVEMBER 29, 1862

Saturday. The 15th North Carolina Regiment came this day into our brigade. I sent Tom to Fredericksburg with my horse for sugar, tobacco, rice and candles, $8.00 paid.

## DECEMBER 1, 1862

Sent to my wife Minnie, by John Gorden, Esq. $200.00 and sent to Major F. S. Wiant for pay as captain for April and 15 days in July $195.00 and pay as major from July 15th to 20th Oct. $475.00. Total six hundred and seventy dollars less fees paid Joe McCoy for making out papers. My wife to pay Wiant $668.50. Total sent to my wife and Wiant $868, by Godwin.

## December 3, 1862

Reviewed by Cooke and Ransom (very poor review). Gen. A. P. Hill's Division and some of the others of Gen. Jackson's Corps passed through here today. Saw Billy Kerr, Bivens, etc., much the larger part of the division were North Carolinians, generally quiet, with medley suits and rather dirty looking.

## December 4, 1862

Began battalion drills. Major A. A. Hills's forced drill very well.

## December 5–9, 1862

Regiment up, drill by battalion every day.

## December 11, 1862

We are ordered to Fredericksburg where we land about 10:00 and take up our positions on the left. At 2:00 p.m. we fall back and rest and look at the enemy bombarding. Saw Generals Lee and Longstreet, the latter very common looking man. About 8:00 or 9:00 p.m. we are ordered forward in front of the heights by a cemetery where we have a cold night. Few had clothing and very little fire. The enemy was driven back in the morning by Barksdale Mississippi regiment from making their bridge at the time, they then shelled the town and made their bridge in evening and numbers crossed over.

## December 12, 1862

We expect to fight today but the day passes off without anything more than picket firing.

## December 13, 1862

A bloody day for the 48th North Carolina but gloriously sustained by the gallant boys. The battle rages furiously before us and we must soon go. It began on our right this morning, Jackson and A. P. Hill are on our left and the enemy are repulsed there. They are now attacking our left, occupied by Gen. Longstreet's Corps. Cooke's Brigade on the extreme left, Cobb's Brigade in front, behind a stone wall. The balls and bombs are flying thick and heavy over us in a hollow. At about 1:30 p.m. we are ordered forward to occupy the heights. Our boys move forward in a gallant style to the very brow of the heights under a merciless fire and storm of Minie balls and shell. Our right rests on the Washington Battery, and our men fall thick and fast, but open a destructive fire upon the enemy with great spirit and affect. When we left our camp in the hollow and ordered the boys to cap their pieces, Gen. Cooke ordered them forward, but I kept them until they capped their pieces, being myself in front of the men. This movement of order from Gen. Cooke disarrayed slightly our line of battle. But when they had capped their guns they soon got into a good line again as we advanced and I fell to my position in the rear. The boys and officers began a determined and incessant fire as soon as they reached the heights around Marye's Hill.[103] It was by far the most exposed and dangerous position on the left wing. I moved backwards and forwards along the right wing and center encouraging and cheering up our men and seeing our men falling as they stood firing and exposed their whole length to the sight of the enemy's sharpshooter below. I immediately ordered then to lie down and fire from that position, which they did with great coolness and deliberation. I myself went from right to center looking after and cheering the boys and was wounded in right hip, a flesh wound not very serious. I still proceeded along the lines for some time and then lay down to watch the progress of the fight and the movements of the enemy. Our men were entirely too deep in files. I made many of them move forward and frequently cautioned those in front. But those in the extreme rear were not apt to shoot much, they were rather cautious and cowardly. The whole fire of the thousands of Yankees in the railroad cut, and behind it, in the plain below, and from the windows of houses in town were concentrated upon our regiment, ours being the only forces exposed to their fire. Those of our forces at the foot of the hill, between us and the enemy and behind a stone wall (which was filled level to the top of the wall on the side next to the enemy and dropped off like a step to the road in which our foes lay) were concealed from the view of the Yankees, by reason of the rolling ground between them, unless when the Yankees made a charge from the railroad cut and began to use the ground, when they became exposed to the destructive fire of those behind the stone wall, as well as to our fire from the summit. The distance from us to the railroad cut was about 250 yards. The stone wall about 25 to near 100 yards closer to the enemy. The Yankees received frequent reinforcements of fresh troops and were frequently driven back, when fresh and larger numbers would move forward in dense masses and they would renew the charge and come beyond their position only to be driven back with much severe losses. Their very number made their courage more awful. They came up by acres and our boys fired into the dense masses without the fear of missing and with a fair prospect of cutting down two at a time. Some of our officers were severely wounded. Lt.

William F. Beasley, Co. H, came running by me and said he was wounded. I asked where, he said in thigh, and told me to tell his mother he died like a true Southern soldier at his post. I told him he had only a flesh wound, no artery was out and he was not dangerously wounded, and told him I was also wounded and passed on. Then came Lt. Bitting[104] of Co. K and Lt. Stafford and Banner[105] of same Co. K, then I saw poor Irwin Simpson,[106] Co. F, bourn away from the field mortally wounded and I felt quite sad, for I feared from his looks that his wound was mortal. Lt. Heitman,[107] Co. H, was carried off, his right arm broken. Lt. Smith, of Co. H, was also struck by bomb in face, several privates were killed and many more wounded. I took my post behind Captains Turner and Laney's camps on right wing and soon saw Lt. Plyler, Co. E, lying dead before me, and again my soul felt sad and again nearly in front of him soon after, Jim Osborne Thomas,[108] a brave and civil soldier of Co. A was killed and there close by him to his left and in front of where I lay, Presson,[109] Co. A, was killed and on the right wing in Co. I, Sgt. John A. Long[110] whilst gallantly fighting falls, pierced in the throat and close by him Capt. John E. Moore,[111] Co. I and Adjutant J. R. Winchester, Lt. of Co. A, keep up a continuous and deliberate fire of over 100 rounds each. Sgt. B. F. Hilliard,[112] John Yarborough,[113] of Co. B, do the same though not many of the company or Co. G venture a deliberate shot. Co. A and C have many who fire well and several who act the coward as have the other companies. McManus[114] of Co. I behaves quite gallantly, Sgt. Krimminger[115] and Joseph H. McCoy[116] (a boy from Philadelphia) act with much gallantry in Co. A. A young boy 16 or 17 years old named Ellison Hays[117] and a young Alvin Parker,[118] both of Co. E, display the courage and coolness of veterans, loading and firing with great deliberation over 100 rounds. Hays is at last wounded in the left arm, flesh wound, and I order him to retire. About this time the 8th or some other South Carolina regiment charges up gallantly and plunge forward through us to the stone wall in front, some 50 yards which is quite a secure place but some of their number fell as they pass our fatal point and in going down the hill. Here Daniel Harkey[119] of Co. F was mortally wounded and rushed down the hill after the South Carolina regiment, his brain being shot out. Sgt. McInnis[120] of Co. F also falls and Lt. H.A. Grey[121] of Co. F is wounded in the shoulder and leaves the field. Sgt. William D. Howard[122] of Co. F wounded and James Vickory[123] killed, several others are killed in numbers 17 and 7 mortally wounded. Our total losses in killed and wounded through the day amounted to 209, including myself and Major A. A. Hill, all the field officers in the engagement. The Major was wounded in the right shoulder not severely. Of these about 90 were slightly wounded, many of them receiving only mere scratches or bruises not unfitting them for duty, and leaving the field in consequence and never returning during the fight and many not until next day, having gone four miles where our wagon, tents, sick, cooks and barefooted men were left. Many left with wounded men who failed to come back to the fight, or even until next. Some of whom were found secreted in a ravine and had to be forced back and several left without receiving any wounds at all. Thirty-one names are marked off by their officers as having acted cowardly and I had them paraded publically, and also had the names of those read out who left generally with wounded men and did not return, as having acted contrary to military discipline and censurable. We took into the action 387 men, commissioned officers and privates and had only 135 at our camp at night and next morning we had 26 commissioned and two field officers engaged in the fight and both officers were wounded and 15 of the commissioned officers of whom one, Lt. Plyler, was killed and Lt. Banner was mortally wounded and perhaps also Lieutenants [Sugar] Dulin and [William] Austin. The regiment remained until dark when the firing ceased. We then gathered up in groups and were looking for our wounded and removing from the dead any valuables they had about them and I ordered the wounded who could not leave to be assisted to the rear to the surgeons' quarters and those who could leave without help to go back and the balance to remain until the enemy opened a brisk fire upon our whole left in front of us and lie down and be ready for any emergency. But I fear many of them left and went back to the old camp at this time, which gave rise to the false rumor that our regiment had broken, circulated by Gen. Ransom, but which report is false and slanderous. Not more than a dozen could have left at that time, and even if they had left the other regiments had, some of them gone back and ours was the very last which left the field. The firing soon ceased and we again began to go on as before, examining our dead and seeing if there were any wounded who had been overlooked or not cared for. During the interval before the first firing an aide of Ransom's passed and said we would soon be relieved and soon after Col. Hall, who had commanded our brigade as Lt. Col. (Gen. John R. Cooke having been seriously wounded above the right eye by a rifle ball) came to us and told us the same thing and to gather up our arms and dead. We were doing so when an aide of Gen. Ransom came up and wished me to send an intelligence officer to Ransom's quarters to give an account of the condition of our regiment. I sent Capt. Turner who, after over half an hour absence, returned with orders for our regiment to go back to our camp, which we did. It was near two hours or nearly so after night and all the regiments in our brigade had been in camp some time, so that we had been on duty at least five or six hours, four of which we were under a terrible fire. We got back to [camp] and had to send for cartridges and it was 12:00 before we retired with sad hearts for our lost friend and the widows that day made in our regiment. Some of our bravest and best and most beloved officers and men were killed and severely wounded. We were told by Col. Hall, who commanded the brigade, that we must occupy the same position next day, and I begged to have entrenching tools and throw up a slight breast works, but they could not be had, and I was determined to shield my men by moving them further to the rear and right.[124]

### December 14, 1862

This day passed off without any fight. We stayed in camp and many of our stragglers came in. We buried our dead and put head boards giving their rank and names. Sixteen were buried and [Daniel] Harkey's body could not be found and was supposed to have been buried by the South Carolina 8th or 25th North Carolina, among whom he was lying. Our other dead, Simpson and two others, Jack Phillips and Clodfelter, were buried at the hospital when they died. On Sunday night, the 14th, we got entrenching tools [and] with logs, rock and dirt, threw up a pretty substantial breastworks and made a ditch about two and one-half feet wide and felt ourselves quite safe for another fight.

### December 15, 1862

Passed off without any demonstrations beyond occasional picket firing. We found our stragglers coming in, many slightly, some not wounded at all. At night a brisk fire opened about the time we lay down, upon our working party, and the Minie balls flew thick and fast around us, but we got into a hollow and escaped danger. Several of the 35th North Carolina had been killed at the same place the day we fought though it was a quarter [of a mile] behind our lines of battle. Our left was in a most exposed place. The firing continued but a short time, when we broke into a laugh and went back to bed. It rained on us this night and next morning when we were relieved by Col. Bratton 6th South Carolina. I saw William Cowser here and we talked awhile.

### December 16, 1862

We winded around to camp on the side of a hill shoe deep in mud, then changed the camp to a piece of woods behind a hill and built a fire and fried. When we were ordered back to this our old camp, about four miles and got there safely.

## December 17, 1862

We were ordered out suddenly into line of battle, but soon found that it was false alarm and were dismissed with orders to subscribe for the needy in Fredericksburg. I gave $20.00, our regiment made up $189.00.

## December 20, 1862

Major F. Wiant came to us this day. Reviewed by Ransom, my salute quite cute to him.

## December 22, 1862

Tom Clutts left for home and Major Wiant also.

## December 24, 1862

Received present of dried peaches, apples and rolls from Mr. Jenkins, brother-in-law of Major Wiant and had apples today.

## December 25, 1862

Had apple toddy for breakfast Christmas and a fine dinner of squirrel and partridges well prepared by Stephen Timmons. Had been sick for some days, burning at pit of stomach and severe cough, pneumonia or dyspepsia.

## December 27, 1862

Received of Capt. L.C. Hanes[125] for three months service from Oct. to first of January 1863—$510.00.

## December 28, 1862

Sunday. Determined to try and go home, from hospital in Richmond, if possible. Got to Richmond 10:00 p.m. No supper.

## December 29, 1862

Dick Stitt[126] sent home deed by Wiant. I failed to get off. Orders came to Dr. Peebles to grant no more furloughs one-half an hour before I applied. Drawers $3.00, handkerchiefs $2.00, cap $12.00, hat $14.00 or $20.00, suit $195 to $222.00, $135.00 and [with] stars [insignia] $147.00

for coat. They ask for oranges $1.00 each. My box was taken by White, bought hat for $10.00 and paid $8.00 for hotel bill and two railroad ticket to Hamilton Crossing.

## December 30, 1862

Inspection of companies of 48th Regiment, very cold, had eggnog with Sheriff Austin and got new suit of military from Dr. J. M. Miller, Charlotte and two pairs of flannel drawers $137.00.

## January 1, 1863

Eggnog. Sent $300.00 to my wife by Austin and $140.00 to Dr. Miller by C. Austin in letter, total $440.00, on hand for self $40.00. With intense suffering, trial and glory for the South, for North Carolina and for the 48th Regiment North Carolina Infantry: French's Farm around Richmond June 25th the opening of the big fight, when we were dubbed "The bloody 48ths," City Point, Malvern Hill, Coggins Point, Maryland, Harper's Ferry, Sharpsburg Sept. 17th . Fredericksburg Dec. 13th are days never to be forgotten by the 48th. First French's Farm 18 killed, 105 (wounded), Sharpsburg 750, or about that, engaged, killed 33, killed and wounded 228, Fredericksburg, engaged 387 private and non-commissioned officers and 26 commissioned officers and two field officers, killed one officer and 16 privates, wounded and killed 209 of whom 17 were officers, 90 severely wounded. Almighty God be praised that so many of us still survive to begin the New Year 1863 and His direction and protection devotedly invoked for the incoming year and for Peace.

❖ Letter from Walkup at camp near Fredericksburg to wife Minnie:

My dear Wife,

I write by C. Austin who is here and who slipped off [without] learning how you and my family were or letting you know he was coming for fear, I suppose, that you might want to send something with him to me. Mrs. Turner however wrote by him and informed Turner that our blessed little darling Lelia had had spasms and I am very troubled by it. Whooping cough, teething and spasms all is too great for a delicate child to bear at once and I fear the worse and feel more for you than I do myself in that sad event. My dear wife write to me and relieve my mind from suspense. I can bear easily like a philosopher having been trained in the school of adversity but it would be a terrible blow to even my stout frame. But you a young and delicate female, in loneliness with only this ray of light to delight you and [provide] exciting scenes to divert your mind, the effect would be much more severe and shocking on your nervous system and therefore I fear more for you than for myself my fond, dear and affectionate wife. Let me hear from you and let us bear the rod like Christians and like Cross. But I will still hope, though I have fears in my hopes, of better news.

I wrote to you from Richmond and left here day before yesterday and got back to this camp when I found all in tolerable health. My own is pretty good. I am taking good care of myself for fear of that dread disease pneumonia. But upon arrival at camp I found our boxes had come and with them my overcoat and three pairs of socks, including that warm, neat and elegant present from Sister Rebecca, all wool and very fine. God bless her for it. I found also at last my famous mess chest with the veritable jug of wine and brandy, and molasses and five pounds sugar which my good friend H.H. Potter gave me. That was the whole contents. There were no socks or paper in it. The paper was not doubt ruined and the socks got misplaced somewhere. I have been using blackberry liberally and am getting up an eggnog this New Year's morning. Oh that I knew that you and Lelia were well.

I found upon my arrival at camp that Dr. C.M. Miller had sent me a coat and pants of light Confederate grey cloth very well made and trimmed, which cost me only $115.00 less in fact than a cost of heavier material would cost in Richmond. A coat there costs $125.00 to $147.00 and a full suit $195.00 to $222.00. I came very near having a suit ordered, without knowing Dr. Miller had ordered one. He ought to have had sense enough to have informed me about it. But he said he did write. If so I never received his letter. However, no harm was done, and I am very glad he sent me the suit. I wrote to him from Richmond to have it made for me. He also sent me a couple of pair of fine flannel drawers, made up by Eugenia and well made too. They were the very things I needed most and I have on a pair now. So you need not send my old woolen drawers by Hall,[127] nor need you send anything else by him as transportation on the railroad is very difficult to get through. Eat the crout yourself, as it could never reach here. I hope to help you eat it at home when the winter comes.

I wish you to look out all the notes I have against Jim Richards and get H.M. Houston or C. Austin, or someone to take them to William H. Simpson, Clerk of Superior Court and have a writ issued on them against Jim Richards for me as I learn he was closing up his business without making provision for settling my notes. I don't remember whether I have more than one note against him or not. If there is more than one, let them all be consolidated into one suit and take Simpson's receipt for the notes.

I hope you will keep in wood a plenty and provender for Fanny and the cows, and if anybody will bring Fanny to me I will pay all expenses for the trip and pay him $25.00 besides. If there can be no one to bring her to me, just keep her till I get home. But don't undertake to drive her. Col. Austine, Shoote, H.M. or J.P. Houston can probably assist you in finding someone who will be coming out here and can ride Fanny to our camp, get a bridle at home and some old or common saddle which will do to bring her here. Some of our returning soldiers, such as either of the above named men or Major Wiant or Covington would recommend, might bring her here.

If you can loan out the $300.00 paid in by Joe Adams on the Burleyson's estate note, do so taking good security for it. Perhaps Clement B. Curles would borrow it and he is very good. I would prefer to have it loaned out and make interest for the estate.

Now I believe I have written to you fully, but can't promise when I can come home. I think from some indications making, that a system of furlough will begin, which may let some of us and perhaps all get home during January or February or March.

C. Austin says he will fix up the yard fence and the papering upstairs which I have urged him to do. I am very glad you got the house as you did. I would not try further to buy it.[128] Give the Hymms tract and the three Negroes, Jinny, Betty and Charlie, and nothing else.

I will try and enclose some vaccine matter, if I can get it and would advise you to have yourself and all the family, black and white, vaccinated, to secure against the smallpox. Dr. Miller says Mr. Spratt and Monroe Anderson have it in Charlotte.

I enclose you $300.00 by C. Austin in this letter and sent Dr. Miller $140.00. I have enough left to do me until I draw again. I drew $510.00 and got $60.00 for my pistol which makes $560.00 and have left $30.00 or $40.00. I spent some in Richmond for and cap and hotel and railroad bill.

My love to Brother William, James Houston, Stephen and families and respects to Miss Lizzie, her brother Stuart. R.S. Stuart came here Monday and brought my suit from Dr. Miller.

Kiss our dear Lelia and be cheerful and believe me in reasonable health and spirits and anxious to see and hear from you.

Your devoted and loving husband

## JANUARY 2, 1863

G. Laney and Conrad Plyler came to camp.

## JANUARY 3, 1863

We leave camp for a movement south on Saturday, January 3.

## JANUARY 4, 1863

Sunday we began by daylight our march and got to Hanover Junction by 3:30 much fatigued and took up camp. Ransom cut up some extras, arrested Max Webb of 27th North Carolina because he said a man whom Ransom had shot was out on a call of nature.

## JANUARY 5, 1863

Monday got near Richmond nine miles and camped near Spring Run on Chickahominy. I walked five miles hard today and sweat freely. Got letter from Minnie of Dec. 26th telling of Lelia's spasm, not mentioned in letter of 29th received by Rev. C. Plyler, Jan. 2nd.

## JANUARY 6, 1863

Tuesday, passed through Richmond with thanks to God for our safe return this far again, soldiers all say cheerful, because returning towards North Carolina, got to winter quarters and staid all night seven miles from Richmond, had rain in evening, wrote a letter to [Minnie] and sent by John Irby[129] and lost it. Saw Gen. Cooke in Richmond and gave him three cheers.

## JANUARY 7, 1863

Wednesday. Got within three miles of Petersburg, Virginia and took up camp, seemed like getting to familiar place and boys all anxious to visit Petersburg. I have been quite unwell for three days past with dyspepsia.

## JANUARY 8, 1863

Still at camp waiting for transportation by railroad to North Carolina I suppose. Am still quite uncomfortable with dyspepsia. Wrote again to my wife and sent by mail, wrote also to H.A. Potts of Virginia.

## JANUARY 12, 1863

Monday. I got through to Dr. Hall[130] of 2nd North Carolina Hospital[131] expecting to get home by transfer, but failed after making two or three efforts, fell back on Ransom's clemency, no hopes of success. Paid Jarrott $6.25 for one and one-third day washing etc., $.75 hack, $1.50 Linsey's dinner.

## JANUARY 13, 1863

Began boarding at Mrs. Holdenby's at $3.00 per day for supper, not very attractive.

## JANUARY 14, 1863

Got bottle of peach brandy $5.00, wrote to wife to come here. Capt. Hanes loaned me $85.00. Feel better.

## JANUARY 15, 1863

Thursday. I am almost regretting that I am getting well so fast. I have less opinions of my boarding house. They stint me with food, grudgingly given, of poor quality, badly prepared. The son drinks more liquor than would pay for all I have eaten. I will suspect the Scotch-like Junius, when I hear them boast of being Presbyterians, that they have some designs to make money out of me. It looks like hypocrisy. I rather hear them speak of being Christians than any sort of sectarian, and love any creed or person who loves God and shows it by their actions and deportment.

## JANUARY 16, 1863

Our regiment left for North Carolina yesterday, Goldsboro, the wagon train leaves today. I will try again to get home. The weather is turning colder.

## JANUARY 17, 1863

I was feeble and listless yesterday, but am better today. I have one-half gallon of oysters and hope to improve my fare by them and gain strength.

## JANUARY 18, 1863

Still improving. Fare good, weather clear and cold.

## JANUARY 19, 1863

Still improving, fare good, weather fair, beautiful and cold, got whiskers and hair dressed by John Shore $.50 and took a walk to Dr. W.H. Hall's and post office, telegraph and Potter's.

## January 20, 1863

Saw Dr. Hines, got cakes $1.30, paid bill of Mrs. Holdenby's for one week, $3.00 per day, $21.00, paid for oysters $2.00 and papers $.35, Eliza for washing ten pieces $.19, pants $.25, [total washing] $1.15, Hack to carry trunk and self to hotel, $.75 and put out trunk, [total] $1.00, railroad fare to Weldon, $3.00, pudding $.40.

Got furlough for 14 days to go home.

## January 21, 1863

Missed connection at Weldon and had to stay over. It is a dirty horrid place to sleep at, no comforts, $5.00.

## January 22–23, 1863

Railroad to Raleigh from Weldon, $5.00. Got to Charlotte morning of 23. Railroad from Raleigh free. Miss Nancy Hilliard's supper elegant, $1.00. Reached home with Fanny and Hall on Jan. 23 and found all well and beautiful, unexpected arrival home, feel happy[132] James Richards paid me my notes $177.43 and I paid W. H. Simpson costs $3.75.

## April 1863

Sold Fanny to Maxwell for $225.00.[133]

## May 5, 1863

William Utley began to board at my house.

## May 6, 1863

Hall left home for the army.

## May 7, 1863

I left home for the army which I found at Weldon, North Carolina, with cash $13.35.

## May 11, 1863

Received from Lewis C. Hanes, Assistant Quartermaster, 48th North Carolina Troops, three month's pay from first of January to first April 1863, cash $420.00 and note, total $510.00.

## May 14, 1863

Thursday we left Weldon. Turner[134] and myself sent box 52 rock fish to our wives, it costs $23.00 or $24.00. McMatthews to sell balance.

We got to Goldsboro 14th and left 16th Saturday for Kinston where we arrived Sunday, May 17.

## MAY 21, 1863

Sent $30.00 to Adjutant General Fork H. Battle, private secretary for officers commissioned 15 or more [months], sent unpaid R. C. Stills deed, $30.00.

## MAY 22–23, 1863

Our order is just received to "hold our regiments in readiness for immediate action in the field." Don't know what it means, a fight or picket duty or a march toward the army. We go to Gum Swamp to drive back a party of Yankees who surprised and routed two regiments, the 25th Col. Rutledge[135] and 56th Col. Faison's,[136] and took some 100 or 200 prisoners and frightened Gen. Ransom badly. Gen. Hill said it was the most disgraceful thing that had occurred during the war. Both regiments were of Gen. Ransom's Brigade. We charged with 15th on our right and 27th and 46th on right and Ransom's Brigade through Gum Swamp, an impenetrable marsh, the enemy shelling us with one piece of artillery and wounding one man of 27th, leg shot off. They retreat and we passed. Friday, we continue the pursuit under Gen. D. H. Hill toward New Bern. We separate, Gen. Cooke taking the Dover Road with 27th and 15th and we 48th and 46th under Col. Hall[137] and myself going down the railroad. We camp after dark. Hall has my horse and blanket on the Dover Road and I have to lie down without them. The night is cold and I was sitting in a negro hut, when orders came to move three miles further down the road. We stopped about 12:00 p.m. and I slept in the road on ground but getting too cold to sleep sat up beside a fire and got about two hours sleep. Hall arrives next morning about sunup when we are ordered to move forward. We get in sight of Yankees, our pickets fire on their pickets and kill one man. The Yankees continue their retreat. We are ordered to Dover Road to rejoin Cooke's Brigade at Core Creek, where our artillery shell the Yankees who leave. We remain two or three hours and pursue. Thinking we would fight soon, I sent my horse to the rear with Hall and made on foot six or seven miles to battle [at] Bachelor's Creek, where we are drawn up in line of battle, and our battery open a fire and shell from 14 guns. No reply is made. The enemy shell our left and engage our pickets under Col. William Mack, [and] wound four men. Their commander Col. Jones is reported to have been killed by a shell, on our left [or] by a Minie ball. The Yankees burned a house which we passed. After remaining awhile we concluded that the Yankees are trying to flank us and began a retrograde movement, retire four or five miles and remain for the night, fare hard and lie without clothing when about 12:00 p.m. S. Timmons[138] brings my horse and overcoat, Hall having tried and failed to find me.

## MAY 24, 1863

We leave early Sunday morning, arrive at Core Creek and remain until evening at 5:00 p.m. and move forward to Gum Swamp, passing scene of Major Henry Schenk's[139] exploits, where he fought and retreated 5 to 1500. I eat and sleep comfortably etc.

## MAY 25, 1863

We arrive on picket near Gum Swamp.

◆ Letter from Walkup at Gum Swamp camp near Kinston, North Carolina to wife Minnie:

My loving and dear wife:

I received your very grateful letter of the 20th this day and actually wept with pleasure upon reading it. I saw you and little Lelia in her new bonnet and blue fringed dress, with your eyes beaming with delight full innocence and affection upon your return trip home, that it made my heart swell with gratitude and joy to know and feel that I had such "loved and loving ones at home" and that you were well and fondly thinking of me as I roamed. You two are my sunbeams of delight as I journey over this wilderness world and cheer me and gladden my soul as I travel on.

I am glad you visited Steele Creek and happy to hear of Lelia's attractions and fell proud of both her and her mother. I am glad you have the garden comforts and fine prospects and sorry you lost your fish but we heard of it before you did and we were satisfied in as much as you appreciate our good intentions. We hope to have better luck next time. We lost about $13.00 each by the speculation, but had they saved, we would have made the fish sent home free. I got your other letter on last Friday just as we were ordered to Dover Swamp near New Bern. We have just returned from a trip after some Yankees who came within about five miles of Kinston and surprised two of our regiments, the 25th under Col. Rutledge and the 56th under Col. Faison. They took some one or two hundred prisoners and run the balance shamefully, on Friday morning. The Cooke's and Ransom's Brigades made pursuit under Gen. D.H. Hill and drove the Yankees within seven or eight miles of New Bern.

We attacked them at Gum Swamp about half a mile from this place. They fired upon us from a battery of one gun and shot off one leg of a private in the 27th Regiment and then retreated, we followed and our regiment and Col. Hall's 46th overtook a party on the railroad, our pickets fired upon them and killed one Yankee and run the balance.

We then joined Gen. Cooke's Brigade on another road and caught up with a party posted at Gore or Core Creek, where our battery opened upon them and drove them back. We followed to Battle Creek eight or nine miles from New Bern and shelled them there. Our pickets became engaged with their pickets. Col. MacRae's[140] 15th Regiment were part of our picket skirmishers and was engaged with the enemy's pickets. Four of his men were wounded. A Mr. Freeman had one arm shot off and Sandy McClellan received a flesh wound on the ankle, not dangerous. It is said that one of our shells killed the Yankee Col. Jones. We turned round and came back to near this place last night (Sunday). The Yankees are following, but will hardly be bold enough to attack us, or come near here. If they do, we hope to make them rue their temerity. The two regiments who were surprised and who ran so freely belonged to Gen. Ransom's Brigade and Ransom ran faster than any. Gen. Hill says "It was the most disgraceful affair of the war."

Our regiment all got off safely, only their feet are very sore and they are much broken down marching. Hall did very well, but says he was badly frightened at the shelling. Col. Hill started with us but was sick and had a sore foot and gave the regiment in charge to me when the battle began and we charged through Gum Swamp many of them half thigh deep in mud. He afterwards came up, but left and went back to Kinston where he is at present. My health and Hall's continues good. We still hear that we will be ordered to Virginia, and don't much care whether we go, or stay in North Carolina. The sand is so deep and hot and water so scarce and the country so desolate, we rather prefer Virginia. We had to lay out without tents or covering for two nights and eat raw meat and hard crackers.

## May 31, 1863

Sermon from Reverend Russell, chaplain of 15th North Carolina, pastor at Carthage, Moore County, North Carolina. Three sermons, also had Reverend Foley of Goldsboro, and Fairly of Greensboro, North

Carolina, chaplain of 27th North Carolina. We have a feast all at once. We have out two companies each day on picket and tomorrow one more on fatigue duty, with 54 men.

## JUNE 1, 1863

We begin the rifle drill and manual by order of Gen. Cooke. The officers objected to changing the manual, but Cooke orders it and we begin today. Co. F is placed in quarantine for small pox, some three cases of it from that company sent to hospital, two others supposed to have it. Capt. Walker[141] and 54 men sent on fatigue duty to throw up breastworks. Detail continued daily. Mess bill from 24th May to 1st June $23.00.

## JUNE 4–5, 1863

Orders to leave Kinston for Petersburg Thursday and Richmond, to get off June 4 in haste, following 27th North Carolina. Stay at Goldsboro three hours, 11:00 p.m. leave there and arrive in Weldon at 5:00 a.m. and thence to Petersburg 6:00 p.m. Saturday June 6.

## JUNE 6, 1863

Transportation by foot to Richmond, the cars having left us where we traveled ten miles and arrive at Richmond June 7 on Sunday, 7:00 a.m. Saw John Medlin, Jr., and at liberty we fell out. Bynum Small[142] got sick, but I compelled him to march. Hagar of Co. C, S. Ashcraft,[143] Co. A and B. Bigger of Co. I fell out. We are to be placed in Gen. Heth's division with Pettigrew's, Anderson's [Brigades]. Horse shod in Petersburg. $2.50.

## JUNE 9, 1863

Monday. Saw Henry Ringstaff in Richmond, paid $2.50 for two drinks. Saw Gen. Winder about John Medlin's quarters and had him rearrested.[144] Heard of Capt. Turner's foolishness and mischief about making his insolent report of men falling out at Gum Swamp, was surprised and vexed at his folly. Ordered all surplus baggage to be disposed of, had orders to be in readiness to march towards Hanover Junction at any moment.

◈ Letter from Walkup in Richmond to Governor Zebulon Vance:

Dear Sir,

Upon our arrival in Richmond Sunday 7th June from Kinston, N.C. we found John Medlin Jr. who was a deserter from the 28th North

Carolina and who killed William Hosea Little and crippled William L. D. Murchison both of Monroe in Union County, N.C. last winter, whilst they were attempting to arrest him and three others, all of which was reported to you by the militia authorities. Gen. Winder of Richmond had released John Medlin Jr. and he and his father who had come to Richmond, Va., were in our camp, and young Medlin was about trying to get into our regiment. I called on Gen. Winder and inquired how Medlin Jr. came to be let out stating his offenses. He replied that he had no authority over him, that a Confederate court could not try for an offense committed against state authority but wanted me to have him arrested and sent to him and he would send him to his regiment. I did not care to trouble myself about him for that business, but told him (Winder) that he ought to send Medlin to you to be tried by the civil law if the military could not furnish for such offense. He replied that he had written to you time and again that he (Medlin) was here subject to your disposal and he received no reply and that he wants not keeping him here any longer, as the Confederate court has no sequence over the case and therefore turned him out. And remarked further that by Judge Pearson's decision, the civil authorities in North Carolina could try him for no offense, because by that decision, it was held to be no offense in any conscript to resist the military authority-that it made no difference if he was a deserter.

I left the office and met with Lt. Henry Ringstaff who was with the party that went to arrest Medlin and came near being shot himself by Medlin and his band. He (Ringstaff) told me that he had authority from Gen. Smith of Richmond to arrest all deserters and showed me the order. I then went back to Gen. Winder and took Lt. Ringstaff[145] of 43th North Carolina Troop with me, and told Gen. Winder, that he (Ringstaff) had an order to arrest deserters and was with the party when the arrest was attempted to be made. Gen. Winder then wished me to deliver Medlin to him and said he should be tried forthwith as the court was in session. I took a police officer who made the arrest and Medlin is now in Castle Thunder and awaits trial; perhaps the trial may now be going on.

I have very little confidence in Gen. Winder and think justice and law will come through a very foggy and cloudy atmosphere, if he is to be the medium through which it is to be applied. I therefore hope that you will demand John Medlin Jr., after the military power had disposed of him, to make him subject to the cleaner light and purer atmosphere of honest old North Carolina jurisprudence. I don't know what was Judge Pearson's decision, but I feel confident, it was nearer the perfection of reason and right, than any opinion that can be given in the Old Dominion by Gen. Winder, or any of their civil judges.

Old John Medlin is himself a great rascal and ought to have been hung long ago two or three times over. He has a good deal of money too, whether his money has any agency in his son's release from custody I know not. But to turn out a man, charged with such crimes, under such circumstances, is calculated to leave a doubt, whether the parties having him in charge were, like Caesar's wife was said to be, or not.[146]

## June 10, 1863

Ordered hastily to Hanover Junction, two drinks for myself and Ringstaff, $2.00 and three for J.R. Winchester, self and Lawhon $4.40. Got to Junction Tuesday night. Horses got there Wednesday morning. Capt. Turner's company spent Tuesday morning with Col. MacRae, by daylight our picket returned Wednesday evening to camp at North Anna Bridge. Lawhon's[147] Co. D stationed at Bridge, [also] Co. B.

## June 11, 1863

Thursday. Capt. Mabry[148] [Co. B] at Polecat Bridge, John Potts, Co. C, Capt. Walker at Mattacocy Bridge. Co. E, Lt. Stearn's, at church five miles from Junction, Co. F, Capt. Richardson at county bridge North Anna. Went to station pickets [companies] B and C at Mattapony 15 miles from Junction and returned to find camp in motion and regiment ordered back to Richmond. Yankees reported 5,000 strong coming up Chickahominy. We got to Richmond about sundown, balance about 11:00 p.m. under Major Hill, except Co. D, C, and B and two detailed for county bridge, who are to remain until relieved.

## June 13, 1863

Yankees reported as going back from Chickahominy, our camp at Camp Lee, Richmond, Virginia.

## June 15, 1863

Orders to move on Williamsburg Road tomorrow.

## June 16, 1863

Move from Camp Lee, Richmond, Virginia to French's Farm or

near it on Williamsburg Road opposite our first battleground at French's Farm where the bloody 48th was baptized in blood.

## JUNE 17, 1863

Sad feelings hover over our minds. Scenery all changed, though rained yet cheerful and hopeful. Whole brigade present, 27th and 15th and Cooper's [Virginia] Battery all present with 46th and 48th. Great desire to view the battleground. Awkward squad formed today.

## JUNE 18, 1863

Hall home with trunk and clothing. Cpl. D. P. Bell's 11 men furlough for 12 day's home.

## JUNE 19, 1863

Capt. Turner and Lieutenants John Nix and Hart and Perrill furloughed to go home, Nix 20, Turner 14, and Hart 20 days, Perrill 12 days. Allen Richardson takes charge of my horse.

## JUNE 20, 1863

Saturday. This day with D. R. Bonner, Stephen Timmons and Lt. 20th Clegg (Col. E.D. Hart in part). I visited the battlefield of French's Farm where the 48th first experienced the realities of war. It was with a thankful soul I felt how God in His mercy had still preserved me then and ever since my last visit to this place in August last, whilst so many others had fallen around me in battle, and disease. We traveled up or rather down the Williamsburg Road to where the Seven Pines battlefield of 31st May 1862 is said to have taken place and taken its name from the seven large pines at the forks of the road leading to Richmond, one the Williamsburg Road (called Seven Mile Road), the other the Nine Mile Road. This it was at Williamsburg [Road] and not Seven Pines where was a hotly contested field and was, I believe, where Duncan McRae's[149] regiment fought so bravely and fell so thick and where John F. Hoke failed to march up and left McRae to fight alone. Many North Carolinians are buried here, and more Yankees lie shallow and unburied, their bones are lying on the surface and many of our soldiers desecrate them by making rings from them. Dr. Bonner[150] among them acts near Barbarian [in] this. We visited near where the fight was heavy near Fair Oaks on the Nine Mile Road, on the 31st, and Savage's Station on the railroad ten miles from Richmond where the fight also was heavy about 29th June and where was a fight though not very great. I doubt whether any of them were as severe as ours of French's Farm, unless it was at Seven Pines. The country is generally low and flat and had been cross-wayed or corduroyed by McClellan's by-roads. The houses were generally burnt down and fencing gone. Tents had been for miles all over the country and awful desecration of the dead visible in skulls and other bones lying exposed on the surface, mostly Yankees, whether exhumed or never buried. The flesh of one had dried up on the bones like dried beef, he had not been buried, some lay on litters and were left so, what writhing they must have suffered no language can tell, whether starved to death, or exhausted by slow and painful wounds for days they were left to die unknown and only guessed at. Horrible realities follow in the train of civil war. If they suffered thus here, what must have been their anguish at Vicksburg and Port Hudson a few days ago and at Chancellorsville as they burnt in the woods? Rev. Watts, nephew of your Steele Church Presbyterians Pastor Kyrder are here and [Watts] preached for us tonight and tomorrow Kryder. (Watts knows you Minnie.) I urge the claims of John Minor,[151] the widow's son, and rushing to get furlough to cut wheat, and write to surgeons at Hospital, Wilmington, North Carolina for Hoey's transfer to Charlotte, North Carolina and order Lt. Thompson[152] with Pope[153] and his detail in Davidson County to report to me at headquarters. Capt. L. D. Hines arrives in camp.

## June 21, 1863

Rev. William Kryder preached today a good sermon. We are ordered to be ready for moving at any time.

## June 23, 1863

Had three men, two of Co. D and one of Co. B, whipped for desertion today, 25 lashes each, and one of the Co. B to stand on a barrel six days one hour at dress parade and on the seventh to stand tied by trunks one hour, made them all take the oath not to desert and to support government and be true and faithful.

## June 24, 1863

J.K. Potts sent on detail to Richmond for clothing and reported by Cook to be drunk, he and Belk found them sober on their return. Capt. A. M. Walker reported to be examined for incompetency yesterday, is sick today.

## June 25, 1863

This is the anniversary of our first battle when the 48th was baptized in blood twelve months ago and acquired its cognomen of the Bloody 48th. We are in sight of the field of our glory and sufferings. Charges against Lt. J.M. Walker[154] and opinions of his father's competency given. Ordered at 9:30 p.m. to send one company on picket with two day's rations, sent Capt. Moore's Co. I.

## June 26, 1863

Ordered to send one more company on picket, sent Co. K, heard of Yankees advance from White House, five miles toward Richmond. Ransom has come down. Resolutions on E. C. Stewart,[155] Sgt. Major of regiment, passed. Matter of Capt. Walker's son discussed. Captain refused to be examined by board. Son tenders his resignation, refused unless he satisfies some charges, etc.

My account stands as follows: cash on hand: $62.00. Due from C.S.A. from first of April to present time at $175.00 per month to first July, three months $510.00, some notes for borrowed money about $26.00. Mess bill with Dr. Chears and Banner account of my past from 15th June when mess began. Due Turner $.60 fish, due King $.25, Timmons $.25. Due commissary candles one lb. and Hall two day's rations. I owe nothing more here in army.

## June 28, 1863

Sunday. We heard a sermon last night from Rev. William B. Pressley, a minister of the Associate Reform Church, who is an acquaintance of my wife's, and who says she pointed me out to him at the fair in Charlotte, North Carolina. He is a man of clever and pious [character]. We moved camp today about two miles on the Nine Mile Road to New Bridge Church.

## June 29, 1863

Monday. Visited New Bridge where we crossed 29th June last year just after the fight at Gaines Mill or Cold Harbor. Saw Gaines' house, Hogan's house and the place where the battle was fought. Yankees reported as rapidly advancing in force. Great excitement in Richmond. Militia turning out in strong numbers.[156]

## July 1, 1863

Wednesday. Hastily ordered to move our command with shovels and picks and one day's rations.

## JULY 3, 1863

Just returned from march quite fatigued. We went two miles down the Chickahominy, near Mr. Garnett's, close by McClellan's Bridge to tear down some Yankee entrenchments made last year, and we did work until about sunset. We were called up about 2:00 a.m. to work again and did so until daylight, some working very little. Capt. Moore very easy and pipe smoking, lacks energy, and Bob Howie[157] too lazy, Capt. Jones[158] and Tysor ditto but worse. We rested and ate crackers, then marched Bottom's Bridge, passing Jenkins of South Carolina and Ransom's Brigade who repassed us. Jenkins' Brigade was remarkable for dressing like Yankees, for being most ordinary and stolid in appearance and most homely regiment we have seen. We crossed Bottom's Bridge where the Yankees camped the night before on Chickahominy and marched towards "The White House," the Yankees falling back, it was near sundown when we recrossed it. We passed on, soon both parties began shelling each other. One of our men was killed by a grape shot and one of the 49th North Carolina was wounded. We met four Yankee prisoners who seemed to be well pleased that they had been captured, one had no hat on. They were well clad and said that they heard that we were half starved but that we did not look like it. We followed to within about four miles of "The White House," and returned very much fatigued about 10:00 p.m. on side of Bottom's Bridge. We don't know of any casualties to Yankees except prisoner. Their artillery double as effective as ours. I eat one cracker and a small piece of fried ham. I did not want any more, not being well, dysentery slightly. It is now 12:00 [midnight]. We began our march at sunup and camp by rail six miles, but the train did not arrive as early as the baggage train which left when we did. Maj. Gen. D. H. Hill was in command and though everyone feels that he is full of courage as a bull-terrier, yet like a terrier he attacks regardless of numbers, or opposing forces and marches and works unmercifully severe. It was said that President Davis gave him express orders not to engage the foe. If so that may account for our not following them to "the White House," and having to suffer losses and make a disgraceful retreat and hazard the fate of Richmond. This is a second edition of the New Bern trip. Our men are all in camp and well. At sunset received orders for three day's rations and to be ready to move camp. At 12:00 a.m. received orders to pack up for movement at once. Did so, but received no further orders, the 15th moved off, enemy said to be advancing.

## July 4, 1863

Saturday. We are still 10:00 a.m. in camp, with a prospect of remaining here longer. Capt. Turner has returned to camp, brought me a letter from home. The secret is out now, much to my surprise and admiration and joy. I feel like a lover to whom his sweetheart has just responded favorably. It is a glorious Fourth to me. I am a happy man.[159] Glorious news from the army from York Pass to New Orleans, Louisiana to battle Gettysburg.

## July 5, 1863

Sunday. Letter of June 26th received from Minnie also calculated to surprise me, and would have done so but for the letter of July 1st by Capt. Turner.

## July 7, 1863

Ordered to Hanover Junction and on 9th ordered to South Anna Bridge where battle was fought July 4th.

❖ Letter from Walkup at New Bridge near Richmond to daughter Lelia:

My little Cherub Lelia,

As your mother says you are fond of my letters, and I have never yet written to you my much loved daughter, and furthermore as you are now nearly two years old, and may be quite that by the time this letter reaches you, and may find yourself slighted unless some attention is paid to you by your Papa, I write to you for the benefit of you and your Mamma, my charming wife and lovely daughter.

I am well except I have the neuralgia over my left eye, which annoys me some, though it is not severe. Our friends here are all well. Capt. Turner, Lt. Winchester, and Dr. Chears etc. from Monroe are all quite well and in excellent spirits at the unparalleled great news that fills us from all quarters of our army.

In the first place, Gen. Cooke with the 15th and 46th Regiments of his brigade, and the 44th North Carolina and 1st North Carolina Cavalry, and Cooper's Battery, in all about 2,000 men, beat off a force of about 4,000 Yankees from Hanover Junction last Saturday with the loss of only one man killed and only 5 or 6 wounded.

Secondly, Gen. Grant is said to be hemmed in and at the mercy of Gen. Joe Johnston and Vicksburg is perfectly safe. Grant is trying to escape.

Thirdly, Gen. Banks is said to have given up his assaults on Port

Hudson and after sustaining heavy losses, has gone back to New Orleans, with only 5,000 men and Gen. Taylor, McGruder and Walker's Divisions more than three times that number or thereabouts, having already taken Brashear City on the Mississippi, which is itself a very strong position with immense army stores.

And lastly, but not least, a telegraphic dispatch has been sent to Mr. Morris (who has control of all the telegraph lines in the Confederate States) stating from a Martinsburg Dispatch that Gen. Lee has completely defeated Gen. Meade at Gettysburg, Pa. and taken from him 40,000 prisoners, and is pursuing him towards Baltimore City, Md. and has Washington City within his grasp. Cities that your beautiful Mamma and I passed through in the days of our honeymoon, and where it is not improbable that our brigade may be sent before long to reinforce Gen. Lee. If so and you and your Ma could be there, I think, if we could take those places, we might spend our honeymoon over again with greatly increased delight. Ask your Ma, my very delightful daughter, how she would like to spend the fall in Washington and Baltimore. Perhaps we could extend our trip to the City of Brotherly Love too.

If neither you, nor Mrs. Walkup can come, and if we do go there, it may be well for you to let me know what things you and your Ma would like for me to buy you, as things will be very cheap there and I may have a chance of sending them home. If we do go, it may be a long time between our letters, and may be uncertain whether we can hear from each other in less than three or four weeks after our letters shall be written, and that would be a great cross to us all. But write and let me have a list of at least fifty or one hundred articles and things you would like me to buy, and it may be I can have a chance of getting and sending them to you. Tell your Aunts Jane, Martha, etc. and Uncle William to send in their bills too, and if I have a chance to fill them cheaply, I will do so with great pleasure. If you and your ma conclude to come yourselves, you will have to walk one hundred miles or more, as there will be no railroad communications.

Everything looks more favorable for peace now than it has ever done before and by the Grace of God, we have been more triumphant in this campaign, so far, then in any other, and have been seldom equaled by any the world has ever known.

"Dood my Ma I go to see Papa." Well now darling, will you leave Mamma? You had better stay my dearest baby and eat those good things you have at home-watermelons, peaches, apples, roasting ears, beans, Irish potatoes, butter, etc., etc., and go and visit your Uncle William and Cousin Harry and it may be I may pop down among you about August and help you to your good fare and fine cheer. That would be glorious, wouldn't it, my little rosebud, to be with you with you and your fascinating mother, who is even sweeter than you.

Give my love and several kisses to your Ma for me and squeeze her hand a little too for your Papa, dear daughter. You must also give my respects to Miss Alice and Miss Maggie and don't be too fond of kissing the little boys, Frank M. and Mr. Joe McLaughlin's and Major Covington's and the other little boys. Make them stand at a respectful distance and let them champ their bits, till you please to favor them with a smile. Then do it, like your Ma used to do your poor Papa, as if it were a special act of charity and grace, and not that you cared much about it yourself.

If we go off, I will write to you and Ma and I would be glad to hear from you both at your leisure.

Again I say, smother your Ma with kisses for you both from your kindhearted and deeply loving father and husband.

## July 10, 1863

Friday. We received telegram from D.H. Hill to be prepared for movement immediately from South Anna Bridge, where to, we can't imagine. Probably to reinforce Gen. Lee, now suffering a worse than Antietam or Sharpsburg defeat in Pennsylvania and who will scarcely be able to recross the Potomac without fearful loss, if not the destruction of his whole army. Meade, Couch and French etc. are after him like a pack of wolves elated with victory, enraged by invasion, prompted by hate and national pride and rush upon him with double or terrible force for his annihilation and nothing but the favor of God, great generalship and hard fighting can retrieve him and his army. Our reported successes were fabricated by dispatchers, from men who did not know or care what news was sent, perhaps was sent to deceive us. Our news from the rest is worse if anything than from Lee. Vicksburg fell on the Fourth July and that day has been for us a day of mourning and bitterness.[160] The picture looks gloomy and casts a smoke and frightful shadow over coming weeks. We can only look to God and hope for the best. He can inspire us and our weary Lee or his army with courage and wisdom and cast down the arrogance of our jubilant foes.

This is the darkest hour we have yet felt, beyond question, and there is no telling what may be the result of our bad luck. Cash on hand:

$79.00. Joe J. McNeely's note not paid $10.00 or $15.00. Capt. Walker and son J.M. leave of absence yesterday and left today, from Co. C. Rev. Moretz[161] resigns and claim of Moretz for pay. He having received no appointment in writing as chaplain of regiment claim pressed on Secretary of War. Gave unfavorable opinion to Moretz on the morality of buying Bibles $.50 and selling them at one dollar. The soldiers gave him a dollar each to buy the books, which first sold for a dollar each, though he [got them for $.50].[162]

## July 11, 1863

Today heard the sad news of the death by Battle of Gettysburg of Capt. William Wilson,[163] Lt. Richardson,[164] McWhorter[165] and others of 26th North Carolina Regiment, but nothing from brother Henry C. Walkup. We are still here. Army news more cheering or less discouraging. Rev. Moretz makes an honest statement of Bible speculation and offers to refund, remarks in good taste and Christian spirit. I will write to Brother Henry. Lt. Hugh Grey leaves for home thirty day's furlough disability. I am sending by him $55.00 to G.C. Baker, his pay for five months from 31st January to 30th of June 1863, sent to Lt. Grey in care of Dr. J.J. Williams.

## July 12, 1863

Rev. C. Moretz preaches his farewell address. I feel sorry for him. Tonight the camp sounds like a camp meeting singing and praying in several companies going on. I wrote to Brother Henry today.

## July 13, 1863

Gen. Lee asks for Cooke's Brigade so says Cooke. No doubt Cooke's ambition has thrust his brigade forward, hoping to push himself forward by the blood of his brigade. Ambition will wade through slaughter to a throne and shut the gates of mercy on mankind.[166]

## July 14, 1863

I have just heard by letter from Lt. H. A. Grey that Brother Henry Clay Walkup was wounded at the Battle of Gettysburg, Pennsylvania, but don't know when or what extent nor where he is. The regiment and his company suffered terribly in the fight, nearly all killed, wounded or prisoners. Heard today of the death of Lt. Henry Ringstaff by Battle at Gettysburg. Poor fellow, he was I fear unprepared for death and leaves a dependent family. He owes me a note of which I believe about $170.00 I will probably lose.

Received of Capt. Lewis C. Hanes my pay from 31st March 1863 to 30th of June 1863. There being three months at $170.00 per month, [total] $510.00. Total on hand cash today, $590.00 and $15.00 note on J.J. McNeely, after paying mess bill and for two chickens, leaving cash $5.70.

## July 16, 1863

Brother Henry lost his right arm amputated. Don't know where he is. I wrote to Stempa today whilst I was taking a chill, took calomel and afterwards quinine and Dover's powders, got a letter from my beloved Minnie and was so badly confused, stupid and deranged could not understand it. Though it was more tender and enduring than common and had more news to interest me, telling of Hall's coming with the prisoners,[167] of my congressional candidacy, etc. and dearest of all, herself and Lelia. I must have been in a profound lethargy and far worse than had supposed.

## July 18, 1863

I read the letter with astonishment. It was all news. Wrote to Minnie telling her of gloomy prospects of an early fight as Lee and Meade were in line of battle opposite each to be prepared for any sort of news, but anticipate the worse. "Nil desperandum Deo Duce."[168] That bloody riots prevail in North opposing conscription and cause Gen. Seymour to recall the orders to draft and that other places were doing so likewise (I think it doubtful though).Feel pretty well but very weak.[169]

## July 19, 1863

Feel quite well. Supply of six chickens, three dozen eggs, two dozen onions, two lbs. butter and one and one-half dozen guinea eggs, [traded] for nine pounds sugar within a day or two past and fare quite well, cost about $1.25 in sugar, worth at market price $13.00 to $14.00, we pay $12.50 lb.[170]

## July 20, 1863

Monday. My boy Hall arrives from home bringing with him my valise and pair of drawers and collars, ten lbs. butter from Jane Walkup, one-third of peck of Irish potatoes, three dozen onions, some beets and sweet cakes, three dozen all round. Loaf and letters from Minnie and William.

## July 21, 1863

Start to Staunton to look after Brother Henry Clay, sent Minnie by Sandy McClellan $106.50 and wrote to Col. Harry.

## July 22, 1863

Passed Staunton by Gordonsville and Charlottesville over rivers Rivanna and South and Mechums, a fascinating country with beautiful scenery, cross Blue Ridge through four tunnels, two of them not over 100 yards long, four minutes passing through the longest, very dark. Charlottesville a quiet, pleasant place, the seat of Virginia University, founded by President Thomas Jefferson whose residence Monticello is situated about four miles from the town and overlooks it and has become classic as the seat of the great.[171] Staunton is the county seat of Augusta in the valley of the Shenandoah where Washington said would be his last retreat. County of Augusta, then the whole valley, a Scotch Irish population, zealous, Whigs, hardy, in a rich valley surrounded with mountains with few passes and easily defended against a larger force. The hospitals are well constructed and especially the General Hospital, deaf and dumb asylum with shady groves, neat walks, beautiful shrubbery, fine water, an artificial lake with jet from duck's bill, and fare varied and excellent. The building is a beautiful piece of architecture.[172] So are the university buildings at Charlottesville, the seat of Congress in 1778 which Tarleton came near capturing. I could learn nothing of where Brother Henry Clay Walkup was but his right arm was amputated and he was doing well next day. Some doubt as to the necessity of his losing his arm and that he was probably left behind and captured by the Yankees who would treat him well.

## July 23, 1863

Returned bill at hotel $8.00 per day, one and two-thirds day $14.00, railroad fare to and from $16.00, liquor and three snacks, $2.00, papers $.23.

## July 25, 1863

Brother William Walkup arrived in camp with letter.[173]

## Nov. 13, 1863

❖ Letter from Walkup to Governor Zebulon Vance:

| By favor of Dr. B. Chears I drop you a few lines to beg you to aid me

in purchasing a suit of the best quality of cloth. I am getting too ragged for a North Carolina Field Officer and feel that it is due to the service and the respectability of North Carolina that I get a genteel suit. I have filed my application in the Quartermaster of Confederate States in Raleigh, N.C., but almost despair of getting it filled.

If you can aid me in procuring the imported best quality enough to make a coat and pants and vest, I shall feel under grateful obligation to you for it. Dr. Benjamin Chears will take the cloth to Charlotte for me and have it made up by my tailor there. If 1st quality cannot be had the 2nd will answer.

Dr. Chears is even more needy than myself of which you can judge by personal inspection. I hope he too will be accommodated if possible. The money shall be forwarded as soon as required at my risk.

Our regiments 48th North Carolina and 15th North Carolina are in great need of blankets and shoes.[174] Many of them being barefooted. We get none of the shoes and blankets sent by the Quartermasters of the 27th and 46th North Carolina, only a very slight and insignificant surplus after helping themselves in Cooke's Brigade.

We are daily receiving conscripts from Col. P. Mallett and would be very glad if no more were permitted to be sent to the 48th which is now larger than either of the other regiments in this brigade. The 27th and 15th North Carolina need them and deserve them and I hope they will be forwarded to these regiments, particularly the 27th which is very little over as full as the 48th North Carolina.[175]

Ours and Kirklands Brigades were shamefully sacrificed at Bristoe Station. Our regiment lost 9 killed, 116 and 47 taken prisoner. The men all fought well but were overpowered, and were in a very disadvantageous position.

Our request for the Roll of Honor will be forwarded as soon as the papers can be made out. Many of the captains are absent sick and wounded and have their muster rolls with them which are needed to make a complete report.[176]

We are now under marching orders. I suppose toward our right, or maybe to the rear. The men are in good spirits and reasonable health. I am commanding the regiment still.[177]

## Dec. 9, 1863

◆ Letter from Walkup at camp near Orange Court House to wife Minnie:

My own Loved Minnie:

What a glow of satisfaction flows over me as I write your much loved name and to feel that you are comfortable, as I believe, at home as I am here with cheerful fire in my tent and with perhaps better fare than you and my little Lelia and her tiny sister have at home. Oh how deliciously could we melt into each other's embrace and gaze with rapture on each other as we meet. One such glorious meeting would repay months of tedious marching... But let us hope as the French say: "Le contemps insendre"—the good times will come! I read one of your loved and cherished letters when on picket duty in front of the enemy with Yankee pickets within gun shot. It comes sheering and hopeful and sent the blood pure and streaming through my veins! Oh how tenderly we think of those most dear to us upon the eve of some great and expected battle. We seem to take a first fond, lingering look before we rush to carnage and death.

Our wives and infant children and brothers and sisters stir within us a holier love. Our innermost soul clings around them as if taking its last look on earth. How grateful was the reception of a letter from you, always so gladsome, at such a time as that. Soldiers have an insatiable craving at all times to hear from home and receive letters from their loved ones there. We are all selfish and would not be forgotten by those we love. Do they miss me at home? Do they miss <u>me</u>, crowds through the soul day and night and oh, oft how we wish we were there. We gaze on the silvery stars at all hours of the night and think how they look down on our loved ones at home. Whether in camps, in the bivouac, on the march or some dangerous outpost, our thoughts may roam through the heavens or on the earth, but its most frequent and holiest and sweetest emotions will kindle with joy as it turns to a lover or a friend, but so sublimely more thrilling when it is the husband and parents...

Your letters have come frequent of late, but still my soul is insatiable and looks and longs for letters from Sweet Minnie and sweet home. Ask Lelia, that little sweet lump of glory, whether she would know her father or not. I guess she would sell me for a nice red apple. The great mother of us all sold Paradise for an apple and who would expect a child to do less. Well, I shan't stand to the trade if she sells me, unless we all belong to the same master. Kiss her little fat cheeks, dimpled with innocence and joy and tell her Papa's love for her through his precious Mama and keep her warm through the cold nights. Kiss little Minnie [Jane] too, for she is a sweet little girl and just keep my dearest, finest person that comes in kissing distance, for him who can't kiss at this distance.

My own Minnie, I think you are managing better than I could if at home. You will have meat and bread enough to do and I hope you will have opossum, potatoes, molasses, etc. enough too.[178] You can hire Hall at $350.00 and [equip him with new] shoes and clothing, blankets and cap, unless Brother William buys the Carnes [possibly Cains Creek] plantation for me and wants to put in my hands to work there. Nothing would please me better than to own that place and have one year's supply and horses and stock and farming implements to begin with. I have telegraphed William to buy it if it sold for less than $30.00 to $35.00 per acre today. The sale comes off next Monday the 14th. I fear our bonds and money will depreciate greatly and prefer investing it in land at a high price. One year's products on it, with my forces, at present prices, would come near paying for it and supporting us besides.[179]

As to Stephen,[180] I would rather not hire him [out] at present as I may need him to stay with me next year. There is an order not to use white men as cooks or ostlers, and we cannot get Negroes, only from home. Therefore, I prefer not hiring Stephen at present. I may decide by the 1st of January, if I do not get to come home by that time. If I can get Tom Clutts, I could hire Stephen out and would rather Winchester have him than anyone else.[181] But if we get the Carnes [possibly Cains Creek] place he may be needed there. William wants Sally and says he will give the highest price for her. Margaret[182] is as good a hand as any.

If I do not get that land, you and William can hire Hall to whoever gives the most, McMurray, Stone or Harden. First of January will be time enough to determine. Walker Hellus must give $50.00 for the rent of my place or the usual rent in kind and if anybody wants my houses on lot no. 12, they must pay $100.00 for each except Mrs. Brown who can pay $25.00 and pay in work at the same rates, catching turkeys, etc. If she will find someone [to help you as a nursemaid], she may have the house for nothing and I will make Abram a present of a suit of Yankee britches and coat.

I sent my old coat back the same day it arrived by Eli D. Stewart's boy Sampson. He took the box William sent me with my coat and vest and silk sash in it and Dr. Chears coat pattern also, to be left in Charlotte in care of Dr. Miller to be sent by stage to Monroe. I suppose my coat and pants have reached you. Dr. Miller said Phillips cut them out and could not get any vest. I think he cabbaged off that if he cut the cloths (coat and pants) right. I will forgive him. You can send to Phillips or George Caldwell for thread or anything for trimmings that you need to make the coat and pants. I don't want any lace on it, only the buttons and stars from my old coat.

Dr. Miller sent me a bottle of brandy, and some person, Eugenia, I suppose, sent me an excellent jar of catsup. Your cabbage and sausage are splendid, and William's ham and potatoes. We had molasses, but yours is better—equal to New Orleans. We don't need the crout, nor any more molasses. Brother Henry, I regret, could not get here but went to Macon, Georgia. I have written him today and if he doesn't like to stay, I think he can easily get discharged.

We are all well and in winter quarters unless we go south or west. I feel rather gloomy about our cause. William Stough is still with me and well. We keep fast day tomorrow. Capt. Turner and Arthur Winchester took dinner with me Sunday. All well, love to all. Glad you have Dr. Alexander. He will do. Hate to lose Chis. Hope he gets his coat. Respects to him and love to you and friends—no more good byes.

God bless you

## Dec. 18, 1863

❖ Letter from Walkup at Headquarters near Orange Court House and Rapidan Station to wife Minnie:

My own dear wife:

This will reach you about Christmas and will, I hope, find you and my family and friends enjoying good cheer and in health.

I received your affectionate letter of the 10th on yesterday whilst out on picket beyond the Rapidan. We had had a cold night just before and the frost on the trees and weeds, but it turned warmer and melted during the day. We returned to camp last night all well and this leaves us generally quite well.

You will see by my last [letter] that I hired out Stephen to John H. Winchester (a son of W.) for 400 lbs. of pork next Christmas. You can hire Hall as you and William think best, but I think he ought to bring $500.00 or you had better wait and hire him out publically next January.[183] The prices must rise or we must suffer. Labor should bear some fair proportion to provisions. You will surely have enough of pork now and must take good care of it and the salt, for both will rise greatly unless money gets better. The Yankees will soon have our salt works, and salt will be higher than sugar. Try and get that flour from Howard as soon as possible and as much as you can.

If William can hire me an active boy for $200.00 or $300.00 to come to the army, I would be glad to get one to take care of my horse and to cook. An old sound Negro woman 45 to 50 years of age who could cook and work, might be of service to me if I had one, and she could make wages here. I fear William and all the men at home will have to come to the army and if so, I can't tell how you women will get on.

Dr. Chears ought to be here, his time is out. I sent his cloth in the box you received with my old coat, by Lamp. I think Mrs. Bowen can make my coat, but if it is not made yet and you can send to the tailor at Wheeler's Store, it will be better. I suppose you could furnish trimmings at home from some of your old cloths and some of my old coats as I wrote before. But you no doubt have fixed that some way before this. I am glad you received the $100.00 sent by Broom and hope you also got that sent by Forbes ($100.00). Our little rolling cherub with her beautiful glee and fiery locks must name her little white calf Albano and I give it to her for a Christmas gift. Little Minnie Jane shall have the next or Margaret's next baby, I don't care which. Lelia may have Harriet and Sue or Sarah [and] ought to have one for you, but they are all yours anyhow, and me besides.

I have just stopped to eat some cheese and biscuit and found cake brought by our Chaplain William Plyler,[184] and they are fine and I can only think of you and Lelia, and miss you and wish I could be home to eat there. I suppose little tiny Minnie Jane could not eat it if she would try. I hope your apples have come by this time from Charlotte.

If Dr. Miller and Brother William have to go into service I should like to give them some position and will do all in my power to do so, but don't know what I can do yet. They may command my services to the utmost extent. I should like to know what was done about the Carnes [possibly Cains Creek] tract or the [W.J.] Curaton land, in your next. Tell Lelia she must kiss Uncle William for that nice calf, and for his kindness to her and Mrs. and Jean and call him her good "grandpappy" and love him as such. For my part, I'd rather fight in two battles than to have him in one. For next to you, my dearest and my beloved children, my beloved brother comes foremost in my heart.

Don't forget to send my boots and socks, with my new coat and pants, if you have socks and tell me if you got the $100.00 sent by Forbes, and if the apples have come and get yourself some twenty gallons of molasses. I have surely said enough on clothes and things and will not add any more only to say do as you please and can will them all. I will stop here until Harget leaves for home and send this letter by him or Ficher or Deason.

December 20th (Sunday) Last night I read yours of the 13th by mail and Brother Henry surprised me at night by his presence with a letter from you of the 14th. He looks very much improved both in manner and appearance (save the top of his right arm) since I last saw him and I think he will no doubt get his discharge. He will apply for one today and will likely return in a few days.

I was greatly shocked at the unfaithfulness of the beautiful Mrs. Lou Alsobrooks and her treacherous uncle, Dr. [William M.] Timmons. Their incestuous intrigue is shameless, horrible. Poor Stephen is so ignorant of it and will nearly go crazy when he hears of it. He is a good boy and I have not the heart to let him know of his sister's disgrace. I am not quite well today—diarrhea and a touch of the dyspepsia troubles me.

I am glad Brother William did not buy me that land as it would have left me in debt and it would be the worst policy to have owed anything in these changing times.

Send my coat to White's Store to Mr. Bowman to make, if you think the women can't do it. Mr. Joe McLaughlin can probably send it down. If neither chance will do, send it to Phillips in Charlotte to finish, but send no more trimming than is actually needed, or he will keep them. My love to you and the children and friends.

In haste, your ever loving and devoted husband

## JANUARY 1, 1864

The New Year comes in beautifully, but rather blustering and cold in evening. I determine to resign my commission as lieutenant colonel rather than silently submit to the indignity of going for examination before a board organized expressly to reject for incompetency and rid the army etc. but drawing up the resignation, unless Major Hill too joins me, will consider further the movement.[185] But there are still suspicious circumstances against him. His old company and friends favor it. He refuses to resign with me and has studied so hard for some time for it.

JANUARY 3, 1864

I am field officer of the day and have command of the brigade today. Received 91 pair shoes and 140 blankets and distribute to regiment to most needy. Furlough comes back for Plyler and eleven men today. J. S. Bickett brings wife's letter.

JANUARY 4, 1864

Capt. L.C. Hanes returned last night, five furloughs to 100 men allowed, sent detail of 40 men under Lt. Reed[186] and Sgt. Thomas to build tents. Howie and Hix leave.

JANUARY 7–8, 1864

Hanes gave a lemon punch 7th. For the last few days Major Hill and myself have studied most assiduously on tactics. Capt. Mabry, Bitting and Lowry left. Dr. Chears and good things, coat, etc. arrive.

JANUARY 14, 1864

Loaned Dr. Smithers my horse to visit Davis Brigade and Stone, Col. 2nd Mississippi Regiment.

JANUARY 15, 1864

Major Hill furious at Moore's petition, I retort fiercely in its favor as a means of condemning the falsehoods of those who pretend to speak for the majority.

JANUARY 17, 1864

Refuse to let Lt. Jim Hix[187] go to Lane's and Scale's brigade two days to slander me and prejudice the mind of Lane[188] and others by malicious statements and we allow him after inspection to go today.

JANUARY 18, 1864

Dr. Chears off at Col. Faribault's[189] Headquarters, passed through rain and mud and arrived 2:00 p.m., too late for examination. Col. [John Marshall] Stone [2nd Mississippi Infantry] advised me to summon witness, that want of discipline would have to be met. Sullen to Major Hill and all around me. Had to go back the next day and that vexed me. Studied late, so did Hill. Got up mad, out at Hill and all suspected of agency in my going before Board.

## JANUARY 19, 1864

Very cold and windy, sick. Had Chears, Adjutant Winchester, Capt. Moore and Richardson, Lts. Stewart[190] and Stitt [available as witnesses]. Capt. Turner and Lt. Hamner[191] bring suit against me. I pass a very credible examination on tactics before the Board, answering correctly the questions except not clear on deploying battalions as skirmishers. I correct the President of Board Col. Stone 2nd Mississippi informing left into line rear companies into line faced to rear in centering the march. Col. Faribault said I learned him something in drill and all said I had proven a gallant and good fighting qualities. Capt. Turner did me full justice about rallying the men at Richmond and Sharpsburg when Col. Hill failed but erred in saying his company and Co. E were all that were rallied at Sharpsburg. Richardson's and Jones's parts of nearly every company were there and rallied instead of only 40 men. I think there were over 100 men rallied, 125 I would say. He said I was "only tolerable on drill or discipline," as good as many others and better than some, that I made frequent mistakes, such as when men were at an order to command a movement without shouldering and at Gordonsville when battalion were at column by divisions right in front gave order right into line wheel. Left companies on right, into line, guide right, march. That he supposed I knew better, but got men into confusion often, yet that they would not move when wrong command was given. Had no personal ill feelings, that we had a little difficulty but it was settled and he had none now. Moore and Richardson [testified] discipline good and very good drill. Richardson said I made some little mistakes sometimes. Board well satisfied with my conduct, examination and proofs of witnesses.[192] Did not examine balance [of witnesses], not necessary. Evening cold. Took drink in Orange, self, Adjt. Winchester one-half pint for $6.00.

❖ Letter from Walkup at Orange Court House to wife Minnie:

> My own Sweet and Darling Wife Minnie:
>
> How joyfully my pulse bounds and the blood rushes through my veins and my heart throbs with tender emotion as I write your cherished and much loved name. My memory recalls a thousand pleasant incidents of the happy past and the prospective future of bliss.
>
> The parlour at I.B. Kerrs where a glance from your enchanting eyes, just swept my soul from the moorings of bachelorhood and when "your fingers witched the chords that passed along and your lips

seemed to kiss the soul in song." Or when your angelic grace and prettiness swept the last ray of hope from the dull grey eyed, red haired, twisted lipped, but rich Miss — to whom I had almost sold myself at Pleasant Grove Camp Ground and from whom I beat a glorious retreat. Or to the parade ground at Morrows Turnout, where you bought me with a quarter and bound me with a soft look and gracious smile that sealed me your own forever; to Kerr's parlour again at the event of the November Companions, and at the Agricultural Fair in Charlotte where your agreeable form and loveliness made me feel then that:

"Yours were looks and tones that dart an instant sunshine through
  the heart.
As if the soul that moment caught, some treasure it through life had
  sought.
Or if your very lips and eyes, predestined to share all my sighs,
And never be forgot again.
Sparkled and spoke before me then."

And finally, I think of Uncle R. McDowell's parlour, when the whole matter that made me love you, dear Minnie and wife, sealed my enthusiastic devotion, and then our trip via Chesapeake Bay!! to Elmira, Niagara, Saratoga, New York, Washington, etc., pass in glorious review before my enraptured gaze, and the eternal incidents that have so constantly occurred since which bind me link by link to you forever in the forms of Lelia and little teeny Minnie Jane, make my very arms itch to fold you to my fond bosom and smother you with kisses and look myself away in your beautifully fascinating eyes.

You will probably get this upon my birthday, 22nd of January, and if so, make yourself and family happy and congratulate me as Col. Commandant of this regiment.[193] I have today been before the Examining Board and passed a very credible examination, not missing a question and proving even by the witnesses against me a better character than most colonels can prove by their own selected friends—

"A man of undoubted courage and gallantry on the battlefield"
"Rallied the regiment when the Colonel gave way"
"Was always present with his men in the thickest of the fight"

I even corrected the Examining Board in a false proposition they made, and convinced them of their error, and one of them, Col. Faribault, said he was obliged to me for learning him something he did not know and that I had established a reputation for undoubted gallantry in fighting. I have no doubt, as I never had any, of my being appointed colonel of the 48th North Carolina.

But now I wait to hear from you my love and brother William if you think I ought to resign and come home. I feel that I can do so quite consistently, for it was an insult to me to order me brought before the Examining board. It implied a doubt of my capacity and efficiency, and I feel like resenting it by resigning. My own feelings of self-respect demand it of me, and if you and William say so, I will resign and come home.

The only difference it will make is that I have no business to go at if I get home to make anything to support us. But the coming campaign will likely be a bloody one and it seems that our regiment can never get credit for anything it may do beyond what other regiments are lauded for.

I expect to be home about the last of February or the first of March. I may not have more than 18 days to stay, which will give me only 12 or 14 at home. I am in quite fine health at present and am still on picket and will be so for about ten more days. We have pleasant times enough except that our rations are getting short. The soldiers get only one-fourth and even less beef as meat rations per day.

Adjt. Winchester and James Stitt, my particular friends, and Lt. R. L. Stewart also, are all well and Dr. Chears is tolerably well. Lt. Henry Howie[194] is not well and is trying to get home. Stephen M. Simmons[195] has chronic inflammation of the stone and will probably be sent home or to the hospital. He is not to blame for his misfortune as it did not arise from any misconduct and has been coming on him for years. He is as amiable, honest, virtuous and clever and modest young man.

I have heard with much surprise of the marriage of Cousin Nancy Hough with that blank piece of a man William Dillon. He is a do-less act unworthy of Elisha Stansill's daughter, let alone the widow of the amiable and honest, clever Joe Hough. Widows will marry almost any piece of a man who offers now-a-days. Joe Hough would groan from his grave (if the dead could groan) over such a marriage. How does the Widow Stitt and her Methodist preacher come on? Who was it who wrote to her from our brigade? I will speak favorably for her to him, if he is worthy of her, and she will let me know his name.

I am sorry to hear of Mr. Joseph McLinn losing his money. You had better keep your meat and money well locked up in these times of robbery.

I also heard of Mr. D. Bryun's and Mrs. Griffin's losses. Kiss my little Fatty and Leany both for me and tell them to look for me in about six weeks more.

Mr. G. W. Short will bring this letter for you. He leaves in the morning on 18 day's furlough.

It is quite cold and windy tonight. Make Susan take good care of her fires. My love to brother William and brothers and sisters, etc., but much more to you and the children.

God bless and protect you and us all.

Your fondly loving husband

## January 20, 1864

Sent Major Hill before Board. Col. MacRae tells of my calling him young Napoleon and seems touched at it seriously. Regiment generally rejoices at my passing successfully the Examination Board. Several officers (Adjt. Moore) spoke of resigning if I was refused. Fuzz, Hilliard of Co. B much pleased etc., much prefer me to Major Hill.

## January 22, 1864

This is my 46th birthday, fair and beautiful, thank God at I still live in health of body and mind. I received a cheering letter from my dear beloved Minnie, the life and soul of my existence, last night by Thomas McCauley. Today with my friends Dr. B. Chears and Col. William MacRae I enjoy an eggnog.

## January 25, 1864

This day received [official] report of my having passed the Board of Examination satisfactorily. This day also our regiment witnessed the execution by shooting of Augustine Crouch[196] from Davidson County, North Carolina for desertion, by sentence of Court Martial.[197] I tried to have it put aside as sentence did not state two-thirds of court concurring. He was unprepared and much concerned. Being busy in leaving for the Board of Examination when he was sent to Provost I did not tell him his fate and knew nothing of it till Saturday 23. Pinkney White[198] gave me a brandy and honey and pies, pond cake, chicken, apples, butter, sweet cake and some dried peaches. Major A.A. Hill and 19 men on furlough left today, William Delaney[199] steals 12 plugs tobacco from Sutler Hart. It grieves his father and myself.

Torrence case vexes me, a returned deserter. Rushing ditto. Accused of gross neglect by Lt. Gen. Hill for not informing Crouch of sentence of death against him. He kills 1000 by carelessness viz. see Bristoe[200] and because I do not inform [Crouch whom] his minions murdered [through] Court Martial he blames me.

## JANUARY 26, 1864

This day sentence against Bean, Michael, Imbler, Croft, Long began to be executed. Sent off Cook and Croft to Richmond sentence.

## JANUARY 27, 1864

Officer of the day. Some of our cavalry pickets on Robertson River captured. Yankees advance closer to us. Received from Capt. C. Hanes two months four days pay at Lt. Col. to 4th Dec. 1863, $22.66 and pay as Colonel from Dec. 5th 1863 to 31st Jan. 1864, $364.00, of which sent $200.00 by Lt. William O. Stearns to my wife.

## JANUARY 28, 1864

◈ Letter from Walkup at camp near Orange Court House to wife Minnie:

My own darling Wife,

I expected a letter from you by Sgt. George W. Howie,[201] but you failed to write. He told me you were all well and that you were at his house a day or two before he left. But I would have preferred a letter. You know "insatiable of assurance love is." We are still on picket until the 3rd of February.[202] Major Hill has gone home on a furlough of 18 days. He will probably be back about the 20th or thereabouts of February. I expect then to try to get off about 25th February for 18 days only, as that is the longest time the authorities will allow officers as well as [enlisted] men (who are capable of duty) to be absent.

I send these lines and $200.00 to you by Lt. William O. Stearns.[203] If he spends any of it in getting home he will replace it before he returns. If he happens in about dinner time, you might ask him to dine.

We are all well as common. My health is quite good and Dr. Chears, though always complaining, is well enough, if one is to judge by the quantity he eats I think he comes near being a glutton. Capt. Turner will try to get home when Lt. Lowrie returns. He is well and so are Winchester and Lieutenants Stitt and Harward. The latter has an application to go home too. He has not quite recovered from his sickness yet.

The weather is quite mild and beautiful as spring, but it is too warm and enervating after so much cold. It is entirely too relaxing on the system and makes me listless and stupid. It would be a good time to have your garden and patch plowed by Sam Blount, and prepare for your real spring.

We had an unusual scene last Monday. One of our regiment was shot for desertion by sentence of a Court Martial and several men have been sentenced to hard labor, to wear ball and chain to the leg, to solitary confinement on bread and water diet, etc., to forfeit pay for from six to twelve months, etc. One poor fellow was sentenced to work five years in some military post without any pay. Another to forfeit all that was due him (nearly a year's pay) and to work hard and engage in all the drills, marches and fights without any pay for two years to come.

I was officer of the day yesterday and had charge of our pickets, which comes to my turn about every fourth day. Some of our cavalry pickets on Robinson River were captured by Yankees yesterday morning and the Yankees have come closer to us. We can see their camp fires about two miles off from our picket lines. Some dozen Negroes escaped over the Rapidan and went to the Yankees two nights since.

Minnie, my love, this unnatural war keeps thousands of loving hearts asunder and scatters so many ills and horrors around that it seems to me liberty, as it is called, will be purchased, if at all, at too dear a sacrifice.[204] Every heart yearns for peace and the comforts of home and family and would prefer less liberty for peace and the comforts of home and family and would prefer less liberty and more domestic peace and happiness. If we were not in the war this would be the sentiment of almost every person. But now we can't help ourselves and we are in a dilemma, where we must risk everything or lose all. We must fight through or be degraded and disgraced. We must continue to fight for self-preservation, for existence. If death or mutilation nearly as bad comes, we are worsted. But if we escape both and find our families safe and secure our independence the price will not be too great for the prize we seek. I look forward to the day when we shall have a snug little country seat, with a little farm and orchard and garden and some flowing stream, with cows and calves and a diary filled with some milk and butter, hogs, sheep, chickens. Patches of potatoes, watermelons, fields waving in green or gold, with harvests, orchards of choice peaches, apples, cherries, plumbs and other fruits, bee hives laden with rich honey comb and wine, cider and something stronger. When cards and wheels, looms and sewing machines shall be busy and invigorate the health of us and our own dear owes at home. When neatness, cleanliness and good fare and cooking and fine cheer and mirthful hospitality and good nature shall surround us and cause happiness to beam in every countenance and be felt in every fiber of our frames.[205] That is a glance at my hopeful future for us and our family; to see little Lelia, Minnie Jane and all the rest dancing with delight around us and climbing upon us and running to meet us and glad at everything. Busy with the chickens, lambs, pigs, in the garden, kitchen diary, loom house, sewing, spinning, playing on the piano, visiting kind friends or entertaining them, bouncing, laughing, singing, working, playing, coquetting, doing every harmless and innocent thing from a full flow of spirits just for the sake of variety and healthful enjoyment. In fine, doing just what we used to do when we were boys and girls and living ourselves again, except where we did wrong, and in that respect I wish none of them would follow my bad example, but all that was good. Kiss the little cherubs and tell them that their Papa will try and get home to see Mama first and them at the same time, about from the 20th to the 28th of February if nothing happens. And if he could do so, he would never wish to leave them long at a time again.

I enclose you a slip containing the view of "a philosophic darky" on the war and patriotism. Read it to little Lelia and Minnie [Jane] and see if it does not make them laugh.

On next Saturday, probably the day you receive this letter, we will have three more men from the 46th regiment in our brigade shot for desertion by sentence of Court Martial. It is much more shocking to me than in battle, for in battle the blood is up and men excited and as no one expects to be hit positively, he feels a hope. But in these military executions the blood is cool and the doom of the victim certain and it freezes the blood to witness it, though it is necessary to enforce order and obedience. Without which an army, like a government without law, would be a reckless and unmanageable mob. Many of the worst cases such as the Medlins, Shannon, Small and others frequently escape.

I wish you to tell Mrs. Brown that she must not cut down any tree in my yard where she lives. Her son asked me about two growing in the edge of the garden, which his mother asked to let her have cut, but I cannot permit her or any other to have them felled. I told her son that his mother might have the house this year and it made no difference about her giving any notes. You and Mrs. Brown may regulate that yourselves. She might make a well rope, and help you in spinning and weaving, catching babies, black and white, etc. to pay rent. Deal kindly and liberally with the old lady, for she is a kind and good old soul, and if she pays nothing, it won't hurt us.

My love to any of my brothers and sisters or Stephen or their families you may see and particularly always to Brother William. Many kisses from me to you and the children. May God bless you and all of us. Good bye, your lover still in the honeymoon, which if it wanes becomes new, fresh and often.

Your husband truly

## JANUARY 28–30, 1864

Was arrested by Col. MacRae under order from Lt. Gen. A. P. Hill, for not informing Crouch of his fate. I had no order to do so and am to be Court Marshaled for gross neglect of duty. Ordered to have three day's rations prepared for moving and men brought in from new camp. Day like spring [as were] four days past. Three deserters from 46th North Carolina shot Saturday, Jan. 30. I did not go to see. Told Lt. Hamner, Co. B, of his company's spite on me which he disclaimed, told me my rash censure of himself at Fredericksburg. I apologize as unjust to him. Capt. 26th North Carolina said I knew more English Court and stood superb examination.

## JANUARY 31, 1864

Sunday. Lt. Hix's leave disapproved by Gen. Lee on my endorsement. Yankees cross Robertson River. I released from arrest to take charge of regiment. Yankees are driven back by our cavalry, or go back themselves, more probably.

## FEBRUARY 1, 1864

I am again arrested and charges preferred for neglect of duty, to be tried tomorrow. Have Chears summoned for and Adjutant [Winchester] and Butler.

## FEBRUARY 2, 1864

Trial before Military Court over. We leave for new camp and winter quarters tomorrow. Sent by J. R. Winchester, Adjt., to General, $10.00 fees for commissions for Lawhon, two Cleggs, Stitt and Lowry. Bitting returned today being absent from 13 January.

## FEBRUARY 3, 1864

Wednesday. We moved to new camp today and went into winter quarters.

## FEBRUARY 6, 1864

Orders about 9:00 a.m. to have one day's rations cooked and to be prepared to move regiment at any moment. Regiment moves before day. I remain at camp glad to be under arrest. About 8:00 to 9:00 a.m. artillery and musketry heard in direction of Liberty Mills on our left four miles.

## FEBRUARY 11, 1864

Released from arrest and in charge of regiment.[206]

## FEBRUARY 12, 1864

Brigade reviewed by Gen. Cooke and inspection. Lt. Col. Hill returns, MacRae leaves 13th.

## FEBRUARY 13, 1864

Receive my leave of absence for 20 days leave 17th or 18th to 10th March. Received from Capt. L.C. Hanes Feb. $195.00.

## MARCH 10, 1864

Returned last night about 1:00 in the night, left home Monday 7th got to Gordonsville, Virginia 8:30 a.m. walked to camp seven miles. Expenses home and back $48.75. Total payments at home and on my way besides above $600.00. Left with my wife $52.00 in paper, brought with me from home $102.00 to camp, $550.00 specie and $100.00 with Laney.

17th, 18th, and 19th February were remarkable for the intense cold weather of those days. The water in the pipes conducting water to the engine became frozen near Gordonsville and at Richmond the thermometer fell to 17 degrees below freezing point, some say to within 4 of zero, whilst I was on my way home and we missed connection at Petersburg and at Raleigh and I missed connection with the stage at Charlotte and rode to Dr. Miller's house to Four Mile Creek and walk home from thence 14 miles, arriving home at 3:00 a.m. Sunday, 21st February very weary. But cheered by the sight of my wife and children. Commanding Cooke's Brigade as [Acting] General Colonel.

## MARCH 14, 1864

Large chapel, 44 feet by 57 feet, built. Rev. Jacob Smith preaches for one month. MacRae relieves me of brigade command 13th. I sent by Major W.W. Hart $5.50 specie to pay $2.50 for par cotton or $60.00 Confederate and to get from my wife gold and silver to invest in buying Confederate at 100 [to one] or less [up] to 50 for one in Confederate bonds and to divide profits.[207] Rev. Mr. Smith leaves today.

Nothing [final] of Brigade to invite Governor Vance to speak. I am chairman of committee, report resolution tomorrow.

## MARCH 15, 1864

Ordered to begin deploying skirmishers to front and posts and to rear, during battalion drills from center and from left and right groups. Frank Cuthbertson becomes troublesome. Been absent since Bristoe fight from a light wound in left arm. Wanted to substitute about Christmas, wanted transfer to cavalry, wanted detail on quarter or post in North Carolina. Always nosing around for a change and needs close watching. I told him of it, and ordered him back to duty. Dr. Chears examined him yesterday and says he has nothing the matter with him. Col. William MacRae becomes Napoleonic and finds fault with 48th North Carolina.

## MARCH 16, 1864

Inspection, best condition yet seen, day very cold. Lt. Hart inspects, addressed [as] chairman of meeting to Governor Vance.

◈ Letter from Walkup to Governor Zebulon Vance:

I have the honor of forwarding to you the enclosed preamble and resolutions adopted by the soldiers of Cooke's Brigade (comprised of the 15th, 27th, 46th and 48th North Carolina Troops.

I hope it may be consistent with your arduous duties to comply with the cordial invitation embodied in the 5th resolution of the meeting, that we may have the pleasure of personally greeting and old fellow soldier who has done so much for us, your brethren in arms, and for our families and fellow citizens of North Carolina at home. It is made my agreeable duty to earnestly solicit Your Excellency to address this brigade upon the subjects which have now engage the attention and interest of all North Carolinians, and which are of special interest and concern to her soldiers in the field.

I trust that it will suit your convenience to comply with the wishes of our brigade and if so, that you will designate the time, at which you can be present to address us.

## MARCH 17, 1864

Thomas W. Dial of Co. K sentence read, to be shot next Thursday, seems stupid, indifferent, young, fat, half dead, thoughtless and ignorant. I learn today nomination for Senate, North Carolina. Begin officer drill and sergeant drill [on] 18th.[208]

## MARCH 19, 1864

Saturday. R.L. Stewart, Lt., returns, excitement at home about conscripts. Army Northern Virginia composed of Ewell's and Hill's Corps, and Stuart's Cavalry. Ewell's Corps 1st. of Rhodes, Johnson's and Early's Divisions. Hill's 3rd of Heth, Anderson and (Pender's) now Wilcox's divisions. Stuart's Cavalry. Heth's Division, composed of Cooke's, Kirkland's, Davis' and Walker's Brigades. Cooke's Brigade of 15th, 27th, 46th, 48th North Carolina. Kirkland's of 11th, 26th, 52nd, 44th and 4th North Carolina. Davis of 55th North Carolina and Mississippi. Walker's of Tennessee. Wilcox's Division of Lane's and Scales' Brigades. Lane's of 7th, 18th, 33rd, 37th North Carolina. Scale's of 13th, 22nd North Carolina.

## MARCH 22, 1864

Intense cold and windy, freezing at 10:00 a.m. in tent. Snow and wind very cold, commenced snowing at 11:00 a.m. and continued until after 10:00 a.m. with high wind. Snow very dry and drifted from two feet to three or four, average about 12 inches.

## MARCH 23, 1864

Wednesday. Warm, calm and sunny. Kirkland's Brigade attack ours [with snowballs], who turn out and drive the enemy home. A truce is called for, and challenge to fight at 2:00 p.m. Both brigades turn out, Col. MacRae commanding Cooke's and Gen. Kirkland commanding Kirkland's four or five regiments. We take position, 48th on right, 46th on left, 15th right center and 27th left center. Regimental colors out. 44th and 26th attack our left and drive them back, capturing the colors of the 46th and their Lt. Col. McAlister and our reserves. 48th drive back 52nd, capturing their colors and many officers and men. Our commander is captured (Col. MacRae). Our center maintain their position.

## MARCH 24, 1864

Thursday. This day begins new volume of a diary or journal kept by me for the year 1864 from April 1, 1862. We draw rations free from this date, equal with privates.[209] On this day the snow rapidly vanished, the day is warm and beautiful, the snow which yesterday morning was 12 inches deep has vanished from the south side of the fields. We had great sport yesterday between the regiment and Kirkland's Brigade in a general [snowball] battle.[210] Our brigade had overcome Kirkland's in the forenoon, they having assaulted our camp without notice which ended in their having to defend their own and having suffered a loss of several stands of colors. They challenged us through Gen. Kirkland for general engagement, in the evening. We all accepted the challenge, Gen. Heth was present and several ladies. Our left were driven with our reserve back in confusion by the 26th and 46th. The 46th on our side acted shabbily and its Col. McAllister and his columns were captured. But our right wing drove back the enemy with great loss. The 48th literally demolished the 52nd and drove them from the field, capturing the commanding officer and his colors and then wheeled in on the flanks of the 47th and 11th and gave effectual aid to our center 15th and 27th enabling them to drive back the foe and save the honors of the day. Our General MacRae was captured in a general melee after the flag of truce was shown. But the 48th runs Gen. Kirkland from the field and he owes his safety to the speed of his horse.

On this day Private Thomas W. Dial,[211] a condemned deserter from Co. K in this regiment, was shot by sentence of Court Martial and order of Lt. Gen. A.P. Hill, and two from Kirkland's Brigade.[212] Dial met death quietly and stolidly, professing to be changed and willing to die, of which the evidence was quite feeble. He died like a sick man takes medicine, by nerving himself to the act. I doubt his capacity to know what death meant, he seemed so indifferent.[213]

## MARCH 25, 1864

I visit Military Court [for] three army corps today to defend Hirmen Williamson of Co. D for desertion. I think Col. D.M. Carter rather overbearing in remarks about quibbling. Lt. Col. Whittle with one arm, and Col. Hill, brother of Lt. Gen. A.P. Hill, composed court. A sharp and energetic but severe court. Had a disagreeable duty to perform. William J. Shannon and wife come to regiment, had a petition written by Col. J.M. Stewart and signed by many of our best citizens, sheriffs, clerks,

H.W.H., D.F.H., D.A.C., etc. to Jeff Davis, Gen. Lee, myself and the Court Martial in behalf of Shannon. A letter from myself and the commanding officer of the company of the facts of the case, which I gave pretty freely and firmly as in duty bound. I feel sorry for his wife and for him too, but must strike though I weep.

## March 28, 1864

Visited Ransom's Brigade, saw Governor Vance review the troops and Daniel's Brigade and make a speech, saw Col. Bennett of the 14th North Carolina regiment, Lt. Col. Still of Daniel's staff, Gens. Ewell, Early, Stuart, Gordon, Rhodes, Ramseur and other officers. Vance made a tolerably good speech, but had too little seriousness and too much buffoonery in it for a Governor on so solemn an occasion.[214] Most of his audience will soon be engaged in bloody battle and many will be killed. If our arms suffer reverses he will be defeated for Governor, if we are victorious he will be elected.

## March 29, 1864

Very rainy all day and constant rain in evening and at night. Vance could not speak. No review called on Vance at Kirkland's headquarters. Met with Gen. Heth there who says he thinks Lee will [launch] spring campaign, says he knows Gen. Grant in old service. He was not promising then, took a ride with Grant on Grant's fast trotting pony, turned over the buggy, ran against cow, threw Heth into a cranberry thicket, broke Grant's collar bone. Pemberton said Grant had raised siege of Vicksburg but ordered back by Gen. Thomas and took it, say also Grant ain't much.[215] Governor calls [with] J.F. Taylor, dilapidated young gentleman know the middle names of all the young ladies, ruffles and stove pipe hats, agent for N.C. Botany & Co. in West Indies islands. Mrs. William Shannon called on me early this morning, was blackening my boots, did not have on coat and hair uncombed.

## March 30, 1864

Wednesday. Governor Vance addresses Cooke's and Kirkland's Brigades.[216] Just before he begins he tells me, "Well Colonel, we used to be good old Whigs together. I want you to Amen for me when I say any good thing." I told him I would do it at a venture whether at the right place or not. He made a good Vance speech, but it was scarcely dignified enough for the Governor of North Carolina before Generals J.E. B. Stuart, Heth and others of our own state. Sent off today four men to Navy

Department from this regiment—Frank Fincher,[217] Cpl., Co. A, Jesse L. Parker,[218] Co. F and Spence Murray[219] of Co. G and Sgt. Nading[220] of Co. K. Sent charges and specifications against William Shannon for desertion and advising and permitting others to desert.

## APRIL 1, 1864

Snow follows the rain. Sickness increases in our camp.

## APRIL 3, 1864

Sunday. Day clears off fine. Begin the sublime and rapt poem of the Prophet Isaiah. Pope might well invoke "Oh Thou my voice inspire, who touched Isaiah hallowed lips with fire." Got knife today, paid Shepherds Raines, free Negro, $10.00 for a sorry job and James Smith ground [blade] for $1.00, total $11.00.

## APRIL 4, 1864

Rainy and sleet and snow all day. Sent knife to Major Pickard's to have fixed. Rain, snow, sleet, followed by hard wind. Sickness in camp increases. Sgts. Correll,[221] Nat Hendrix[222] and Lt. Fulp[223] resign.

## APRIL 5, 1864

Lt. W. D. Richards shows W. Gills political death warrant. Sgt. R.R. King deposed.

## APRIL 6, 1864

Twice today to drill company officers. The first attempt I ever made to drill a company. Made a miserable failure, quit in confusion. But will try again. Capt. Richardson finished the drill. I would almost as soon fight a battle.

## APRIL 7, 1864

Tried the company drill again with a little better success, but still indifferently done. I know it well theoretically, but have no practical knowledge. But will make a spoon or spoil a horn trying. Fast day tomorrow recommended by President, Gen. Lee and myself.[224] Private Joe Medlin[225] of Co. A brought by courier this evening and sent to guard house.

## APRIL 10, 1864

Gen. Cooke assumes command of the brigade today first time

since his wound at Bristoe. Heard Rev. Mr. Bell of Rowan Presbytery in chapel. Col. MacRae called with Capt. Foxhaw.

## APRIL 11, 1864

Called on Gen. Cooke, pleasant enough and very communicative, urges the forming a band for music. Friday a tournament comes off at Gen. Heth's headquarters. Sent witness against William Shannon. His statement to James I. Richardson[226] to desert but none stuck up except his brother John B. [Watson] and Robert Watson[227] and a few others. How he had planned, talked and mapped it out. Joseph McNeeley[228] wanted to go because he would stick up as well. Nathan E. Baker,[229] Evan Watson,[230] Allen Gordon,[231] William Vickory,[232] Ace Phillips,[233] Thomas Adams[234] all promised and many others. Shannon not tried today. To be tried tomorrow.

❖ Letter from Walkup at camp near Orange Court House to wife Minnie:

My ever dear wife:

I drop you a few lines by Mr. Hunter who is going home from Co. I on 30 day's furlough having furnished a recruit. I have just written to you a day or two since and have no news of much consequence to add, by Mr. Moeser. We are still in camp here as you will perceive and have had more rain and more sickness. My own health is good and our officers etc. from about Monroe.

We held a tournament today at Gen. Heth's headquarters. I did not attend it. Many of Virginia's chivalry and fair ladies graced the occasion and feats of horsemanship and arms were displayed in the old fashioned way of the times of the renown Knights of La Mancha and the rueful countenance and perhaps several windmills charged with less danger than Don Quixote encountered. Adjt. J. R. Winchester was there and much pleased with the performance.

Gen. Cooke has returned to camp and assumed command. The band is now serenading him. We are ordered to have seven day's rations on hand at all times and to be ready to move. All our trunks and extra baggage is ordered to be sent back and all visitors to leave camp. Some women are here and sick. I don't know how they will get off.

I will send my trunks with Mr. Hunter and a few things in it and carry the balance in my saddle bags and with my bed roll until my valise arrives by Richardson[235] if we move before he comes. I think the roads are so bad we will not leave for a week and expect him back by that time. My trunk and key will be left with Squire Mac Matthews and Dr. Miller in Charlotte until you have an opportunity of sending for it. It has very little in it and you need not be in a hurry about sending.

Shannon's case comes on tomorrow for trial before the Courts Martial, and will be pretty strong against him. I would not be surprised if they sentence him to be shot, though Gen. Lee or Jeff Davis may petition him on his wife's account. Joe Medlin is quite penitent and will not fare so well, though not so bad a man. Wives are a great benefit oftentimes to very mean husbands. I have known many better wives suffer with unavailing tears for many better husbands than either.

My lovely and gentle wife, how are you and our dear little babes getting on, [as] I have not heard from you very lately? I would like to have them climbing on my knees to share the kissed their mother would be sure to be getting if I were at home. Yes, I would be drinking in your beauty and gentleness through my eyes, and you would be taking in and melting my whole soul through your dovelike orbs, and we would let our hearts and souls with thrilling rapture mingle into one. I often almost wish I could look myself away and melt into your eyes, or absorb you through my own! Kiss our flowerets for me and tell Lelia I have not killed dem Yankees yet. I want her and her baby doll to help you to work the garden and potatoes and spin and weave cloth and raise corn and potatoes. I hope you will have strawberries this spring. I should be sorry to learn they were killed. The snow still covers the sides and top of the neighboring mountains.

My love to relatives and respects to Major Wiant, McLaughlin and friends. I will bring these few lines to a close. May God bless you and the dear children and all I love, and protect us henceforth and forever.

Your devoted and loving S. W. Walkup

P.S. I send: one woolen shirt, one woolen drawers, 24 cotton socks and pair boots, cap, one-half bottle ink, quire paper and books and psalms in trunk.

## April 13, 1864

Began brigade drill today and battalion drill tomorrow. Held election Seventh Congressional District. Leach 147, Porter 40, Ramsey 8 in the 48th Regiment.

## April 14, 1864

Joe Medlin tried for desertion today, whipped hard today.

## APRIL 15, 1864

Cooke's Brigade as above Kirkland's [experience] revivals flourishing in this brigade. One sad private touched my heart at his distress.[236] Twenty-two were immersed by Rev. Howerton Sunday, six sprinkled by Plyer of 48th.[237]

## APRIL 18, 1864

I inspected 46th North Carolina and visited Montpelier[238] and President Madison county seat and burial ground, scenery enchanting. Mountains covered in snowing point west. Velvet green lawns slope in graceful undulations on all sides and curves steep or gradual, magnificent grove of black walnuts, refreshing walks of spruce pine, huge chestnut oaks sunny side and well laid off with gardens, ice house covered with red painted tin, two wings [main house], front like White House in Washington City, rear six iron pillars, five chimneys to large part and two to the wings. Gravel walks as President's house, which was no doubt the model. Country mountainous but picturesque and soil dark. It needs river to complete the picture. The burial ground contains an unpretending granite monument inscribed "Madison, born March 1751, died 1836" and near it a neat marble monument "Dolly Madison, wife of Madison, born 1768, died 1849" with others of the Madison and other families, showing they were of great longevity. I plucked some boxwood from the yard and some ivy from the graveyard and sent home by letters.[239]

## APRIL 20, 1864

W. J. Shannon sent to Richmond under sentence to be shot. Preferred to President Davis and his voluntary surrender, wife in tears, and he stubborn and pragmatic. I prepared a statement of the case but willingly abandoned it at Col. Hill's suggestion. It stated the case strongly against him, but my promise strongly in his favor.

## APRIL 21, 1864

Improve 7th attempt on battalion and brigade drill considerably, appoint sharpshooters for watch tomorrow. Broxley Morris and N.E. Baker of Co. F who make the best.

## APRIL 22, 1864

Average shots by regiment in brigade [match] 22. I beat Gen. Cooke and the field shooting 7 1/4 at 140 yards one shot, Cooke's nearest 18 inches. Cooke, Anderson, Dr. Hart and captain of 27th shot and myself, 24 in 3 shots, the best average by marks 15th Regiment, 27th Regiment, 48th Regiment.

## April 23, 1864

Orders arrive to cut tents and flys and make shelter tents for the company.

## April 24, 1864

Cancel receipt by Surgeon Montgomery.[240]

## April 25, 1864

Hear Rev. Grandberry[241] of Norfolk preach brigade revival, many join churches. Eli N. Henderson and others immersed.

## April 27, 1864

In command of brigade. Kirkland's Regiment moves camp. I will form squares in four ranks and columns against cavalry.

## April 30, 1864

General inspection and muster of all the men.

## May 1, 1864

Visited Col. Lane[242] of 26th North Carolina and saw Rev. Howerton immerse a great many men.

## May 2–5, 1864

Severe storm of rain and wind blew our tent partly down, gave us a run from general drill with a broken rain. Sergeant George W. Howie[243] of Co. F declines the appointment of ensign. I will leave for North Carolina on the 5th instance for 12 day's absence unless circumstances change. On the 4th day of May we are ordered to move and do so. General Grant having crossed the Rapidan,[244] I do not go home but continue with the regiment determined to share its perils. On the 5th we opened fight, Cooke's Brigade and Davis sustaining heroically the whole shock of battle.

## May 4–6, 1864

...Retreating slowly and orderly, passed General Doles. Forming in line in road. They were only in part there. Halted my regiment and asked

Cooke where to form. [I was told] "To left." Went there and found it filled with other troops, reported to Cooke, [was directed] "Go to where the troops are not in line and form to the left of those in line." Did so, met Capt. Heath and General D. B. Stewart and Capt. Butler told me to form in edge of old field. We overtook 27th who had gone before, close by road and told them to form twos. They did so and I was placed in command of brigade and Gen. Lee told me to get with the balance of the brigade or to get the rest of them to my command and to hold that point at all hazards.[245] [I remained in command of brigade] until Cooke came up soon after I sent for him and took command. My whole regiment and 27th were there and a company of about 30 and 25th and 6 or 7 men from 46th We went out (48th) and picketed.

... Were about sending for rations when the enemy made an assault upon our lines and came within 200 yards of our battery when we were just getting into position and had stacked our arms to get our rations and to throw up with bayonets we raised some temporary breastworks. McGowan's South Carolina Brigade gave back in great disorder and confusion and could not be rallied, hurdled together and paid no attention to the General who urged in vain to form them. They had parked behind us and formed at last in our rear. Yankees had us entirely surrounded and if South Carolina [Brigade] only had defended us we [would] have had our battery and position. But Longstreet and Anderson came up in time to drive them back with great loss on both sides.[246] The field was stubbornly contested. We finished our works and found of our own 18 were wounded, two or three mortally, among them were G. Norman of Co. A and Sgt. B.F. Hilliard[247] of Co. B and Piper of Co. B. We went out in the evening and formed line of battle. Some received wounds.

## MAY 7, 1864

Saturday. We remained to defend battery there. We had fighting that day also and at night all were placed on picket finishing posts about 12:00 midnight.

## MAY 8, 1864

Sunday. We moved along the lines of work and I visited destruction [and the dead], finding them on battlefield [and the] railroad cut and more dead in front in front of where our brigade fought and especially the 28th and 48th. We moved south last night hearing firing south in evening and found a line of battle but did not become engaged. Took up camp late.

## May 9–10, 1864

Monday. Moved early to Spotsylvania Court House, hard fighting. We were not engaged but put in breastworks. Early on Tuesday we moved by old Spotsylvania Court House to prevent a flank movement by the enemy—48th being on the left and about 4:00 p.m. were drawn up in line of battle and marched through fire, shell and attacked the enemy on Po River and stormed a battery but fell back. 48th falling back after balance of brigade [withdrew in] both skirmishes. We again moved forward under heavy firing of battery grape and came through with 2 men killed and 28 wounded, some of them mortally.[248] Late in the evening after dark returned and were withdrawn and placed on our extreme behind breastworks.

## May 11–12, 1864

Wednesday. We rested all day and fortified. Thursday the 12th we manned the works on our left, fighting very hot, but just to our left in the morning we were gratified by a sight of a flank movement by Wilder's Division and the fire of artillery and capture of 400 Yankee prisoners and three stand of columns and a most beautiful exhibition of the splendid colors on horseback of the prettiest flag afloat, but were on a fool's errant.[249] Cooke's and Martin's Brigades [ordered] to flank the Yankee batteries by Drunken General Early,[250] under protest of our officers Cooke and Mebane and had two men wounded by shell and rifle and others suffering little except Martin's Brigade who lost two privates and a major. We encamped late and went into camp on our right behind the breastworks.

## May 13, 1864

Friday. We again manned the breastworks to our left, wet and raining, sleep on ground and trenches. Spent a most uncomfortable night with occasional alarms of picket firing fearing an assault by Grant. Rained during night. Col. Hill and myself slept by breastworks on a bench eight or nine feet long.

## May 14, 1864

Saturday. We worked on entrenchments and dodged shells. One man in Co. I wounded by a Minie ball in foot.

## May 15, 1864

Sunday. We were in suspense all last night [as we] lay in the trenches behind the breastworks with accouterments on and arms in reach expecting a night attack by the enemy as was the case for two nights previously. It rained too. I set up or lay on a bench doubled up within four and one-half feet. The morning came and all was quiet, the day cleared off and was pleasant. The Yankees moved south and have been kept at bay. They have been rather worsted at all points and have tripled our losses in killed, wounded and prisoners and missing. Sabbath—first day of peace.

❖ Letter from Walkup at Spotsylvania Court House to wife Minnie:

Dearest Minnie,

Knowing your anxiety to hear from me I write again today having written on yesterday. This is the eleventh day of the fight and it is still progressing. We have not been actually engaged since the 10th beyond Po River three miles from here, though we have been under fire of shells, solid shot and musketry every day and were close by Wilson's division when they caught the 11th [North Carolina Regiment], saw the fight and under a portion of the fire. We also were sent on a dangerous excursion to the front and center to draw out and flank the enemy and if practicable to storm a part of his breastworks. It was full of peril, but we escaped unhurt, only two or three being seriously wounded. From that time to the present we have been behind breastworks and doing picket and skirmish duty and strengthening the works. We have been in expectation of night attacks from the enemy and for the last two nights have lain in the trenches with our accouterments on, lights all out, arms in reach, one man in each company up to give warning and wake up the balance of companies if attacked and advanced posts some two or three hundred yards in front, about two from each company. One man, Crotts[251], was wounded yesterday by a Minie ball through the foot. He was in Co. I and from Cleveland County.

We have a good deal of fun among the boys dodging cannon balls and shells. When we see the flash of the enemy's gun a mile off and give the alarm and every man strikes for the trenches. Wright's Georgia Brigade was engaged somewhat yesterday. We have been quite uncomfortable on account of wet and mud for the last four days. I have not had off my boots since last Wednesday, a week (from 4th to 15th) and that is the case with about all the others. The day now is apparently clearing off and the band is playing some splendid music. I saw Captain Cureton last night and he is quite well. Our officers are all well and in fine spirits. Captains Turner, Laney and Richardson and Lieutenants Stitt, Henry B. Howie, Lowrie, Belk, Starnes, Austin (James K.), Robert J. Howie, Hart, N. Stuart, William D. Howard, and the men and non-commissioned officers are generally in better health than when in camp. Some diarrhea in the camp from wet and night air but not bad. I have a slight touch of it, but it is not inconvenient. In fact, we have a pleasant and jolly time to be surrounded by actual war—much more so than any of you at home can imagine. Man is so constituted fortunately, that he can adapt himself easily to circumstances and be quite comfortable, in fact enjoys himself better than if idle and secure. Often "the choicest rarest flowers of bliss are plucked from danger's precipice."

I had provisions and bed clothing along, but they were in the rear with the wagons and I got along well without the bed clothes or cooked provisions. I saw your nephew Samuel Neal and Ardry and Jim Dunn, the 49th [North Carolina Infantry] Regiment men with us. They are all well except Capt. J.T. Davis who is at home sick. Capt. Turner is well. Lt. Winchester is quite fatigued and has been a little unwell but is improving fast. Lt. Stitt is well. Dr. Chears is quite well and in fine spirits, His brother, Vachel, is here today. I am glad Mrs. Chears visited you and that you enjoyed yourselves so finely. I am glad too, that you have been visiting freely, and that Mrs. Julia Winchester called on you and hope you will cultivate her acquaintance. Give Mr. McLaughlin my best respects for his kindness to you and my congratulations upon his new daughter. I hope Mrs. McLaughlin will do well.

I am glad to hear that my Steele Creek friends made kind inquiries for me and feel grateful to them for it. I hope you and Lelia will have plenty of those fine strawberries to eat. Kiss her for her Pappa and get her learned to talk. Tell her me and Hall have been fighting the Yankees. Hall seems to take pleasure to hear from you all, and says to tell you he is well. He writes to Miss Margaret Winchester about once a week, has acquire paper and envelopes and makes some money washing and selling cakes.[252] You can do as you please about Watson Reid's grave. Perhaps it would do as well to send it to Uncle Robert and let him receive the money for us and he can keep it until you can get it. Reid paid Dr. Bell for giving Shoute [money, to be] repaid to him, if it was more than he owes for Jinny's hire last year.

I'll take good care of myself in battle and [should] I fall, will get some friend, Dr. Chears, Turner or Winchester, to care for me.

We had a military execution last week—a man was shot for desertion in Ransom's Brigade.

My best love and prayers for the safety of you and Lelia. Respects to friends. May God bless you and Lelia and protect us and preserve us for each other for many years to come.

Your kind, loving and affectionate husband

P.S. We had a case of smallpox from my old company. He was sent to a hospital. We don't think it will spread any further.

## MAY 16, 1864

Monday. Yesterday was the first quiet day we had without fighting since the 5th. We expected an advance last night as we had done 12th, 13th, 14th and 15th and had thus one man up from each company—men lay on arms and until last night in trenches. Dysentery begins and some pneumonia. Capt. Lawhon, Lt. R. J. Howie figure [in] sickness as Capt. Bidding did and shirk the expected fighting. Many men begin to return with seed tick wounds. Officers, none were wounded as badly as myself. My boots and clothing have not been changed since the morning of the 4th. The Yankees moved on our right last night. We received General Order from General Lee congratulating us on good conduct and favorable prospects all around.

## MAY 17, 1864

Tuesday. We were ordered up at 3:00 a.m. and remained all day up, but did not move. Got cup of milk for cup of coffee and made me sick. Visited Col. Lane of 26th North Carolina and Capt. T.J. Cureton and got news from papers. Lt. Col. Rufus Barringer called, of 1st North Carolina Regiment. Looks well. Enemy's pickets advanced on our right and front of us at about this time 3:00 p.m.

## MAY 18, 1864

Wednesday. Opened about sunup by heavy artillery firing on left. Picket firing and musketry followed and continued for from thirty minutes to an hour, and heavy shelling along our whole front until 9:30, which continued after a short interval until 11:30 a.m. Cooke's Brigade among the thickest of the shelling. Our batteries replied occasionally under the cool aim of Lt. Col. Pegram.[253] Very few men wounded.

## MAY 21, 1864

Saturday. Sharp fighting on our front after sunset. Shells short fired near breastworks. Cannonball came near killing Adjt. Winchester who dodged in time to save his head. It rattled around yards further. After dark we began march and go eight miles rapidly and start early next morning.

## MAY 22, 1864

Sunday. Lee is outwitted by Grant and let him get the start of him to Richmond.[254] We begin at 5:00 to march to North Anna River. I'm sorry for my horse.

## MAY 23, 1864

Monday. Arrived Little River, 398 men, 25 officers, total 428. In endeavoring to advance back to North Anna, we got two men killed and six wounded. Captains Turner and Cureton[255] of the 26th wounded. March back and begin attempting at railroad cut and then abandon it and go to Little River. Entered next morning near river and Doswell's house and Anderson's Mill.

## MAY 24, 1864

Rest all day and night. Ewell said to be engaged on right successfully.

## MAY 25, 1864

Wednesday. Opens fair, some firing to front and right.

## MAY 26, 1864

Thursday. Opens with some sharp picket firing and some shelling, get first letter from my wife during the month of May, and she had not on the 18th instance heard from me since the 1st of May.

## MAY 27–28, 1864

Friday. We leave Doswells and march about seven or eight miles occupying the whole day until 11:00 p.m., a most annoying thing after night with equipment waiting in wagons. I lie down, do not even spread my blanket, double up over my saddle and sleep well until 3:00 a.m. when we are ordered (Saturday 28th) to move forwards towards Aydletts Station near Mechanicsville and harbor on the Chickahominy. We arrive at Old Church and camp late into evening (3:00 p.m.) not far from Central Railroad at Shady Grove Church near Mrs. Crump's Farm where Adjutant got in a good mess of greens and nice lettuce. We got an increase in rations—one-half lb. of bacon.[256]

MAY 29, 1864

Sunday. All day at Shady Grove Church where Lt. Gen. Hill kept his headquarters. He is a proud, haughty, old maidish son, and selfish-looking misanthrope and loves to be a tyrant and vexish, snaps and snarls at everything and everybody. About an hour by sun we are ordered to the point two miles to Carter's farm, passing the 4th South Carolina Cavalry where I meet my South Carolina friends Darling, Andrews, Belk, Porter, Crockett, etc., also Lou MacGill. They had been engaged on the evening before, about 15 out of the company, so Dr. Belk informed me, 9 of whom were captured. We are a long time selecting a bad position and ground seems to be fit only for being skillful to make one uncomfortable and doing anything in the worst possible manner. Old Mr. Carter very well fixed. Beautiful rows of cedars, the wide avenue to his antiquated mansion and centurian sycamores proclaim an old family residence and garden surrounding. House well stored shows comfortable living and indicates Virginia hospitality. But rural tranquility and felicity must give way to the stern realities and necessities of war and ancient and honorable families must yield to its onward and rude footsteps. The weapons of war not only destroy human life, but everything and vegetation in its range. Desolation marks the track of an army like some fiery blast consuming everything and leaves the rich and poor in one common ruin.

It is pleasant to see how generally comfortable Virginians live. They nearly all are of fair standing in houses, orchards, gardens and vegetable patches and all the concomitants of good fare and comfortable living—cows, butter, bees, honey, neat houses and genteel families and the generous result and a Virginian is prima facie a gentleman. This war has broken rather unfavorably for Virginia—courage through time, so misfortune will never conquer the pride and self-conceit of that and its sister state of South Carolina. They are as proud as Spaniards and will admit no superior, and rarely an equal. No matter how much they may be [excelled by others], they importantly boast of their superiority. Their vanity makes them disgusting and causes them to underrate and slander better men and drives for quantities that they want themselves. They "raise their own mortals to the skies"—they bring "angels from other places down to their levels." Their glory is in the past and all except their sun is set. Their Stonewall Jackson and Lee are their only redeeming great men of the present. Tis grace still but [Jackson] living [would] grace still more.

## MAY 30, 1864

Monday. We began vigorously to form earthworks last night after marching and countermarking until we were fatigued and sleepy in hunting the most unfavorable position and have done such great things in fortifying, having very few tools. The Yankees are nearby about our outer works. General Cooke called on me today and was gracious and complimentary, in high glee, praised the Regiment, Brigade and Adjutant Winchester. General Heth[257] also called and was very sociable and clever. Some cannonading at night, more now, but on our right.

## MAY 31, 1864

Tuesday. All is quiet. We fear the enemy will flank away and not attack us in our works. We are itching for an attack in these works by them and think we can ruin any assault they may send. We have to leave our works and move to the right to Mac's Hill or Taliaferro's where Gen. Breckenridge with his Virginia troops let the Yankee's picket run them out of their works (rifle fire). We are compelled to build new works behind the front works under fire, in doing which our brave, gallant and ready William D. Howard, lieutenant of Co. F, is shot though the head and I had twice been where the works were to be constructed. Once before we began and another time to set the party to work and the balls rattled ominously through the woods, one of which came near striking me. Lt. Howard was not sent by me, but accompanied Capt. Potts[258] without my knowledge. No officer in the regiment would be more useful or more missed; few would be more gallant, prompt and efficient as my personal friend and associate Lt. William D. Howard. No one also, save a private in Co. H, was [killed] all that day, I had him [Howard] buried under a large cherry tree near Privates Hill and Tolines, one and one-half miles of Atlee Station, two miles west of Mechanicsville at the Haw's [Shop or Aenon] Church Road, in coffin and head boards up. This sad scene spread a gloom for the day over us. We finished our work late at night, temporarily, only half done.

## JUNE 1, 1864

Wednesday. We finished our work pretty well and have a defense erected for myself and Col. Hill when heavy firing is heard about 6:00 a.m. toward our right. We are ordered there, and in leaving James W. Hancock[259] is enrolled private of Co. E. We arrive where no breast works are up and after lying exposed for some time, and some of our men being wounded, Sgt. Pink White[260] of Co. C and one of our pickets from Co.

G, we leave a line to build where the enemy fire upon us from the rear as well as front. We protect it from both sides and are told to quit work, when a vigorous assault is made by the Yanks on Kirkland's Brigade on our right, who repulsed two or three assaults made by them. They were very determined and wished to come on but our men prevented them by firing at them—some 75 or 80 did come on and things settled quickly down, the enemy gradually working his way to our right [near] Yorktown and the White House on the Pamunkey. I met Col. (Gen.) Hoke today, brother of John F.

## JUNE 2, 1864

Thursday. All quiet and enemy moving to right. We also move in the evening having taken some 76 prisoners by out-skirmishing some of the Yankee line of breastworks and moving two miles within their rear: are shelled and fired upon, two or more men wounded and lie in the woods in the rain until about 9:00 p.m. and return wet and without rations, only what we had left at noon. Every man to the road and camp, thoroughly fatigued; begin moving up entrenchments which we were told could not be moved. Sleep without covering and it raining, a little to the right in an exposed place, the 48th being on left flank.

## JUNE 3, 1864

In the trenches, a picket of 20 men in front of them.

Friday is an unlucky day. The enemy advanced in force at 6:00 a.m. We have no cannon in position, three pieces on left were trying to get into position. Col. Rose, Lt. Smith of Co. H, a brave and gallant officer, and two men of Co. H just in my front, and Ferguson,[261] Color Guard, and several other good men killed and wounded, among them Capt. Marby[262] of Co. B wounded. The fight is still progressing and it is nearly sun set; the Yankees slip in very close and a few men were with their heads above the entrenchments. I dig my own hole for safety, and it is much needed. Thank God that it is no worse. We were flanked on left and annoyed the enemy much from a house in front of our left. Our regiment sustained the brunt of this day's fight. Killed: 9 (1 officer and 9 men); 2 officers and 35 men wounded, ten missing, making a total of 56. We fought from 6:00 a.m. until after 7:00 p.m., in fact until dark with a constant stream of balls piping over us. We left the battleground at 11:00 p.m. and camped as day broke, having done without water and food all day, 13 or 14 hours, greatly fatigued, our flag shot in four or five places and colors over 200.[263]

## JUNE 4, 1864

Saturday. We leave camp and go towards Gaines Mill. Co. A: killed, Shelby Polk[264]; J.T. Laney[265] one bone of leg broken; Bryant dead and Arab Clarke[266] [captured]. Co. E: Isaac Sims[267] killed; Churchwell Horton[268] mortally wounded in back of head; Abraham B. Hays'[269] forehead, very serious; J.I. Richardson, back, slightly. Co. F: John Fincher,[270] left eye, dangerously. Co. I: A. McCall,[271] June 2nd, leg broken; Sam Hagler, June 3rd, right arm broken, Samuel J. Blount, wrist; John E. Caseby, injury.

Gaines Mill. We arrive here yesterday evening. There was picket firing on our front. Shells came unpleasantly near. It began to rain in the evening. We are now blessed with too much rations, bread and meat. We get coffee and sugar and molasses and have a good night's rest. Heavy musketry and some artillery are heard during the night and cheers by our men.

## JUNE 5, 1864

Sunday. We are at 10:00 a.m. in camp. Quiet all day. Washed up, put on clean cloths, slept. Heard preaching. Got abundant rations, good and sound. Got coffee and sugar plenty. About an hour after dark Yankees feign a charge, fired off small arms, booming cannon, shells fly wildly and furiously and hissing like some huge serpent all around us.

## JUNE 6, 1864

Monday. We slept till 1:30 a.m., when we move to second line of Deep Port, Martin's Brigade of Hoke's Division, and arrive only two miles against daybreak. A constant hammering of rifle keep up a monotonous music of death and funeral elegy during the whole morning, and death dealing Minie balls rattle rudely over and around us. We are on the position the Yankees occupied at New Cold Harbor 27 June 1862, and are at the moment encamped in the second line, precisely where Branch's North Carolina Division and the South Carolina Brigade fought, where many of them fell, among Capt. Mathews People and Col. Campbell [who] lie at the edge of the cornfield. [We are] lying on the very graves of our friends and where also the New York Zouaves fell and which was one of the most awful fights of which I have yet seen except Second Manassas.

## JUNE 7, 1864

Tuesday. Frequent firing, often from the line, was heard last night. Picket firing continues brisk this morning. News arrives that Stanton is captured, Gen. Jones killed and that Grant is moving to the right to cross James River from White House. We get abundant rations including sugar, coffee, onions and cabbage. Number of arms bearing men 311. Total for rations 373. Regimental loss in killed so far 27, of who two, Lt. W.D. Howard and E.H. Smith, are officers. Others will die.[272]

## JUNE 8, 1864

Wednesday. Last night just before sunset a truce was allowed Grant to bury his dead in front of our works.[273] It [originally] ended by dark and we were ordered to occupy the front works where the 23rd Georgia of Colquitt's brigade had been posted for eight or nine days and from where Clingman's Brigade had previously been in. The truce continued all night and until this morning at 9:00 a.m. It is mutually kept, neither party being disposed to halt the quiet, though the Yankees are advancing their works, already within less than 100 yards. Some papers have been exchanged this morning, and both parties freely expose themselves above and about the works unmolested. By tacit consent both parties remain quiet and easy and passed freely along the works unmolested until 2:00 p.m., when one of the enemy's guns began throwing shells over our lines beyond us at I suppose a working party in our rear of Gen. Davis' Brigade. No firing of small arms and our artillery did not reply. All things quiet again in evening and soon twilight gray had in somber livery all things clad. We begin fixing abatis or otherwise refresh [breast] work, in our front and rested quietly for the balance of the night, maintaining a strict watch, one-half the company being up all night.

## JUNE 9, 1864

Thursday. All quiet until about 7:00 a.m. when we received orders to fire a signal gun for all to get within entrenchments and stop the careless and easy condition of the men. Upon the signal every man of both parties let off at full speed for the breastworks, like frogs when a snake is after them, or sheep strike for home when dogs are working pressing them, or Tom O' Shanter at Halloween with haunted kirk with the witches after him. Some half clad clothes in hand, some with breakfast half eaten, some laughing and others with consternation in their faces.[274]

One of Gen. Davis' Sharpshooters[275] came into our lines with a No. 2 Whitworth globe sighted gun[276] presented to him (Gen. Davis) by his uncle Jefferson Davis, President, C.S.A., imported from England, worth $400.00, shooting 10000 yards and fired at the artillerist and others in the second line of the enemy's works [and so] pressed them to lie low.

Our boys began operations at the first line and the Yankees kept up a brisk response. Their sharpshooters are skillful and terrible and make us cautious and vigilant. At night we form a more complete abatis and enlarge our works and strengthen them.

## JUNE 10, 1864

Friday. We again open fire first. One of our sharpshooters are wounded, William Granbly, in the front hole near me, and others have narrow escapes. We are to be relieved by Colquitt's Brigade tonight.

## JUNE 11, 1864

Saturday. We come back to our old position behind Martin's North Carolina Brigade last night on the battlefield of Cold Harbor. About 320 guns, 14 ambulances. Colquitt's Brigade relieves us. Brigade lost in killed and wounded to June 3, officers inclusive, 998 and 35 missing, about 20 have been lost since to date. Total about 1050 plus. Mortar firing began this evening.

## JUNE 12, 1864

Sunday. Cool night, quiet morning, considering some picket firing. Brigade partly relieved last night.

## JUNE 13, 1864

Monday. The Yankees having left in our front last night, we are ordered to our right and march down the river, crossing at McClellan's Bridge and [marching] down on south side near Bottom's Bridge, arrive about 1:00 p.m., very dusty, at White Oak Swamp.[277] Cavalry there. Saw Capt. Henry N. Hill,[278] Capt. M. Ray, Jimmy Johnston. We throw up breastworks with abatis on point. MacRae gets prickish because I do not chime in with him and help him to work.

## JUNE 14, 1864

Thursday. The Yankees having disappeared in front we again cross the swamp and move after them to the right. I received letters last night from wife telling me smallpox in Monroe. We move only about one mile and remain all day and at night camp on the ground. In the morning we began making breastworks, but before we had finished, we are ordered forward after some delay.

## JUNE 15, 1864

Wednesday. Our regiment are marched two miles down the Charles

City Road toward Mrs. Gary's. We then are marched perpendicular to our left flank by right flank. We build breastworks in edge of old field. The Yankee skirmishers firing upon ours endanger us within the works, many balls falling near us. No one was hit. The 24th Virginia Cavalry behaved shamefully, braggadocio and poltroonery appear as equally predominant in them. They would bristle up swelling, much bold and forward to part of our works, and then suddenly countermarch back as if they had forgotten something, or suddenly hear something drop. They did this often and made themselves not only ridiculous but contemptible. Our skirmishers were in front. We are ordered to advance through very thick undergrowth of woods, worse than the Wilderness. Our right rests on the road. The enemy's skirmishers fire persistently upon us at close range. The skirmishers of the 27th North Carolina behave badly and break through our ranks, causing some of our Co. I to break also. They are with difficulty urged forward by Lt. Jones [through] a swamp, but lag so slowly that our line of battle perceiving them in front sustain a heavy fire and are afraid to return it least they hit some of our own skirmishers. The enemy are obliquely on our left flank. I break off Co. B to deploy on our left flank and Co. G, H and E to march by their right flank perpendicularly to our rear, to prevent a flank movement from the enemy on our left. Co. B gets lost? We are shelled, lose 7 men killed and 32 wounded. Some of our best men fall. The regiment came near breaking. [An officer] behaved badly. Capt. Potts anxious to get to rear on account of lead, only wound appears his hand was hit. My shoulder received a glazing shot which cut a hole. We built and threw up some slight works. Gary's Cavalry and Hampton's Legion and 7th South Carolina come up and we retire to camp. Six in 27th [North Carolina] and two in 46th [North Carolina] killed, seventy wounded in all. Two in 5th [North Carolina] wounded, some killed. No enemy near [at this time]. They move by left flank in rear of right of 27th and there forward into line. This was called a skirmish, but for our regiment it was worse than a battle. It was dismounted cavalry (Wilson's Division) we fought. They had Burnside breech loading carbines and some Spencer and some revolving rifles and pistols and were lying in ambush.[279] I think we lost more than we gained. We took some few prisoners and some rifles and got several carbines. We came back from Mrs. Gary's to camp about a mile west of our camp of the previous night.

JUNE 16, 1864

Thursday. We remain in camp throwing up a line of works in a field.

Col. Galloway,[280] 22nd Regiment Seales Brigade, visits us. I feel uncomfortably annoyed by venison we eat all day.

## June 17, 1864

Friday. Still in camp. I take a bath and feel better. Day worsens, disagreeable and dusty. I take a second bath in White Oak Swamp and feel refreshed. We are ordered to move about 5:00 p.m. and go about four miles.

## June 18, 1864

Saturday. We continue the march, cross James River at Drewry's Bluff on pontoon bridge before we rest. The strong entrenchments there are cheering news from Petersburg about victories and slaughter of the enemy which are greatly magnified. We continue to Port Walthall Junction where the Yankees take up the railroad track. Our armies are very much fatigued. We march 18 miles, and there was more straggling by other regiments (Walker's and Kirkland's), not so much by ours. Picket firing is heard by division on left. Left Port Walthall Junction and came to Petersburg (left one mile), [where] as we lie until the other regiment [comes] late at night and take position and bivouac for the night. My horse did not arrive and I lay uncomfortably without covers.[281] Hear of death of [various acquaintances] of wounds. Picket firing through night. 1100 Negro [troops] said to be slain yesterday and 200 prisoners taken.[282]

## June 19, 1864

Sunday. The day opens quietly. We begin to assemble to hear preaching by Rev. Granberry but we are ordered to the left down river Appomattox to Fort Clifton[283] where we spend the day two and one-half miles northeast of Petersburg. Some shelling and fighting to left across river. 1400 Negroes said to be captured yesterday and two got away!!![284] High banks on bluffs to river in front, short three-quarters mile to front.

## June 20, 1864

Monday. Change clothing and have my [soiled] one washed and put on cotton clothes and a pair of cotton socks, but apart for first time since I came to war, though carried all the time, [not preferring] cotton vs. woolen clothes.[285] We are ordered to our left seven miles towards Richmond above Port Walthall Junction and arrive 11:00 p.m. or 1:00 a.m. of 21st.

## June 21, 1864

Tuesday. We are behind Pickett's much whuffed division. Old Lee makes himself an undignified paternal fussy-puff for his petted and spoiled darlings. We camp at lower pontoon bridge over James River at Chaffin's Bluff.

## June 22, 1864

Wednesday. We move towards Malvern Hill and stop at our old position near New Market, move towards river, entrench, in sight of pickets, come near being bit by copperhead snake. We retreat one-half mile and entrench in woods six feet apart as skirmishers. Receive a post shelling from gunboats. Eat some Irish potatoes and my bowels much affected and seeping blood.

## June 23, 1864

Thursday. Remain in line, post pickets.

## June 24, 1864

Friday. Sew my pants and while engaged thus, pants off, [a] lady comes to complain about depredations in her potatoes. Consulted with much nonchalance sometime before leaving, part of the time quite pathetically, sympathizing sincerely and promise we will set a guard over the patch but cannot find the thief who took them.

## June 25, 1864

Saturday. This is the anniversary of our first battle two years ago at French's Farm near Richmond, Virginia. This is a hot, sultry day. Men begin to sicken. Everything quiet. Beans today for dinner, garden snaps. Buttermilk for supper and some gooseberries for morning. Cavalry return from pursuing Sheridan. Regiment goes out to flank some Yankees. 1st North Carolina and 6th South Carolina Cavalry camp near us.

## June 26, 1864

Sunday. Hot and sultry morning. Everything quiet. Cavalry pass us to cross at Drewry's or Chaffin's Bluff. I see Winchester and Chamby's Brigade pass. We catch a squirrel and cook with snap beans and bacon for dinner, rich treat. I keep Sabbath much better than usual having my Bible with me. Read 53rd and 54th Isaiah and 1st and 17th Judges and five chapters in 2nd Corinthians, some Psalms and Galatians and [perform] vigil. Orders to make abatis. We hear report of the capture of 2000 prisoners and of 1600 and 500; the last only is true.

## June 27, 1864

Tuesday. Arise before day and graze my horse and heat the refreshing bustle of morning song: the cock's shrill alarms, the warbling songsters. Enjoy the breezy calls. The magisterial Glory of lovely morning is lost to the sluggards. We finish our abatis and thereafter our sharpshooters make a term of observations and everything remains quiet.

## August 18, 1864

I remained with it [regiment] until 18th August when I received a sick leave of 30 days and went home.[286]

## Sept. 2, 1864

◆ Letter from Walkup at Monroe, North Carolina to Governor Zebulon Vance:

Dear Sir:

Col. Brown of the 63rd Bat. Home Guard has been in this county from Mecklenburg for three or four days—and Majr Ashcraft has the Battalion out of the Home Guards from this county—I also learn that a Battalion from Anson Co. is ordered here. Now there is but six deserters reported present in this county. Two of them have come in under your proclamation and two others I am informed will be in in a day or two—So that there appears to be no call for any forces here for purpose of arresting deserters. There are none to arrest. There have been no depredations made by any of them in this county for some time past. Those who had committed any have all been taken and sent back to their regiments sometime since.

If the purpose is to put the Battalions under organization so as to be ready for any emergency, that objective has already been accomplished. They are now organized and will be in a state of readiness for meeting and moving at short notice.

I would most respectfully bring to your Excellency's attention, with great diffidence the citizens of the county—Our county (Union) has very few slaves and the few white men left here are the laborers who are necessary to save the growing and matured crops. It is now in the beginning of tine to save fodder and the Sorghum Molasses are now ready for manufacturing and there is a considerable quantity of it planted. Neither can be saved unless these men are left at home—and this is, I learn the case in Mecklenburg and other places—Our county had to rely for its supply last year beyond its limits for some of these necessities of life and it behooves them to use all their resources to keep from suffering.

I hope you will therefore take the premises into consideration and have the home guard released from active service until they can collect their fodder and Sorghum—or until some greater emergency arises for their surmise and when they can be more conveniently spared—this is the general wish and cannot desires of all concerned in the prosperity of the county & its necessities—whatever may be the condition of the county in other sections. I feel sure that there are not ½ dozen if more than two, deserters in Union County—Nor do I believe there are any worth notice in any adjoining counties fewer in fact than ever before.

You will please excuse me for making so free as to suggest these remarks.[287]

## JANUARY 1, 1865

This day cold and clear, very cold and freezing. Gen. Cooke leaves for two days. I am in charge of brigade and Capt. John E. Moore of Co. I of the regiment. I got a small box of provisions from my wife, three balls of butter. Mrs. Hailey and Mrs. J. P. Belk sent [package], and one backbone sent by Major Covington, also one opossum, a pound cake and sweet cakes, sausage and molasses, which last was lost by the bottle breaking.[288]

## JANUARY 2, 1865

Monday. I visit picket line, excessively cold but clear and calm. Have a good dinner, opossum and potatoes, pie etc. Dr. Smithers said a colonel of 18th Mississippi would visit me today and borrow a plate and fork for him but he failed to come.

## JANUARY 3, 1865

Tuesday. Received part of shoat, three pounds killed by scout Tupsey in front of picket lines, also four eggs, one-half pound butter, hind quarter opossum, dried beef and sweet cake and tart from Chaplain Plyler. Read books of romance and Scott's novels,[289] visit pickets daily and have charge of brigade today and last night heaviest and most constant rain of the season and thunder. We were ordered to be ready to move on 7th as the enemy were reported moving on the Vaughn Road to our right.

## January 15, 1865

Brigade drill. Col. Hill visits Miss. Southerland. Applications for leave of absence for 25 days. Received it for 18 days.

## January 22, 1865

Birthday, 47 years old. Took a glass with Col. Hill and Adjt. and S. Timmons.

## January 23–24, 1865

Heavy cannonading in James River at night by our ironclads. Rumors of good news about peace propositions from Lincoln through F. P. Blair, and of English and French recognition.[290] Gold comes down from 80 to 35 for 1.

## January 25, 1865

Capt. T. K. Potts drunk on dress parade and falls down.

## January 26, 1865

Visit Capt. McLane, Paymaster, to receive pay for November and December 1864 and January, $390.00.

## January 27, 1865

Expect to leave for home for 18 days with Gen. MacRae. I will not leave until 29th Sunday morning for fear of missing connection to stage. I visited paymaster McLane yesterday and received pay for only the month of November and December to 1st day of January 1865, $390.00.

## February 16, 1865

Returned to Brigade Hospital and on 16th returned to camp. The regiment had been engaged on the 5th of February in front of works in a fight with the Yankees, one officer, [Acting] Lt. H.W. Laney, and five men killed on the field, three mortally wounded, 14 severely and 20 slightly wounded and seven missing. Our regiment suffers some more than the whole brigade. The 55th Regiment North Carolina and Mississippi Brigade were added to Cooke's Brigade only a day or two before the battle.

## February 18, 1865

Sent by Sgt. Eubanks to Dr. J.M. Miller for E.H. Britton advertisement bulletin $27.00 in full of his account for publishing deserters August 17, 1863,[291] and $13.00 to W.J. Yates for Minnie's paper. Received of Capt. Potts for deserters published $5.00 from Capt. Turner for two ditto $5.00, B. F. Richardson for $20.00. From Capt. Moore ditto $15.00.

## FEBRUARY 20, 1865

Four men deserted last night, Hugh Starnes and Therrell from Co. A. and W. Vickory and Evan Watson from Co. F. Five men of Co. C, Sgt. Scroggs and L. Litton were accidentally severely wounded by Sapp of Co. K whose gun was loaded on drill. Sent my trunk and quire of paper to wife by Jack Griffin.

## FEBRUARY 21, 1865

Columbia and Charleston have been evacuated in South Carolina. Sherman approaches North Carolina. The hearts of the people and soldiers begin to sink.[292] Deserters increase and commit many desperations about home, our prospects getting more gloomy fast.[293] We had three more desertions last night: McRae and Moore of Co. K and Griffin of [Co.] E. Rev. Wiche has horse to go to Petersburg today.

## FEBRUARY 22, 1865

The birthday of General Washington, President United States, a fine and promising day. At 5:00 a.m. we had orders to be ready to move on shortest notice and that the enemy were moving on our right. There was great rejoicing in Yankee's camp over fall of Columbia and Charleston. Three men deserted last night from Co. G.: Abram Cross, D.W. Snider, John Lomax.

## FEBRUARY 23, 1865

On last night 17 men deserted, many of them to the Yankees, some of them home. Other regiments in this brigade have exceeded us. On yesterday I received a short address of my own in the shape of a pencil order to the regiment on the subject of desertion, which pleased the officers and men very much as appropriate and in season. Many of them wish to have it published.

Sent up resignation of Capt. J.W. Bitting, Co. K and Lt. Shaw, Co. D. Received news by Capt. James McNeely of Sherman's approach to North Carolina, being at Chester, South Carolina with Beauregard's army in rear, Hinds fortifying in front at Nations Ford. They move in three columns, one to cross at Laud Ford, one at Nations Ford, and one at Tuckaseegee Ford or thereabouts.

## FEBRUARY 28, 1865

We had whiskey rations today and by request gave at dark rousing cheers to shoo off the Yankees. The boys were merry and called upon myself and other officers for speeches. I gave them a short talk flattering the regiment. They carried me in corn shucking style to my tent on their shoulders, were in fine glee. They visit Gen. Cooke with the band and several from the other regiments and had a speech from him and others and again called on me. I responded and all retired well pleased. We hear Grant is massing his forces on our right.

## MARCH 3, 1865

Two deserters from picket line last night.

## MARCH 4, 1865

Last night we had orders to move as the enemy were expected to move on us in the right of us. Did not move, heavy rain on night of 5th Co. H has nine deserters. They stuck a paper giving reasons for offense if any and asking pardon, to take 60 days furlough and do no crime.[294]

Thus ends the first term of President Lincoln and begins his second term of blood. Our cause looks gloomy in the extreme. Those men who thought the securing of our independence so easy a matter, who precipitated the South in so disastrous a war, who owe their greatness to their country's ruin, are or have reaped those bitter fruits that like Sodom's apples tempt the eye, but turn to dust and ashes upon the lips. The plan was feasible and the prospect at one time flattering, but the best laid plans will fail. We behold a still lower deep yawning which threatens to engulf us. We have been decimated and more than decimated by desertion.[295] But it may be like [a] Gideon test, that only the faint hearted are sent back and those who are left may be sufficient. We are too far committed to turn back honorably, so, trusting in God for results, forward, guide center, march to victory or to death, glory or the grave![296]

## MARCH 6, 1865

Review today by Gen. Heth, day fair. Cooke's [throat] a little raw and [he] does not give all the usual commands. I wrote home by A.C. Phillips to wife and William and also on the 7th of march to wife. I am in agony of suspense to hear from home. It has been nearly a month since

I left them and have received no letter since. The Yankees were there between them and our forces. I can only look heavenward for comfort. Whatever God permits and wills must be submitted to with patient resignation. The terrible ordeal which will soon come, must be born with meek grace. If Brother William and I escape ruin and death it will be miraculous, or if our army escapes it must be by providential interference. We are forsaken by all the world and our friends deserting. The enemy are exultant and number five or six to our one. An army against an unarmed, unorganized mob. The sea before us, the mountains on each side, behind us a mighty and desperate enemy. Where can we look for help but upwards?[297]

## MARCH 7, 1865

Five men from Co. H deserted last night, two with arms from picket line to enemy, three from camp. Received Hon. John A. Gilmer's letter and Attorney General Davis opinion and note from Secretary of War on examination etc.

## MARCH 9, 1865

One deserter, Andrew Brown of Co. G, off picket line last night. Received today news of capture of 1500 men and three pieces of artillery by our forces near Kinston, North Carolina on yesterday, a good set off for Sheridan's capture of Early's forces near Staunton, Virginia and a fair test of North Carolina and Virginia fighting.

## MARCH 10, 1865

This is fast day and we endeavor to keep it as such. I sent off box to Greensboro, North Carolina. I send up recommendations for Richardson and Turner for promotion whichever is senior in rank. Three deserters from picket last night.

## MARCH 12, 1865

We were called out before day to the trenches this morning upon report of a Yankee deserter, that the enemy intended to attack our works by daylight, remained a couple of hours and permitted to return to camp.[298] Then received orders to be ready to move at shortest notice. Enemy unusually quiet in front this morning, perhaps gone to Stony Creek where we may be ordered. Capt. J.K. Potts of Co. C, who was cashiered for drunkenness, his besetting sin, left us today. I let him have my horse to ride and carry his baggage. This Company's officers are unfortunate. One is a drunkard, one a rogue, one a coward, two killed, two resigned from disability and incapacity, none left.[299]

## MARCH 17, 1865

Four desertions left from pickets line last night. William McWhorter returned bringing terrible news. Plundering by Yankees in Waxhaw and Cane Creek, Lancaster, South Carolina, insult and murder of Abel Belk.

## MARCH 18, 1865

Lt. William Austin, Co. I, Sgt. Eubanks, Co. E and all furlough men returned 18th.

## MARCH 20, 1865

We have orders to have two day's rations cooked up and to be ready to move at daylight this morning. I think we will leave this time out right and many of us will never see this camp again. I feel very sad upon the condition of our country and especially at home. Farewell, my beloved friend, I fear I shall never see you more. I think the campaign will open from here today. Oh, bloodiest picture on the roll of time, how many of our best men will soon fall victims to this bloody Moloch of war. May God protect us and prepare us for our fate.

❖ Letter from Walkup at breastworks at Hatcher's Run, Virginia to sister Sarah N. Walkup Belk:

(date uncertain, between March 8 and March 30)

We are all well and still quiet in winter quarters, but are looking every day for the fierce storm to burst over us. Our men are deserting, half of them or more go to the Yankees and those who go home will, I greatly fear, be very troublesome there. They are just the sort of men to commit cruel and wanton outrages and insult the unprotected.

I feel very much inclined to resign and come home to protect my family.[300] But even that I could not do if there. I might add to the dangers as no place is safe now. The army is about as safe as to be home.[301]

The conflict will be short and terrible. If our people will be aroused and rush to our rescue, we can prevail, but if their spirits are crushed down and they are apathetic our cause is lost.

I am willing to fight desperately to the end, if the people will rise up and do what they can. But if they lie down and submit without a struggle ours would be a useless sacrifice. It would be useless for a few to struggle with over-whelming odds and under all imaginable disadvantages. Oh! that the able bodied men of South Carolina and North Carolina would unite, if only for one hundred days or even half that time and rush upon Sherman's army they could cut it to pieces. But unless it is a general thing, a few could do very little good and might as well stay home; for only the bravest and the best would have to suffer without effect.

My dear sister bear your hard lot with meek and patient resignation, Bow to the will of Him who does all things for some great and wise purpose, and does it well for those who love Him.

Poor Abel's death may show that we are often in the greatest peril when we think we are most secure. He may probably not have been murdered at all, but in trying to escape may have been fallen into the creek and been drowned by not being able to swim with his clothes on. He would otherwise very likely have had some marks on violence upon his person.[302]

Keep his poor orphans for me and tell them how sorry I feel and how sad I am to hear of their good and kind father's death.

Give my love to your Ma, Julia, Martha, William and families and if we never see each other again, let us try to be prepared for death and judgment where I hope we will all meet in peace.

I wrote to Brother William and Minnie lately and gave all the news. I have nothing more than you can learn by the papers. I send this to be mailed in Charlotte, North Carolina and hope it may find you and your family and friends well and unmolested further by additional troubles and that Our Heavenly Father will take us all in his protection.

Farewell, Your affectionate brother

## MARCH 23, 1865

Here yet in charge of brigade for last three days. Gen. Cooke gone to Richmond to return tonight. Glad of it, as we received orders today that Yankees were moving to right and to be prepared to move. Hear favorable reports from North Carolina, fight at Bentonville between Sherman and Johnson. I think it very little to crow about either way. I suppose Sherman will entrench there and flank us as usual, or await attack behind his works. Their forces are said now to be ready.

## MARCH 24, 1865

Friday. Unlucky day, we begin our march tonight to north of Richmond on James River. We to perhaps reinforce Longstreet, who it is said expects attack [having only] two brigades.

## MARCH 27, 1865

We, Cooke's, M. Comb's Brigade, left after 10:00 p.m. I never like to begin anything or enterprise on Friday. It is a common and vulgar prejudice and this day's operation has verified the superstition of its ill omen. We were all night until 4:00 p.m. dragging in weary impatience to between Petersburg and the trenches where we bivouacked on the old ground behind a bluff. The city had a gloomy, desolate, haunted appearance like some plague had depopulated it and spread its deadly still over its remains. We began to conjecture that we were sent to the trenches for our frequent desertions, where the continuous firing of both parties would prevent us going over to the enemy. But we were told that we might expect a fight in the morning. When we were awakened just after daylight 25th we were told that our forces at Gen. Gordon's suggestion had captured three-fourths of a mile of the enemy's and one fort or more with a loss of only 50 in all, taking many prisoners and killing and wounding very many, making a grand surprise of the enemy and doing a most marvelous thing which was just the beginning of much greater. That we had cut the enemy line in two and would roll back their left and capture it from the Appomattox to Hatchers Run. We were sent into the trenches between the Crater and beyond creeks on right of it. We were shelled and mortared some little before we took our position, heavy firing was heard on the left and in sight. We saw our forces in the Yankee fort recoiling and the Yankees retaking possession. They had in fact renewed all their ground, killed, wounded and captured more than they had lost in the early part of the fight. As one of the officers told me we had split a horn instead of making a spoon.[303] I regret that my friend and companion Lt. Col. James Taylor Davis was here mortally wounded. I saw him at Fairground, he died soon after. He was suffering severely and did not expect [to live]. [We] spoke of Yankees being in Monroe... I could do nothing for him and left [as]there was fighting at our right from whence firing [came], promising to call again if possible. We had to leave the road and zigzagging our way along [trying to] keep out of view of the Yankee's lookout which overlooks the whole country and must be 150 or 200 feet high. Such was Gen. Lee's order. Shells were falling beyond us, and we were double quicking to get out of the way. When we got within less than a mile of an old quarters the firing hurried us up and we got informed that the enemy had captured one picket line and most of our pickets. Our regiment lost five by desertion and Lt. Reed.[304] We manned our works immediately and began firing upon the enemy in our old picket one. We then sent sharpshooters on their left flanks and drove the Yankees out of our pickets, without much loss-two killed, four wounded, and we (48th) captured some 17 men and many more killed and wounded. We sent pickets to remain [on] the line under Capt. Richardson and Lt. James Austin[305] of Co. E . This last gallant, brave and most efficient officer was killed heroically leading his men forward and is a very serious loss to the regiment, being one of the very best in it.

About 10:00 a.m. the Yankees made a determined effort to recapture the picket line but were repulsed with a loss by our pickets. Since that time all remained quiet and last night we occupied our old quarters leaving two companies to guard the line. This morning Scales and McGowan recaptured the lines lost by Thomas last Saturday near Battery Gregg. Gen. Lee passed here today. Report of New York Herald of execution of two deserters from Yankees.

## MARCH 29, 1865

The Yankees under Sheridan are moving to our right and some fighting is going on the south side of Watlings Creek. I have just heard that Lt. Col. James T. Davis[306] is dead.

## MARCH 30–APRIL 1, 1865

❖ Letter from Walkup at breastworks at Hatcher's Run, Virginia to wife Minnie:

My own best beloved Minnie:

Your kind favor of the 21st reached me all right and afforded me much pleasure. The assured welfare of you my dearest and of our charming children always revives and reinvigorates my soul. I wish I could drop in for a short while and help you plant your garden and patches and eat fine turnips, mustard and lettuce salad, and far more to gaze with rapture on your delightful faces and hear your cherished conversation and silvery laughs, more delightful to my ears than the sweetish music. We have returned, as I wrote to you in pencil on the 27th, from our trip to Petersburg and have been resting in our old quarters comfortably until yesterday, when Sheridan passed around our right and is probably tearing up our railroad towards Danville, as our cavalry under Fitzhugh Lee is very inefficient. There was some sharp fighting and skirmishing on our right yesterday and our pickets were all driven in on the south side of Hatchers Run. They had all been driven in on this side last Saturday, but Cooke's Brigade on its return recaptured our lines. MacRae, Davis and others [picket lines] are still held by the Yankees.

I gave you an account of the death of our much esteemed Lt. James Austin of Co. E and of the capture of Lt. Robert Y. Howie and some 36 of our pickets whilst we were gone to Petersburg. I learn that Capt. Sanford Howie of 35th North Carolina was also taken prisoner in the right at Petersburg. Your cousin J.L. Davis I learn is dead. He must have died in a day or so after I left. I intended to go see him again, but could not get off, before I heard of his death. It will be a terrible blow to his kind father and sisters and friends. I don't know whether they, or any of them came out before, or since his death or not.

You speak of getting someone to stay with you and of Cousin Jane Howie. If I cannot get back in April, I would be glad if she or someone were with you for company. But if I come, I do not wish any person else to be there as it is close work to live ourselves without encumbrances. I don't think our Jinny can be let out for her victuals and clothes and I would prefer giving someone $50.00 to keep her and child, if they will do so, to keeping her ourselves. I suppose Brother William has gone off with the home guards and am glad he is elected captain, but sorry to learn that he will go. I fear we will not see him and our excellent Brother John Harry again. I am glad you heard from Sister Nannie and that she was going to Texas. That is the best place I know of, and I should delight to be with you and my family and William John Harry and a few other good friends out in that country, if not before, after the war. Write to Nannie and tell her so and give her my brotherly love.

Sgt. John M. Thomas will return about 9th of April and I wish you to get William E. Irby to send me a certified copy of my election with certificate and seal of court attached to it—viz., if I am elected county solicitor and if you can get me 100 or 200 pounds of flour send by Thomas even if you have to pay $2.50 or $3.00 per pound, or 100 or 200 pounds of bacon at $5.00 per pound send either or both with him in boxes. I can sell them at good profits here as bacon brings $10.00 and $12.00 per pound and flour $5.00 per hundred weight. Send my cloth too by Thomas. If you get these things you can send them up to Charlotte to care of Hart by stage and it will not cost over $30.00 to $50.00. I can get my clothes made better for provisions than money. If you can send me a jug of molasses (gallon) it will be very acceptable, but if you hear that the railroad is destroyed, you need not send anything.

Plant all the potatoes, Irish and sweet, you can, and be sure to have the ground plowed up deep and well turned over and put all the manure you can scrape or buy on the grounds. Be prepared for raids and rogues and secure your valuables and eatables where it cannot be found or known by any other person as much as possible.

We are all quite well and comfortable as could be expected. I told James Stitt about going home and if he applies I will do what I can to get him off, but fear that there will be no more chance to go as he is still under arrest for staying away before. He enjoys himself better than anyone else, as he stays comfortable in camp whilst we have to move and fight. There was fighting last night towards Petersburg on our left, and there is fighting just now across the creek and rather in our rear this morning. We were sent out to the breastworks last night and stayed there in some houses all night. It began to rain in the night and has not yet ceased. I think Grant has sent Sheridan around our right flank to cut the Southside Railroad and draw our attention there, whilst he is sending reinforcements to Sherman by his left flank down toward Weldon, North Carolina. We are expecting an advance here upon our works and fear the Yankees will also come in on our right and rear. Our force is very weak. Grant must have from three to five to our one, whereas Johnston in North Carolina has as many men as Sherman, if not more. It is true we have entrenchments before us, but we generally have to fight outside of them as we are too few to man them against a strong assault.[307]

I was much grieved to hear of brother Abel Belk's death, but wrote before of how I feel proud to know that my letter afford you so much pleasure and, however much they give you, I feel still your debtor for the pleasure and satisfaction I receive from the perusal of your letters. I only wish they were a little more frequent. I feel like a weary traveler passing through dreary and arid desserts and the reception of your letters turns it into a delightful oasis, with gushing, clear. Cool water, surrounded with fruits, flowers, and all that the heart desires in such a place. Through these I see all who are so very dear to my heart, present before me. You smiling, Lelia prattling, Alice Jane cooing and rattling and all joyous, innocent and happy. This, my love, is the picture of earthly happiness that comes nearest Heaven of any earth can give. When two that are linked in one heavenly tie, with love near changing, etc., and surrounded with such sweet pledges of affection as ours, who would not be happy and thankful. Oh that we could rest in [sanctuary] of shade, where the war clouds cold never reach us and have our friends around us there. But I still hope to get home some time and enjoy the sweet comforts of my dear Minnie's society and that of our darling children. The greatest comforts I have in life and which makes it more tolerable to me and more desirable to live for their sakes. Kiss the sweet cherubs for me and give my love to all my dear friends and respects to those kind neighbors, who do anything for the comfort of you and my dear family. May God bless and protect you. I may add a few lines before mailing this—if not, farewell my love, your husband truly

P.S. April 1st. We have been fighting and skirmishing ever since I began this letter. The enemy have massed in force on our right; we have had another picket line captured losing 44 men in the 48th Regiment. We have only 98 privates and non-commissioned officers in this regiment for duty and 15 company officers, leaving out those companies sent to hunt deserters (A and B). I send you a list of those captured from Union County, many of whom did not try to escape. Five of the deserters have returned, viz. Hugh Stevens, Frank Cuthbertson, Willie Medlin, Joe Williams, Theo Simpson, Thad Crowell and nine others from Davidson County.

You need not send my clothes, nor flour, nor anything else to me, my dearest; we will either be killed or captured or the road will be destroyed before this letter reaches you. Lee will have to evacuate Richmond or be captured before April closes and perhaps before ten days. Our officers and men are all well, but very greatly discouraged. I have kept this letter back to see if the news would change, but it grows worse every day and I must close. I will add a few lines tomorrow and enclose. Be prepared for bad news from Lee's army. There is no reasonable prospect for good news.[308]

## April 12, 1865

We left camp [after Appomattox parole][309] at 4:00 p.m. and came five or six miles, camped at night. Got cup of coffee and some cakes. Walk left to bridge to Campbell Court House where W. Alexander gave me a julep and dinner. We got a drink and meal and camp five miles beyond. Left day[light].[310]

## April 14, 1865

Beautiful country, saw Peaks of Otter. Failed to cross at bridge because burnt. [Observe Union cavalry].[311]

## APRIL 15, 1865

Going home. We had rain and in bad order came to Buryer's Store and Mornay's Store, zigzag course, and halt at Mornay's getting corn and meat ration. Find our party self-willed, all wanting to be chief. [There are some] who would give or risk their souls for liquor. Camped in old field, got remains of supper.

## APRIL 16, 1865

Sunday. We continue route towards Leaksville which is not on direct way.[312] But food leads and we must follow. Pass over a poor country. Davies of Co. C and Briney and Marsh are with same route. We reach old North Carolina this evening at Cascade River and Smith River, passing William Aikens. Passing large tobacconist, halting at Leaksville, North Carolina. We here got rations to eat but nothing else but beans. Stayed all night with William Wade who treated us well. Col. Hill and I slept in a feather bed. We were not charged anything [by] a brisk old lady who was a "secessionist that never was subjugated."[313]

## APRIL 17, 1865

Monday. We pass Mayo River and Dan at Davistown or Saura Town.[314] Saura Town Mountains and Saura Town have a beautiful, well watered and fruitful grazing country. Press some oats. Mathews gives me some corn. At David Leaks who is amiable and generously attentive and hospitable. Got some of the best apple brandy and supper and camp in sight of Germanton.[315] We pass by Germanton and get rations and sorghum, have bread and corn and buttermilk.

## APRIL 18, 1865

Tuesday. Pass Old Town[316] (Moravian settlement 1755), very dilapidated and poor and quaint, thence to Hall's Ferry on Yadkin. Stop at Jack Boyer of Forsythe County, who is clever and hospitable beyond anyone we met, gave good brandy and dinner. Thence to campground in Davie.[317] Stayed all night with old man and young wife and fared on pressed provisions.

# Chapter Notes

## Preface

1. William S. Powell, "Samuel H. Walkup," *Dictionary of North Carolina Biography*, University of North Carolina Press, Chapel Hill, North Carolina, 1996, online at ncpedia.org, in a 2004 conversation with me identified Walkup as an "important but overlooked" Southern leader of the antebellum, Civil War and Reconstruction era worthy of further research. I had the profound honor of serving with Chairman Powell on the North Carolina Historical Commission, at which time he encouraged and guided my Walkup studies.

2. Ulysses S. Grant, *Personal Memoirs of U.S. Grant*, C. L. Webster, New York, New York, 1885, Chapter 67.

3. We must try to address Ralph Ellison's admonition, "I am invisible, understand, because people refuse to see me... When they approach me they see only my surroundings, themselves or fragments of their imagination, indeed, everything and anything but me." Ralph Ellison, *Invisible Man*, Random House, New York, New York, 1952, preface. See also Erskine Clark, *A Dwelling Place; A Plantation Epic*, Yale University Press, New Haven, Connecticut, 2005. I met Dr. Clark when I participated in his June 14, 2020 seminar as a National Endowment for the Humanities fellow, and was inspired by his directive to "hear the enslaved asking us to tell their story." He stated he tried as "an old white man" to give voice to those oppressed unable to offer their own narratives.

## Biography

1. *The Monroe Enquirer*, Monroe, North Carolina, March 7,1963, reprinting letter from Samuel H. Walkup to his uncle Samuel Walkup in Kentucky dated Sept. 28, 1846.

2. "Membership Applications, 1889–1970," Sons of the Revolution, Kentucky, v.247, no. 49208; Mile Elliott, *Heritage of Union County*, The Carolinas Genealogical Society, Monroe, North Carolina, 1992, 444–445; L. H. McMurray, "Walkup Family Genealogy," Union County Local History Room, Monroe, North Carolina; "Our Heritage," *The Monroe Examiner*, NC, Dec. 18, 1958 and March 7, 1963.

3. See James G. Layburn, *The Scotch-Irish: A Social History*, University of North Carolina Press, Chapel Hill, North Carolina, 1962.

4. See Samuel H. Walkup, "An address on the Bible, its influence, and the duty of the Christian world to extend its influence," *Waxhaw Bible Society*, The Ledger Office Printer, Waxhaw, North Carolina, 1857.

5. John Hugh McDowell, *The McDowells, Erwins, Irvins and Connections*, C.B. Johnson and Co., Memphis, Tennessee, 1918, 81.

6. "Membership Applications, 1889–1970," Sons of the Revolution, Kentucky, v.247, no. 49208; Mile Elliott, *Heritage of Union County*, The Carolinas Genealogical Society, Monroe, North Carolina, 1992, 444–445; L. H. McMurray, "Walkup Family Genealogy," Union County Local History Room, Monroe, North Carolina; "Our Heritage," *The Monroe Examiner*, NC, Dec 18, 1958 and March 7, 1963.

7. Walkup's study of Jackson demonstrated the adept skills of a historian combined with a lawyer's analytical critique and interrogatory. He thoroughly gathered both oral and written primary sources, meticulously documenting narratives in the rigorous format of legal evidence. Although a committed Whig not enamored with "King Andrew's" concept of a powerful chief executive, Walkup remained objective as historian. Such comprehensive, level examination of credible, knowledgeable witness familiar with Jackson's birth and upbringing produced a vetted account consistent with professional and historical standards. The historian biographer James Parton in his *Life of Andrew Jackson* relied extensively on sources Walkup compiled in postulating Old Hickory's birthplace. See Samuel H. Walkup, "The Birth-Place of Andrew Jackson," *North Carolina University Magazine*, New Series, v. X, 1891; L. Blythe and C. Brockman, *Hornet's Nest: The Story of Charlotte and Mecklenburg County*, Library of Charlotte and Mecklenburg County Publisher, 1961.

8. Will Abstract 669, Clerk of Superior Court, Union County, North Carolina. Conveyance of enslaved persons as legal chattel comparable to livestock evidences slavery's profound inhumanity and malignancy.

9. Samuel H. Walkup noted, "My father and we have now a little negro boy, who is very sick of typhus fever, and will probably die in a day or two..." *The Monroe Enquirer*, Monroe, North Carolina, April 18, 1963, reprinting letter from Samuel H. Walkup to uncle Samuel Walkup in Kentucky dated Dec. 20, 1845.

10. Correspondence from Robert Walkup to his brother Samuel Walker, Madison County, Kentucky, July 24, 1838 and Samuel H. Walkup to his uncle Samuel Walkup, Jan. 25, 1844, "Samuel Walkup Letters," Special Collection, Eastern Kentucky University. Samuel related making a "good crop" of cotton comprised of forty bales weighing about 350 pounds each, selling from seven to ten dollars per hundred weight.

11. McDowell, *The McDowells, Erwins,*

*Irwins and Connections,* 87; "Samuel Walkup Papers," Special Collections, Eastern Kentucky University, letter from Robert Walkup to his brother Samuel Walkup, Feb. 23, 1823.

12. Elliott, *The Heritage of Union County,* 444.

13. Correspondence from Robert Walkup to his brother Samuel Walker, Madison County, Kentucky, July 24, 1838, "Samuel Walkup Letter," Special Collection, Eastern Kentucky University.

14. Kemp Battle, *History of the University of North Carolina, From its Beginning to the Death of President Swain,* v.1, Edwards and Broughton Printing Company, Raleigh, North Carolina, 1907, 17–19.

15. William S. Powell, "Samuel H. Walkup," *Dictionary of North Carolina Biography*, University of North Carolina Press, Chapel Hill, North Carolina, 1996, online at ncpedia.org, citing Daniel L. Grant, *Alumni History of the University of North Carolina*, Christian and King Printing, Chapel Hill, North Carolina, 1924. I had the profound honor of serving with Chairman Powell on the North Carolina Historical Commission, at which time he encouraged and guided my Walkup studies

16. Battle, 556.

17. See R. H. Battle, "Hon. Samuel Field Phillips, LL.D.," *North Carolina Journal of Law*, Buffalo, New York, 1904, v. 1, 23–25.

18. The "Fresh Treat" required new students treat classmates to a bountiful feast with abundant alcohol. Rioting frequently ensued, with ribald singing, bell ringing, looting of university buildings, and pranks played on faculty. In response to university disciplinary actions, students created the Ugly Club as a means of resistance and to provide a forum for gambling and drinking. See Battle, 465–466.

19. Battle, 472–474.

20. "Samuel H. Walkup Obituary," *Southern Home*, Charlotte, Nov. 6, 1876, 1.

21. Elliott, *The Heritage of Union County,* 445. He apparently visited north

and middle Florida, St. Augustine and the St. Johns River towns, where his brother Henry Clay Walkup post–Civil War established a medical practice. In regard to the Seminoles he encountered, Walkup expressed a paternalistic, assimilationist empathy, stating that rather than annihilation, they should be shown "Christian charity and benevolence to humanize, to civilize ... by acts of kindness to become our fellow citizens." As Walkup traveled south from Monroe to Florida, he stayed with friends and relatives, and being young especially noted the fine houses and attractive women he encountered. Conversation with Virginia Adams, Walkup's great-great granddaughter, owner and custodian of the Walkup Florida manuscripts, Sept. 11, 2020.

22. "Samuel H. Walkup Obituary," *Southern Home*, Charlotte, Nov. 6, 1876, 1; *The North-Carolina Standard*, Raleigh, North Carolina, June 19, 1844. See also Fannie Memory Farmer, "Legal Education in North Carolina, 1820–1860," *The North Carolina Historical Review*, Department of Archives and History, Raleigh, North Carolina, July 1951, v. XXVII, no. 3.

23. See Lawrence Friedman, *A History of American Law*, Simon and Schuster, New York, 1975, 265–275. Several current or retired members of the Union County bar like Koy Dawkins still have these books in their law libraries with Walker ownership indicated on the flyleaf. Conversation with Patricia Poland, Union County Library, Monroe, North Carolina, Feb. 4, 2014.

24. "Samuel H. Walkup Obituary," *Southern Home*, Charlotte, Nov. 6, 1876, 1.

25. Elliott, *The Heritage of Union County*, 444.

26. Correspondence from Samuel H. Walkup to his uncle Samuel Walker, Madison County, Kentucky, Sept. 21, 1844, "Samuel Walkup Letters," Special Collection, Eastern Kentucky University. Walkup described both his law and agricultural endeavors as "pretty fair business." *The Monroe Enquirer*, Monroe, North Carolina, reprinting letter from Samuel H. Walkup to uncle Samuel

Walkup in Kentucky dated Dec. 20, 1845. See also John G. Saxe's whimsical "A Legal Ballad": The profession's already so full of lawyers so full of profession, That a modest young man like myself Can't make the smallest impression," quoted in Mark S. Steiner, *An Honest Calling*, Northern Illinois University Press, DeKalb, Illinois, 2009, 73.

27. A typical Walkup newspaper advertisement declared his "STRICT ATTENTION" to service. Rather than work solely on an hourly reimbursement basis, he announced a contingency fee where his client would incur no charge unless recovery obtained. Such contingency arrangements were especially attractive to clients with military pension and bonus land claims. See "Advertisement," *The Western Democrat*, Charlotte, North Carolina, July 12, 1859, 1.

28. Patricia M. Poland, Union County Library, has researched the property known as the Stewart-Walkup-Simpson house, utilizing Walkup wills, conveyance deeds, Gray and Sanborn insurance maps, and *The Monroe Journal*. Her work is available at the Union County Library Local History Room, Monroe, North Carolina and online at *Random Historical Notes for the City of Monroe and Union County*, http://monroeunion countynchistorystuff.blogspot.com.

29. Plat preparation was typical of Walkup's real estate and drafting practice. He is credited with rendering one of the first maps of the Town of Monroe. Union County Superior Court Minute Docket, 1866–1877, North Carolina State Archives, v. 1, 1, CR 097.311.3.

30. See E. Lee Shepard, "Breaking into the Profession," *The Journal of Southern History*, v. XLVIII, no. 3, August 1982 and Steiner, *An Honest Calling*, 26–74; See also Fannie Memory Farmer, "Legal Practice and Ethics in North Carolina," *North Carolina Historical Review*, Department of Archives and History, Raleigh, North Carolina, July 1953, v. 30, no. 3.

31. Walkup was Chief Marshall for a festive barbeque solicitation of venture capital for a proposed railroad from Wilmington, North Carolina, to Charlotte.

"Grand Rail Road Rally in Union County." *The Charlotte Democrat*, Charlotte, North Carolina, Nov. 13, 1855, 1. He was designated by the legislature as one of the agents empowered to solicit equity subscriptions. "Bill Incorporating the Wilmington and Charlotte Railroad Company," *Legislative Documents*, North Carolina General Assembly. Raleigh, North Carolina, W. Holden Printer, 1854, no. 13.

32. Elliott, *The Heritage of Union County*, 444.

33. Correspondence from Samuel H. Walkup to his uncle Samuel Walker, Madison County, Kentucky, Sept. 21, 1844, "Samuel Walkup Letters," Special Collection, Eastern Kentucky University, indicating the law practice was then a growing business.

34. Elliott, *The Heritage of Union County*, 444–445. Walkup was a Mason no later than 1866 when he served as an incorporator for the Monroe Lodge Number 224, and he may have affiliated with a Charlotte Lodge in antebellum years. See *Journal*, North Carolina General Assembly, 1866–1867 Session, 344.

35. See "Whig Meeting in Anson," *Fayetteville Weekly Observer*, Fayetteville, North Carolina, June 5, 1844; Marc Kruman, *Parties and Politics in North Carolina, 1836–1865*, Louisiana State University Press, Baton Rouge, 1983.

36. *Charlotte Journal*, July 1, 1846, 1.

37. *The Weekly Standard*, Raleigh, North Carolina, July 28, 1858, 4.

38. *Journal*, North Carolina General Assembly, Raleigh, North Carolina, 1858–1859 session.

39. "For Congress, General S. H. Walkup of Union," *North Carolina Argus*, Wadesboro, North Carolina, July 21, 1859, 2.

40. *Semi-Weekly Standard*, Raleigh, North Carolina, Aug. 20, 1859, 1.

41. *The Western Democrat*, Charlotte, North Carolina, July 12, 1859, 1.

42. "In for the War," *Semi-Weekly Standard*, Raleigh, North Carolina, July 20, 1859, 1.

43. Francis Burton Craige was a lawyer and editor with strong political support by Governor Ellis and large operation planters. Leaving Congress in 1861, Craige was a member of the State Secessionist Convention and primary advocate and sponsor of the disunion ordinance. He served in the Provisional Confederate Congress 1861–1862. J.C. Sitterson, *The Secessionist Movement in North Carolina*, University of North Carolina Press, Chapel Hill, North Carolina, 1939.

44. "Proceedings of the Opposition State Convention," *The Greensboro Patriot*, Greensboro, North Carolina, March 2, 1860, 1.

45. The Constitutional Union Party was unsuccessful in sufficiently dividing the presidential vote to deny a Republican or Democratic majority and force resolution by the House of Representatives. See Don Green, "Constitutional Unionists," *The Historian*, 69 (2), Summer 2007, 231–252.

46. "Gen. Walkup for Senator," *North Carolina Argus*, Wadesboro, North Carolina, June 7, 1860, 2. Clearly Walkup's egalitarianism was limited to white males.

47. See *Journal*, North Carolina General Assembly, 1860–1861 session; *Fayetteville Weekly Observer*, April 14, 1860.

48. "Speech of Mr. Walkup of Union Delivered in the Senate," *Weekly Raleigh Register*, Raleigh, North Carolina, Jan. 23, 1861, 1.

49. McDowell, *The McDowells, Erwins, Irvins and Connections*, 81.

50. Samuel H. Walkup, "An address delivered at the annual commencement of the Carolina Female College," *Pee Dee Star Publisher*, Wadesboro, North Carolina, 1854.

51. See Charles Lee Raper, *The Church and Private Schools of North Carolina*, Jos. J. Stone Printers, Greensboro, North Carolina, 1898, 118–119; Mary Medley, "Higher Education," *History of Anson County, North Carolina, 1750–1976*, Heritage Printers, Charlotte, 1976, 191–193.

52. McDowell, *The McDowells, Erwins, Irvins and Connections*, 78–87.

53. Despite replicating one of the most horrific and traumatic experiences of involuntary servitude, these "slave auctions" have continued in charity fundraising in the twenty-first century.

54. "Samuel Walkup Papers," letter to wife from Orange Court House, Jan. 19, 1864.

55. Minnie wore her fine "Second Day" ash-of-roses dress and played "The Battle of Waterloo." Elliott, *The Heritage of Union County*, 444–445; Powell, "Samuel H.Walkup,"*Dictionary*.

56. See Walkup's characterization of a racially inclusive "family" in his letter to uncle Samuel Walkup, Sept. 21, 1844, "Samuel Walkup Letters."

57. McDowell, *The McDowells, Erwins, Irvins and Connections*, 81.

58. The bright red waist sash, detailed with embroidery, was 7.5 feet long with 5 inch hand knotted tassels at each end. Walkup wore this sash as militia brigadier general and on formal occasions in his Confederate service. Museum of Southern History Collection, Houston Baptist University, Houston, Texas.

59. Samuel H. Walkup, "An Address Delivered at the Annual Commencement of Carolina Female College," Pee Dee Star Publisher, Wadesboro, North Carolina, 1854, 12–15.

60. Walkup, "An Address Delivered at the Annual Commencement," 15.

61. Samuel H. Walkup, "An Address Delivered at the Commencement of the Carolina Female College," Pee Dee Star Publisher, Wadesboro, North Carolina, 1854, 17.

62. Walkup, "An Address Delivered at the Annual Commencement," 20.

63. Samuel H. Walkup, "An Address on the Bible, its Influence, and the duty of the Christian world to extend its influence," Waxhaw Bible Society Publisher, Lancaster, South Carolina, 1857, 13.

64. Walkup, "An Address on the Bible," 13, 21–29. Walkup accepted the deplorable white supremacy narrative that sought to rehabilitate slavery. He appeared completely oblivious to the totally demeaning and denigrating aspects of coerced labor and social marginalization, by supporting the racist notion that slavery was a school for "cultural" and "intellectual" advancement.

65. Walkup's will made March 5, 1864 but not probated until March 6, 1876, referenced slaves but the specifics as to name, sex, age and number were deleted by the County Clerk of Court as a bequest in violation of the then applicable law in light of abolition. The original document in the State Archives Loose Wills File, although redacted by strike through perhaps done post-war by Walkup himself, remains legible and lists Hall, Susan, Betty, Stephen, Margaret, Eliza, Harriett, Fanny, Sarah, Wilson and Jenny.

66. The 1860 census for Monroe, Union County, listing no. 17, stated that Walkup owned $7000 tangible personal property, which valuation included two enslaved, any farm and law office inventory, equipment and stock.

67. Robert Walkup Will, executed Sept. 15, 1846, Union County, North Carolina Court of Pleas and Quarter Sessions, Union County Will Book 1, 33, microfilm at the Union County Public Library, Monroe, North Carolina.

68. See Stephanie Jones-Rogers, *They Were Her Property: White Women as Slave Owners in the American South*, Yale University Press, New Haven, Connecticut, 2019, 18.

69. See Drew Gilpin Faust, *Mothers of Invention: Women of the Slaveholding South in the American Civil War*, University of North Carolina Press, Chapel Hill, North Carolina, 1996.

70. After 1830 free African Americans were not legally permitted to marry slaves, although the law was frequently avoided through informal relationships. See E. Franklin Frazier, *The Free Negro Family*, 38–51.

71. "Samuel Walkup Papers," correspondence to wife, Jan. 1, 1863. Students of history must fully consider how the enslaved were victimized as traded chattel. But equally important, we should look at their assertive agency exemplified through their craft and creativity, religion and family, demonstrating both express and subtle resistance and affirmation of self-worth.

72. "Samuel Walkup Papers," Oct. 17, 1862; June 23, 1863; May 15, 1864.

73. Footnote See Peter Carmichael, *"We are the men": The Ambiguous Place*

*of Confederate Slaves in Southern Armies.*
While the plenary degradation of enslavement and actual or potential violence
experienced by the enslaved were always
present in the American South, real
paternalism by some slaveholders was
also possible and actual. See Peter Kolchin, *American Slavery*, Hill and Wang,
New York, 2003. When considering slavery, forced labor was only one aspect of
the malevolent institution. At least equally
pernicious was the narrative of white
superiority with its legacy extending to
today. A compelling argument can be
made that slavery did not end with the
Thirteenth Amendment, but instead
evolved after the Civil War from a de jure
to a de facto Southern institution. See
Henry Louis Gates, Jr., *Stoney the Road:
Reconstruction, White Supremacy and
the Rise of Jim Crow*, Penguin Press, New
York, 2019, citing Bryan Stevenson, 1.

74. "Samuel Walkup Papers," July 15–
16, 1862 entry. Periodicals of the era
advised that the enslaved nurse be healthy,
honest, good tempered, fond of children
and free of detriments such as drinking, snuff taking and superstition. See
G. Johnson, *Antebellum North Carolina*,
236.

75. See Drew Cilpin Faust, *Mothers
of Invention: Women of the Slaveholding
South in the American Civil War*, 60–62;
"Samuel Walkup Papers," May 25, 1862,
June 12, 1862.

76. See Union County Cohabitation
Registry, entered June 1, 1866 by J. E. Irby,
Clerk. Walkup family tradition related
that Hall assisted in the apprehension
of three of Sherman's forgers in Union
County. A search of wartime court records
and post-war Confederate pension applications and awards has not corroborated the claim. Moreover, Hall's name
is not listed in the Union County memorial to "Confederate Pensioners of Color."
See Commemorative Landscapes," http://
docsouth.unc.edu/commland/monu
ment/353/. Another Union County slave,
Aaron Perry, born 1838, did capture some
Federals. The Union County Court of Peas
and Quarter Sessions Oct. 1864 term
directed "Ten Dollars to be paid over to

a slave of Capt. Wm. Perry by the name of
Aaron for meritorious conduct in arresting some Yankees." See *Union County
Court of Pleas and Quarter Sessions Minutes*, Vol. D (1852–1867), 375; Frances
R. Small, *Union County North Carolina
Marriages*, 391. Perhaps the confusion
arose out of Walkup's July 16, 1863 diary
reference to "Hall's coming with the prisoners." Historian Kevin Levin maintains
that in the post-war South, the narrative
describing the "loyal slave" evolved into
the "loyal and faithful camp servant" and
ultimately, in some instances, what he
deems the "mythical" black Confederate soldier. In contrast, a very few historians continue to assert that some enslaved
workers supported and volitionally served
the Confederacy. Earl James, Curator,
North Carolina Museum of History, purports that some African Americans, both
free and enslaved, served the Confederacy
with some degree of free will. See http://
www.abbevilleinstitute.org/blog/black-
soldier-north-and-south-1861–1865/.
A consensus of historians share the perspective set forth by Levin, *Searching For
Black Confederates: The Civil War's Most
Persistent Myth*, University of North Carolina Press, 2019, that whatever the motivation and volition of the enslaved "camp
servant," "Confederate slave" or "body
servant" at any given instance, his legal
status as property subject to an owner's
authority remained unchanged.

77. See William Byrd and John Smith,
*North Carolina Slaves and Free Persons
of Color: Mecklenburg, Gaston and Union
Counties*, Heritage Books, Bowie, Maryland, 2001, 204–205.

78. A profound twentieth century
American poet using a lyricism tran-
scending the historian's weighty prose,
declared: "Bury the whip, bury the brand-
ing-bars, / Bury the unjust thing / That
some tamed into mercy, being wise, / But
could not starve the tiger from its eyes."
Stephen Vincent Benet, *John Brown's
Body*, 333; Similarly, the novelist James
Lee Burke has his Gen. John Bell Hood
character concede, "Oh, we were always
honorable—Robert Lee, Jackson, Albert
Sidney Johnson, A. P. Hill—but we served

venal men and a vile enterprise. How many lives would have been spared had we not lent ourselves to the defense of a repellant cause like slavery." James Lee Burke, *In the Electric Mist with Confederate Dead*, Hyperion, New York, New York, 1993, 432; Ulysses Grant noted, "As time passes, people, even of the South, will begin to wonder how it was possible that their ancestors ever fought for or justified institutions which acknowledged the right of property in man." Ulysses S. Grant, *Personal Memoirs of General U.S. Grant*, C. L. Webster, New York, New York, 1888, Chapter 12.

79. Walkup, "An Address on the Bible," 15.

80. *The Fayetteville Observer*, Fayetteville, North Carolina, July 7, 1862.

81. "Samuel Walkup Papers," April 1, 1862.

82. W. H. Lawhon, "Forty-Eight Regimental History," in William Clark, *Histories of the Several Regiments and Battalions from North Carolina, in the Great War 1861–1865*, Nash Brothers, Goldsboro, North Carolina, 1901, v. 3, 113–114.

83. "Samuel Walkup Papers," May 23, 1862, May 25, 1862 and June 12, 1862.

84. Lawhon, "Forty-Eight Regiment," 114.

85. "Samuel Walkup Papers," June 24, 1862.

86. "Samuel Walkup Papers," Sept. 11. 1862.

87. "Samuel Walkup papers," Sept. 16–17, 1862.

88. "Samuel Walkup Papers," Sept. 19, 1862.

89. *The Papers of Zebulon Vance*, North Carolina Department of Cultural Resources, University of North Carolina Press, Chapel Hill, North Carolina, v.3, Letter from Walkup at camp near Winchester, Virginia, Oct. 11, 1862. The solicitation was addressed at least in part as the regiment received English manufactured uniforms shipping into Wilmington, North Carolina on the state owned blockade runner *Advance*. See Weymouth Jordan, Jr., *North Carolina Troops, 1861 1865-A Roster*, North Carolina Department of Cultural Resources,

Raleigh, North Carolina, 1987, frontispiece, 363.

90. Samuel H. Walkup, "History of the 48th Regiment," *Fayetteville Observer*, Fayetteville, North Carolina, Feb. 22, 1864. The Washington Artillery, having experienced the withering fire with numerous casualties, had to request assistance in manning its guns from the 48th Regiment. William Miller Owens, "A Hot Day on Marye's Heights," *Battles and Leaders of the Civil War*, Century Company, New York, 1888, v. III, 99.

91. "Samuel Walkup Papers," Dec. 13, 1862.

92. "Samuel Walkup Papers," May 22–23, 1863; May 25, 1863.

93. "Samuel Walkup Papers," July 7, 1863.

94. "Samuel Walkup Papers," July 10, 1863.

95. "Samuel Walkup Papers," Nov. 13, 1863.

96. Lawhon, "Forty-Eight Regiment," 118.

97. "Samuel Walkup Papers," Jan. 25, 1864.

98. "Samuel Walkup Papers," Dec. 9, 1863. Consistent with the repressive nature of slavery, the African Americans were afforded no input or agency in determining what work they performed, for whom, and under what circumstances.

99. Samuel Walkup Papers," Dec. 9, 1863.

100. "Samuel Walkup Papers," letter from Walkup to wife, Jan. 28, 1864.

101. "Samuel Walkup Papers," letter from Walkup to wife, March 30-April 1, 1865.

102. "Samuel Walkup Papers," Jan. 1, 1864.

103. "Samuel Walkup Papers," Jan. 18, 1864.

104. "Samuel Walkup Papers," Jan. 19, 1864.

105. "Samuel Walkup Papers," letter at Orange Court House to wife, Jan. 19, 1864.

106. "Samuel Walkup Papers," Jan. 25, 1864; Jan. 28–30, 1864.

107. "Samuel Walkup Papers," Feb. 6, 1864; Feb. 11, 1864.

108. "Samuel Walkup Papers," Jan. 28, 1864.

109. "Samuel Walkup Papers," Jan. 28, 1864; letter from Walkup to Governor Zebulon Vance, Nov. 13, 1863, North Carolina Archives and History, Raleigh, North Carolina, 9135.

110. "Samuel Walkup Papers," Jan. 28, 1864.

111. "Samuel Walkup Papers," April 15, 1864. Walkup took significant efforts to regularly writing detailed letters. He particularly lamented the logistical constraints imposed on correspondence with an ineffectual Confederate postal service. Unlike many Victorians, Walkup was not inhibited or reticent in expressing to his wife personal emotions and vulnerability.

112. "Samuel Walkup Papers," April 3, 1864.

113. "Samuel Walkup Papers," April 6, 1864.

114. "Samuel Walkup Papers," March 16, 1864; March 28, 1864; March 30, 1864.

115. "Samuel Walkup Papers," April 11, 1864.

116. "Samuel Walkup Papers," March 23, 1864; March 24, 1865.

117. "Samuel Walkup Papers," March 24, 1864.

118. See Drew Gilpin Faust, *Mothers of Invention*, 53–79.

119. "Samuel Walkup Papers," May 4–6, 1863; Lawhon, "Forty-Eight Regiment," 119.

120. Gary W. Gallagher, *The Wilderness Campaign*, University of North Carolina Press, Chapel Hill, North Carolina, 1999, 163.

121. "Samuel Walkup Papers," May 11–12, 1864.

122. "Samuel Walkup Papers," May 15, 2014 letter from Walkup to wife.

123. 'Samuel Walkup Papers," May 15, 1864 letter from Walkup to wife; May 16, 1864.

124. "Samuel Walkup Papers," May 22, 1864.

125. "Samuel Walkup Papers," May 29, 1864.

126. "Samuel Walkup Papers," June 3, 1864.

127. "Samuel Walkup Papers," June 9, 1864.

128. "Samuel Walkup Papers," June 15, 1864.

129. "Samuel Walkup Papers," June 15, 1864.

130. "Samuel Walkup Papers," June 21, 1864.

131. "Samuel Walkup Papers," June 22, 1864.

132. "Samuel Walkup Papers," June 24, 1864.

133. "Samuel Walkup Papers," Aug. 18, 1864.

134. *The Papers of Zebulon Vance*, North Carolina Department of Cultural Resources, University of North Carolina Press, Chapel Hill, North Carolina, v.3, Letter from Walkup at Monroe, North Carolina, Sept. 2, 1864.

135. "Samuel Walkup Papers," Jan. 3, 1865.

136. "Samuel Walkup papers," Jan. 1, 1865.

137. "Samuel Walkup Papers," Feb. 21, 1865.

138. "Samuel Walkup Papers," March 6, 1865.

139. "Samuel Walkup Papers," letter from Walkup to sister Sara N. Walkup Belk, date uncertain, between March 8–30; letter from Walkup to wife, March 30–April 1, 1865.

140. "Samuel Walkup Papers," Feb. 28, 1865.

141. "Samuel Walkup Papers," letter from Walkup to sister Sara N. Walkup Belk, date uncertain, between March 8–30, 1865.

142. "Samuel Walkup Papers," March 4, 1865.

143. "Samuel Walkup Papers," letter from Walkup to sister Sara N. Walkup Belk, date uncertain, between March 8–30, 1865.

144. "Samuel Walkup Papers," April 1 postscript to letter to wife dated March 30–April 1, 1865.

145. "Jordan, *North Carolina Troops*, v. ii 368.

146. Lawhon, "Forty-Eighth Regiment," 123.

147. Lawhon, "Forty-Eight Regiment,"

123; Jordan, *North Carolina Troops*, vii, 368.

148. Samuel H. Walkup correspondence to John Rogers Cooke, Jan. 17, 1866, Virginia Museum of History and Culture, Richmond, Virginia, Manuscript Collection, "John Rogers Cooke Papers, 1860–1894," sec. 2, c7753 a 4–17, record 181844. Walkup was not totally destitute. He owned his residence, law office and lots in Monroe, Union County farmland and agricultural equipment, a buggy, fine watch and rosewood piano. "Excise Tax of United States," *Internal Revenue Assessment Lists, 1862–1874*, Feb. 1866, no. 23, North Carolina M784, div. 1, collection dis. 3; June 1866, div. 2, collection dis. 6, record group 58, National Archives and Records, Washington, District of Columbia.

149. By at least 1866 he secured pro tem appointment as Solicitor, receiving much needed compensation for attending Superior Court. See "Miscellaneous Freedmen's Records, 1863–1872," Bureau of Refugees, Freedmen and Abandoned Lands,1866, North Carolina Western District, Salisbury, North Carolina, roll 63, microfilm m 1909, National Archives and Records, Washington, District of Columbia; *Journal*, North Carolina General Assembly, 1868 Session, 105.

150. Around Jan. 1865 Hall married Mary in a religious ceremony and subsequently legally solemnized their marriage as recorded in the *1866 Union County Cohabitation Registry*, Monroe, North Carolina, entry by J.E. Irby, Clerk.

151. Jonathan Worth was a pre-war Whig lawyer and planter who vehemently rejected secession. During the Civil War he served as State Treasurer but frequently collaborated with William Holden's peace movement in opposition to Confederate authority. Elected governor in late 1865, Worth supported President Andrew Johnson's Reconstruction agenda and opposed the Fourteenth and Fifteenth Amendments and Federal military occupation. See Richard L. Zuber, *Jonathan Worth: A Bibliography of a Southern Unionist*, University of North Carolina Press, Chapel Hill, North Carolina, 1965.

152. William Woods Holden was a pre-war Democrat lawyer and newspaper editor. Like Worth and Walkup, Holden was a Unionist until armed conflict made secession appear inevitable. During the Civil War he championed peace efforts and North Carolina states' rights in opposition to a centralized Confederate national government. Post-war he embraced Republicanism and Congressional reconstruction. Elected governor in 1868 with strong freedmen support he promoted a more egalitarian State Constitution, public education, equal justice, and Northern capital investment in North Carolina. Proactive in repressing Ku Klux Klan vigilantism, he was impeached by an incensed Conservative Democratic legislature and removed from office. See William Harris, *William Woods Holden: Firebrand of North Carolina Politics*, Louisiana State University Press, Baton Rouge, Louisiana, 1987.

153. Max Williams, Ed., *The Papers of William Alexander Graham*, North Carolina Department of Cultural Resources, Raleigh, North Carolina, 1976, v. VI, 448–450.

154. "The Discussion," *Daily Carolina Times*, Charlotte, North Carolina, Oct. 31, 1865, 1.

155. "Col. Samuel Walkup," *Daily Carolina Times*, Charlotte, North Carolina, Nov. 1, 1865, 1.

156. "Col. Samuel Walkup," *Daily Carolina Times*, Charlotte, North Carolina, Nov. 1, 1865, 1. At Appomattox Court House, April 12, 1865, Walkup was listed as a prisoner of war and issued a parole pass. See *Combined Service Records*, roll 191, 48th North Carolina Infantry, Walkup entry.

157. The vote tally was Walkup 3455, Ramsey 3397 and Sloan 1500. Williams, *The Papers of William Alexander Graham*, 449.

158. As anticipated during the campaign, eligibility to take the oath did determine admission. Congress exercised its power to review and accept or reject member's credentials, utilizing its 1862 requirement of an oath that the affiant had never engaged in rebellion or disloyalty to the

United States. On the first day of the 39th Congress, the Clerk was directed by the Speaker to read the member role deleting the names of Congressmen-elect not having taken the oath. Harold Hyman, *Era of the Oath: Northern Loyalty Tests during the Civil War and Reconstruction*, University of Pennsylvania Press, Philadelphia, Pennsylvania, 1954.

159. William Graham, lodging at the Willard as one of the delegation, observed "the table is well kept, but there is great negligence of servants." Williams, *Papers of William Alexander Graham*, 460; *The Western Democrat*, Charlotte, North Carolina, Dec. 12, 1865, 1.

160. "Samuel H. Walkup Papers," April 8, 1866 letter by Walkup to his wife.

161. McDowell, *The McDowells, Erwins, Irvins and Connections*, 82.

162. See *Journal of the Convention*, Cannon and Holden Printers, Raleigh, North Carolina, 1865.

163. See "Samuel H. Walkup Papers," June 3, 1870 letter by Walkup to N. Hart Davis.

164. In contrast to Walkup's failure to publicly repudiate white supremacy and vigilantism was the more commendable example of fellow North Carolina Confederate Colonel William John Clarke. By 1868 Clarke actively embraced Republican civil rights and in in 1870 organized African American state militia against Klansmen. See Alan W. Trelease, *White Terror: The Ku Klux Klan Conspiracy and Southern Reconstruction*, Harper & Row, New York, New York, 1971.

165. Democrats denounced the work product as the "Canby Constitution" in reference to Major General Edward Canby, the Federal administrator of the Reconstruction North Carolina military district, or as the "Black and Tan Constitution' in disparaging reference to its Northern white Unionist "carpetbagger," Southern white Unionist "scalawag" and freedmen authors. The 1868 Constitution was to stand the test of time with its principles of enhanced civic participation, greater transparency and accountability and improved public education. See John Orth, *The North Carolina State Constitution with History and Commentary*, Greenwood Press, Westport, Connecticut, 1993. Dean Orth was my inspiring legal history professor at the University of North Carolina School of Law.

166. *The Western Democrat*, Charlotte, North Carolina, April 23, 1867, 1. Walkup was especially solicitous for the Freedmen who were hardest impacted by deprivation.

167. Samuel H. Walkup correspondence to John Rogers Cooke, Jan. 17, 1866, "John Rogers Cooke Papers, 1860–1894," Virginia Museum of History and Culture, Richmond, Virginia, Manuscript Collection, sec. 2, c7753 a 4–17, record 181844. Congressman Thaddeus Stevens of Pennsylvania, Senator Henry Wilson of Massachusetts and Senator Charles Sumner of Massachusetts were national leaders of the Radical Republicans.

168. See "Samuel H. Walkup Papers," June 3, 1870 letter by Walkup to N. Hart Davis.

169. See "Samuel H. Walkup Papers," June 3, 1870 letter by Walkup to N. Hart Davis. He advised a relative not to become a lawyer unless "very extra smart," counseling instead farming, civil engineering or trade.

170. See "Samuel H. Walkup Papers," April 8, 1866 letter by Walkup to wife.

171. *The Daily Journal*, Wilmington, North Carolina, July 27, 1867, 1; *Journal*, North Carolina General Assembly, 1873–1874 session, 380.

172. See Marshall. Haywood, *The North Carolina Booklet*, North Carolina Daughters of the American Revolution, Capital Printing, Raleigh, North Carolina,1912, v. XII, n.1,18.

173. "Clerks of Superior Court," *The Code of North Carolina*, Banks and Brothers, New York, New York, 1883, v. 1, Chapter 9.

174. Gene Stowe, *Inherit the Land: Jim Crow Meets Miss Maggie's Will*, University Press of Mississippi, Jackson, Mississippi, 2006, 52.

175. McDowell, *The McDowells, Erwins, Irvins and Connections*, 82.

176. McDowell, *The McDowells, Erwins, Irvins and Connections*, 82; An

observation of the "Lost Cause" by poet Stephen Vincent Benet, grandson of his namesake Union brigadier general and Civil War ordnance officer, is relevant: "The beaten cause turns into the magic cause... and the legend has made a stainless host... That stainless host you were not." Stephen V. Benet, "John Brown's Body," *Selected Works*, Farrar and Rinehart, New York, New York, 1942, v. 1 poetry, 166.

177. John Cooke and Edward Pollard were Confederate authors of romantic, non-critical histories of the Army of Northern Virginia whose works Walkup owned, read and noted with handwritten margin comments. See John Esten Cooke, *Personal Portraits* and Edward A. Pollard, *The Lost Cause* and *The Lost Cause Regained*. Virginia Adams of Galveston, Texas, Walkup's great-great-granddaughter, has these books owned by the colonel in her possession. The failure of the Lost Cause narrative to frankly and honestly consider the role of slavery and white supremacy in creating and sustaining the Old South and Confederacy is addressed by Adam H. Domby, *The False Cause: Fraud, Fabrication, and White Supremacy in Confederate Memory*, University of Virginia Press, Charlottesville, Virginia, 2020.

178. J. Griffith and C. Fortenberry, *First Presbyterian Church, Monroe, North Carolina: A History*, First Presbyterian Church Publisher, Monroe, North Carolina, 1973; "Death of Samuel H. Walkup," *The Southern Home*, Charlotte, North Carolina, Nov. 6, 1876, 1.

179. McDowell, *The McDowells, Erwins, Irvins and Connections*, 81, 83.

180. *Private Laws, General Assembly*, Josiah Turner Printer, Raleigh, North Carolina, 1874–1875 session, 1875, 475.

181. *The Semi-centennial Catalogue of Davidson College, 1837–1887*, Alumni Association, E.M. Uzzell Printer, Raleigh, North Carolina, 1891, 9.

182. See "Samuel H. Walkup Papers," March 14, 1876 letter by Walkup to his niece Sarah Elizabeth Davis.

183. Mary D. Beaty, *A History of Davidson College*, Briarpatch Press, Davidson, North Carolina, 1988, 94.

184. *Wilmington Journal*, Wilmington, North Carolina, Feb. 13, 1874.

185. "Charles Phillips Papers," *Southern Historical Collection*, University of North Carolina, Chapel Hill. See correspondence from Charles Phillips to John Kimberly, July 8, 1875.

186. James L. Leloudis, *The University during the Civil War and Reconstruction*, available online at Documenting the American South, docsouth.unc.edu; "Charles Phillips Papers," *Southern Historical Collection*, University of North Carolina, Chapel Hill. See correspondence from Charles Phillips to John Kimberly, July 8, 1875.

187. "Letter from Colonel Walkup's Daughter," Elliott, *The Heritage of Union County*, 37.

188. See "Samuel H. Walkup Papers," March 14, 1876 letter by Walkup to his niece Sarah Elizabeth Davis, 2.

189. "Death of Samuel H. Walkup," *The Southern Home*, Charlotte, North Carolina, Nov. 6, 1876, 1; "Samuel Walkup Entry," *Estate Files*, Clerk of Superior Court, Union County, North Carolina, setting forth Thomas Bickett's billing; "Letter from Colonel Walkup's Daughter," Elliott, *The Heritage of Union County*, 37.

190. *The Charlotte Democrat*, Oct. 16, 1876; "Death of Col. Sam'l H. Walkup," *The Charlotte Democrat*, Charlotte, North Carolina, Oct. 30, 1876.

191. *The Southern Home*, Charlotte, North Carolina, Feb. 6, 1877; "Letter from Colonel Walkup's Daughter," Elliott, *The Heritage of Union County*, 37.

192. McDowell, *The McDowells, Erwins, Irvins and Connections*, 83.

193. McDowell, *The McDowells, Erwins, Irvins and Connections*, 79–84; "Obituary," *The Monroe Enquirer*, May 15, 1880, 3.

194. On Nov. 7, 1871 Martha Ann Walkup, a 33-year-old literate head of household, took her four children, ranging in age from one to 14 years, to Arthington, Liberia, on the American Colonization Society chartered barque *Edith Rose*. See American Colonization Society, *The African Repository*, v. XLVII, American Colonization Society Publisher,

Washington, Dec. 1871, 358. She traveled with other freedman from nearby Clay Hill/York, South Carolina led by Eliza Hill, a zealous educator and Baptist pastor advocate for black civil rights and racial equality. He had been an enslaved of Samuel Walkup's friend Confederate General Daniel Harvey Hill who pre-war had taught Eliza to read. Beaten with a horsewhip and threatened with drowning by the Ku Klux Klan, Eliza Hill adamantly refused to stop preaching against vigilantism and would not renounce the Republican Party. Testifying to a Congressional committee on the necessity of departing the United States, Hill stated "We do not believe it is possible from our past history and present aspect of affairs, for our people to live in this country peacefully and educate and elevate their children to any degree which they desire." See James Martinez, *Carpetbaggers, Cavalry and the Ku Klux Klan: Exposing the Invisible Empire During Reconstruction*, Rowman and Littlefield, Washington, 2007, 76–78; Jerry West, *The Reconstruction Ku Klux Klan in York County, South Carolina*, McFarland, Jefferson, North Carolina, 2002, 126–130.

195. "Walkup Entry," *1870 Federal Census*, Monroe, North Carolina, 5, roll M593 1161, 604A.

196. "Marriage License," *Union County Registry of Deeds*, Union County, North Carolina, Nov. 1874.

197. "Julia Walkup v. John W. Andsey Complaint," *Bureau of Refugees, Freedmen and Abandoned Lands, North Carolina Field Office*, National Archives and History, Washington, District of Columbia, GS 002421014, image 00543, M1909, roll 9, microfilm 2427014, April 30, 1868.

198. "Walkup Entry," 1870 Federal Census, Providence, Mecklenburg County, North Carolina, 43, roll M593 1148, 260A; Marriage License," Union County Registry of Deeds, Union County, North Carolina, Family Search database 133, 83.

199. "Walkup Entry," *1870 Federal Census*, Sandy Ridge Township, Union County, North Carolina, 15, roll M593 1161, 643A; "Union County Cohabitation Records," Union County, North Carolina, J. E. Irby, Clerk, Aug. 25, 1866, item 198,

Family Search database, image 00128, GS film 590483.

200. "Walkup Entry," *1880 Federal Census*, Sandy Ridge Township, Union County, North Carolina, district ED 214, image 007595.GS 1254983; Conversation Sept. 14, 2020 with Taryn Kennedy of Elkins Park, Pennsylvania, South Eastern District Director of the Daughters of the American Revolution and great-great-great-great granddaughter of Dina Winchester Walkup.

201. In 1921 Stephen Walkup, Jr., was one of the beneficiaries of the estate of Maggie Ross, the wealthiest woman in Union County. His testamentary distribution was $200, an amount he deemed inadequate for his services rendered over several decades. White Ross heirs initiated a probate challenge alleging testator incompetency because Maggie Ross bequeathed most of her large estate to an African American household member, Bob Ross and his daughter Mittie Bell Ross Houston. A compelling narrative of legal proceedings in which the all white jury awarded the African American beneficiaries the bulk of the estate is set forth by Gene Stowe in *Inherit the Land: Jim Crow Meets Miss Maggie's Will*, University Press of Mississippi, Jackson, Mississippi, 2007.

202. Steven Bailey, "Klutz Entry," March 4, 2020 posting, *Anson County North Carolina African American Family History*, Anson County Historical Society, Wadesboro, North Carolina. Klutz was a special magistrate in the Wadesboro Mayor's Court, not a justice of the peace elected or appointed by the Governor or General Assembly. For a history of such magistrates, see Albert Coates, "The Courts of Yesterday, Today and Tomorrow in North Carolina," *Popular Government*, University of North Carolina Institute of Government, Chapel Hill, North Carolina, v. 24, 1958, 17–18.

203. See "Klutz Obituary," *The Messenger-Intelligencer*, Wadesboro, July 17, 1890, 3. He was identified as "always voting the Democratic ticket." Superficial appeasement was a strategy to address intimidation, white privilege and

monopoly, particularly in a commercial/ business transactional context.

204. See "Klutz Obituary," *The Messenger-Intelligencer,* Wadesboro, July 17, 1890, 3. The Conservative Democrat orientated newspaper used the title "Uncle Tom." The pejorative title "Uncle" and "Aunt" used to address African Americans promoted a racist naming tradition reserving to whites the use of the courteous titles such as "Mr." and "Mrs."

205. "Assistant Commissioner Records," *Bureau of Refugees, Freedmen and Abandoned Lands, Records 1865–1870,* file 1867, National Archives and Records, Washington, District of Columbia, M 843, GS 1616868, digital folder 004567412, image 00260. "Clutz Entry," *1880 Federal Census,* Wadesboro, Anson County, North Carolina, 58, roll 951, 333C.

206. "Clutz Entry," *1900 Federal Census,* Wadesboro, Anson County, North Carolina, 14, enumeration district 0011, FHL, T623, 1854 roll, microfilm 1241181.

207. Cheryl Ferguson, Archival Assistant, Tuskegee University Archives, indicates the annual catalogs of Tuskegee Normal and Industrial Institute document his preparatory class commencing in 1908 with college curriculum undertaken through 1912.

208. "Clutz Entry," *World War One Registry, 1917–1918,* Jefferson County, Alabama, no. 1260, roll 1509396.3.

209. Steve Bailey, "Kluttz Entry," March 4, 2020; Aug. 11, 2016 postings, *Anson County North Carolina African American Family History,* Anson County Historical Society, Wadesboro, North Carolina.

210. "W. Thomas Kluttz Obituary," *Anson Record,* Wadesboro, North Carolina, July 11, 1968, 3.

# Journal and Correspondence

1. "The Waxhaws No. 2" company was raised in Union County, North Carolina in Feb.-March 1862, then assigned to the 48th North Carolina Infantry Regiment as Co. F. Samuel Walkup was appointed its captain on March 4, 1862 at age 44.

Weymouth Jordan, *North Carolina Troops, 1861–1865, A Roster,* University of North Carolina Press, 1987, v. XI, 432 (hereinafter "*Roster*"). In common with all North Carolina regiments, the 48th was comprised of men exhibiting diverse economic, social and political orientations. Occupations included famer, carpenter, metalsmith, clerk, saddler, cobbler, miner, mechanic, student, teacher, merchant, planter, lawyer, doctors and pastor. Paul D. Escott, *Many Excellent People: Power and Privilege in North Carolina,* University of North Carolina Press, 1985, maintains that such differences hampered unit coherence, morale and military effectiveness. Although such analysis provides some explanation for desertion rates later in the war, Escott does not fully address why so many disparate individuals initially enlisted and continued to fight. William L. Barney, *The Making of a Confederate: Walter Lenoir's Civil War,* Oxford University Press, 2009, 212, supports Escott, stating many rank-and-file North Carolina soldiers questioned whether a war fought to benefit slave owners and the wealthy was in the interests of the ordinary working class. Keri Merritt, *Masterless Men: Poor Whites and Slavery in the Antebellum South,* Harvard University Press, 2017, argues that only a small minority of landless poor enlisted, motivated by unemployment, potential veteran land grants, avoidance of imprisonment for crimes and the enhanced prestige and honor accorded military service. The regiment was comprised of soldiers varying widely in age and physical ability, complicating drilling. "In marching the old men would step too long and slow, the boys too short and fast." See W. H. Lawhon, "48th North Carolina Regimental History" in Walter Clark, ed., *History of the Several Regiments and Battalions from North Carolina,* Goldsboro, 1901, v. 3, 113 (hereinafter "Forty-Eight Regiment").

2. Francis L. Waint. Union County miner enlisted aged 46, Feb. 21, 1862 and elected captain, Co. A. Appointed major, July 15, 1862 and transferred to field and staff. Wounded leg, Harpers Ferry, Sept.

1862. Resigned Sept. 20, 1862 due to wounds. Description by Captain W. H. H. Lawhon, "he was an old man, and won the respect of the whole regiment..." *Roster*, v. XI, 369, 371.

3. John W. Walden. Union County farmer enlisted aged 40 and elected captain, Co. E. Resigned Oct. 3, 1862 due to "feeble health and a condition greatly impaired by hard service." *Roster*, v. XI, 420.

4. Elias C. Alexander. Union County physician enlisted aged 37 and promoted captain, Co. I. Resigned May 22, 1862 due to a heart condition. *Roster*, v. XI, 371.

5. Walkup wrote this song for the community presentation of a flag prior to his company's departure from Monroe, North Carolina. He recounted the Revolutionary War achievements of Waxhaw and his state. The reference "first to come into the bond" may indicate the Mecklenburg Resolves of May 31, 1775, or North Carolina's presence at the Continental Congress as one of the original thirteen participants, although not the first to join under the Articles of Confederation. The reference "last to desert" recalled North Carolina being the last Confederate state to enact a secession resolution, on May 20, 1861. "Glorious Bethel" acknowledged the June 1861 battles of Big Bethel, Bethel Church and Great Bethel where Colonel D.H. Hill's 1st North Carolina Volunteer Infantry assisted in successfully defending southeastern Virginia from Union incursions out of Fort Monroe. With no musical score available, it is uncertain whether Walkup's lyrics were sung to the version of "The Camels Are Coming" based on the Christian revival song or instead to a rendition of the Scots Highland aire "The Campbells Are Coming." A contemporaneous ballad entitled "The Southrons Are Coming" was also sung to the melody "The Camels Are Coming." See *American Song Sheets*, Library of Congress Rare Books and Special Collections, series 2, v. 1. Walkup's lyrics are found in the "Belk and Everett Family Papers, MS0328," J. Murrey Atkins Library Special Collections, University of North Carolina-Charlotte. The regimental flag is in the collection of the North Carolina Museum of History, but requires conservation and is not displayed. The flag is wool, measuring 54 inches by 76 inches, and was surrendered at Appomattox April 12, 1865, with the Army of Northern Virginia stacking of colors. See Collections, North Carolina Museum of History, ascension number 1915.6.1.

In common with most Americans, North and South, Walkup's notion of freedom certainly did not entail African Americans. He did not critique slavery as a central element of the American republic that corrupted and perverted the other founding principles of Constitutionalism, Christianity, capitalism, and home, family and marriage.

6. Camp Mangum was the principal training facility in North Carolina commanded by Daniel H. Hill and Stephen D. Ramseur. The camp was named for Lt. William Preston Mangum, who died at First Bull Run, and his father, William Person Mangum, former U.S. Senator. The site was situated approximately four miles west of Civil War era Raleigh on what was farmland and pine forests primarily comprised of the Horne, Howle, Blake and Tucker tracts. The camp operated until 1864. After the war, the land was returned to Tucker and other prior owners and farmed. In 1870 Jesse Mason, a former slave, purchased a 69 acre portion of the site and created Mason's Village Subdivision, marketing lots to African Americans. Modest cabins or slab houses were erected, giving the community its popular names "Slabtown" or "Save-rent." In 1890 the village was designated Method by the Post Office. In 1918 the balance of the Camp Mangum site was utilized as Camp Polk, for American Expeditionary Force tank training, then re-conveyed to the Tuckers after the First World War. In the 1920s much of the location was acquired for the Camp Polk Prison Farm and later the Polk Youth Center operated through the 1960s. See *Meredith Land History*, www.meredith,edu/library/archivesstory and www.raleighpublicrecord.org, April 6, 2009 article by Kate Pattison, with aerial view of Method neighborhood

1949, North Carolina Archives and History Collection.

Being a training facility not proximate to the Virginia or North Carolina front lines, the encampment probably conformed more or less to Army regulations with grid pattern streets, separate officer, non-commissioned officer, and enlisted men tent accommodations, log/plank barracks for winter quarters, hospital, latrine sinks and guard house. Tents were arrayed in company rows, with company officers separate, and field and staff offers in superior, typically individual, tents. The Camp of Infantry described in U.S. Army Regulations (often replicated in Confederate practice), although most applicable for field conditions and not specific for training facilities, is set forth in *U.S. Army Regulations of 1861.*

While at Camp Magnum recruit instruction commenced at daybreak reveille and concluded with sunset tattoo and taps, with signals throughout the day for troop roll call, surgeon's call, meals, guard mounting and fatigue duty. Recruits learned the forms of inspection and drill and military exercises in the school of the company, regiment and battalion, including weapon training. Rations were flour, pickled beef and pork, peas and rice. When not engaged in inspection, drill and camp duties, camp life was characterized by boredom, somewhat relieved by letter writing, diary entries, gaming, gambling, reading, clothes washing and mending and worship. One sergeant described Camp Mangum as "a very wicked place" with swearing recruits and instructors. Sickness at Camp Mangum, life most military encampments of the era, was endemic, given close living arrangements, water contamination and open latrines. Food borne illness, typhoid fever, diarrhea and dysentery, venereal disease, and particularly measles and mumps, were prevalent. William A. Collins, private, Co. C, stated the regiment did not initially have any shelter and complained of "too much cold and exposure." Those tents that finally arrived were inadequate for comfortable accommodation. The fuel supplied was green pine and did not burn

clean for either cooking or heating. Collins further lamented that "...we have not received the first bit of clothing yet of any sort, not as much as a blanket..." Many soldiers were clothed with only "what they have on their back." Collins did acknowledge adequate provisions of bread, meat, rice and sugar. See Collins' March 1862 letter to his father, "William A. Collins Papers," Collection 05095-Z, Southern History Collection, Wilson Library, University of North Carolina-Chapel Hill; Daniels, *History of Polk Place Property*; Medical history at http://ncmuseumofhistory.org/exhibits/health; Rossiter Johnson, *Campfire and Battlefield*, 495–505; Carlton McCarthy, *Detailed Minutiae of Soldier Life in the Army of Northern Virginia.*

7. Walkup apparently initially had no tent, then had to share with other company officers, possibly an A or wedge type. On April 12, 1862, by special requisition he received a field officers tent for his private use appropriate for his promotion as lieutenant colonel. He stated the tent was absolutely requisite for the public service, with "the Regiment being ready for the field." See *Combined Service Records of Confederate Soldiers*, National Archives, card 2240.

8. Albert A. Hill. Davidson County physician enlisted aged 34 and elected captain, Co. B, Feb. 21, 1862. Appointed major, Oct. 20, 1862 and transferred to field and staff. Wounded right shoulder, Fredericksburg, Dec. 13, 1862. Promoted lieutenant colonel, Dec. 4, 1863. Paroled Appomattox, April 12, 1865. Description by Captain W. H. H. Lawhon, "A good and kind officer. All his men liked him. He made a very fine appearance and was always with his men." *Roster*, v. XI, 369, 383.

9. Arthur M. Walker. Iredell County hotelkeeper enlisted aged 47 and elected captain, Co. C, Feb. 21, 1862. Wounded abdomen, King's School House, Va. (French's Farm), June 25, 1862. Resigned due to wounds, July 9, 1863. *Roster*, v. XI, 395.

10. Benjamin Robinson Huske. Previously 1st lieutenant, Co. H, 1st North

Carolina Infantry. Elected captain, Co. D, 48th North Carolina Infantry, Feb. 24, 1862. Appointed major, April 9, 1862 and transferred to field and staff. Wounded right foot, King's School House, June 25, 1862 and died Richmond, July 15, 1862. His wound was "at first supposed not to be dangerous, but erysipelas followed, of which he died." *Roster*, v. XI, 369, 408.

11. As captain of Co. F, Walkup requisitioned coats, pants, overcoats, shoes, blankets, caps, knapsacks, haversacks and canteens (56 of each) and socks, drawers and shirts (112 of each). The company was also supplied with axes and picks (4 of each), 2 hatchets and 11 tents. These supplies were received April 14, 1862. See *Combined Service Records*.

12. William Hogan Jones. Union County farmer enlisted aged 36 and elected captain, Co. G, March 1, 1862. Appointed major, Dec. 4, 1863 and transferred to field and staff. Resigned Aug. 1, 1864, due to diarrhea and urinary infection. Captain W. H. H. Lawhon's description, "a good man and kindhearted" who "loved his men and was loved in return." *Roster*, v. XI, 369, 443.

13. Jesse W. Atwood. Forsythe County professor enlisted aged 31 and elected captain, Co. K, March 25, 1862. Conflicting reports of location and causation of death, possibly sunstroke and/or typhoid fever contracted June 25, 1862, with subsequent death around July 3, 1862, in Raleigh or Petersburg. *Roster*, v. XI, 484.

14. Robert Clinton Hill. Previously recruiter and staff officer, Artillery Corps and assistant adjutant general (major) on staff of General Robert A. Toombs and General O. B. Branch. Appointed colonel, 48th North Carolina Infantry, April 9, 1862. Died neuralgia, Iredell County home, Dec. 4, 1863. Captain W. H. H. Lawhon's description, "A very fine military man, very strict and much beloved by his men, but being in bad health he was often absent." *Roster*, v. XI, 368.

15. Hugh Wilson. Union County merchant enlisted aged 35, Co. F. Elected 2nd Lieutenant, March 14, 1862, but resigned in favor of Lt. Robert L. Stewart. Wilson then served as sergeant until elected captain, April 15, 1862. Resigned July 9, 1862 due to lung disease and general disability. *Roster*, v. XI, 432.

16. Thomas J. Clegg. Moore County resident elected 1st lieutenant, Co. D, Feb. 25, 1862. Promoted captain April 9, 1862. Wounded right arm King's School House, June 25, 1862. Hospitalized Richmond, where he died of wound July 8–9, 1862. *Roster*, v. XI, 408

17. Henry Clay Walkup. Prior to the enlistment of older brother Samuel in the 48th North Carolina Infantry, 17-year-old Henry Clay on June 5, 1861 joined as private the Waxhaw Jackson Guards that became Co. B of the 26th North Carolina Infantry. Henry Clay Walkup was named after the famous Whig senator reflecting the family's political orientation. He was seriously wounded in the right arm on July 1, 1863, at Gettysburg during the regiment's engagement against the Iron Brigade at Willoughby's Run. Following the retreat on July 4, he was left at Gettysburg and taken prisoner. He was hospitalized at the Lutheran Seminary and his arm amputated, then transferred to Baltimore on or around July 23, 1863. His incarceration continued until paroled Aug. 23, 1865, transported to City Point, Va. and exchanged. Discharged Dec. 30, 1863 due to disability. Known as "a good and brave soldier." After the war he attended his brother's alma mater, the University of North Carolina at Chapel Hill. As a freshman there he was informed that he must use a side door to the lecture hall. He replied that he didn't go through the side door at Gettysburg and he wouldn't go through the side door at the University. After completing the bachelor's degree he earned a medical credential at a New York physicians' college. He doctored around Charlotte in Sharon Township, Mecklenburg County, then relocated to McIntosh, Florida, in the early 1870s where he practiced medicine, operated a drug store and raised citrus fruit and horses until his death in 1908. Henry Clay Walkup was Samuel's half-brother, being the son of Robert Walkup's second wife Dorcas Montgomery. See *Roster*, v. VII, 492; S. G. Hawfield,"Walkup Family Genealogy," *The*

*Monroe Enquirer*, Dec. 5, 1957; Samuel Walkup letter to uncle Sam Walkup, Sept. 21, 1844, reprinted *The Monroe Enquirer*, April 11, 1863; conversation with descendent Sandra Parks of St. Augustine, Florida, Feb. 10, 2014.

18. The horse was a black charger named Tom. See C. McIlwain, "Reminiscences of Upper Union," *Monroe Journal*, May 9, 1905.

19. The legal status of the wife was deemed merged with that of her husband, such that she could not sue or be sued in her name alone and could not hold property without her husband's consent. Nevertheless, as both a practical and legal matter, wives did act as agents for their husbands in business and domestic matters, including debt payment and hiring out slaves. See G. Johnson, *Antebellum North Carolina*, 243.

20. Either Camp Collier or Camp McLean. *Encyclopedia of North Carolina.*

21. The regiment undertook "perfecting themselves in drill." See Walkup's comments, "The 48th N.C. Regiment," *Fayetteville Observer*, Feb. 22, 1864, 2, reprinting *Western Democrat*, Digital NC Collection, www.digitalnc.org.

22. The covering was thought to have considerable efficacy. See *The Military Handbook and Soldier's Manual*, stating: "If disease begins to prevail, wear a white bandage of flannel around the bowels" and citing *Hall's Journal of Health*: "If locomotion is compulsory, the misfortune of necessity maybe lessened by having a stout piece of woolen flannel bound tightly around the abdomen so as to be doubled in front, and kept well in place. In the practice of many years, we (Dr. Hall) have never failed to notice a gratifying result to follow these observations." See *The Military Handbook*, 84, 90.

23. Benjamin F. Chears. Previously private in Co. C, 10th Battalion, North Carolina Heavy Artillery. Appointed assistant surgeon, 48th North Carolina Infantry, Oct. 14, 1862 to rank from April 17, 1862. Reported present May-June, 1863. Reported absent sick without leave, Nov.-Dec. 1863. Dropped from rolls June 15, 1864 due to prolonged absence from duty

without leave. Resigned, Oct. 1, 1864, with resignation accepted Nov. 24, 1864. *Roster*, v. XI, 370.

24. Tom Clutts. Sometimes also spelled Cluts, Clutz, Klutts, Kluttz, or Klutz. He was an enslaved laborer/farm worker, possibly owned by a third party (perhaps Walkup's brother William) and employed under contract to Samuel. He was married to Lelia Clutts, but it is uncertain whether his wife was slave or free, and whether she resided in the Walkup household in Monroe. After 1830 free African Americans were not legally permitted to marry enslaved, although the law was frequently avoided through informal relationships. See E. Franklin Frazier, *The Free Negro Family*, 38–51. The 1860 census for Monroe, Union County, listing No. 17 stated that Walkup owned $7000 tangible personal property, which valuation included enslaved, farm and law office inventory, equipment and stock. Walkup's will made March 5, 1864 but not probated until March 6, 1876, referenced enslaved but the specifics as to name, sex, age and number were deleted by the County Clerk of Court as a bequest in violation of the then applicable law in light of abolition. The original document in the State Archives Loose Wills File, although redacted by strikethrough perhaps done post-war by Walkup himself, lists his slaves as Hall, Susan, Betty, Stephen, Margaret, Eliza, Harriett, Fanny, Sarah, Wilson and Jenny. It is uncertain whether Susan, Betty, Margaret, Eliza, Harriett, Fanny, Sarah, Wilson and Jenny were purchased between 1861 to 1863 or instead originally owned by Minnie and brought into the household. In addition to diary references to Matilda, Stephen, Tom and Hall, Samuel mentioned other enslaved— Jenny and Charlie—in the Jan. 1, 1863 letter to wife Minnie. He later describes a Sally as worth a high price and Margaret as "as good a hand as any." See Dec. 9, 1863 letter to wife Minnie. His Dec. 18, 1863 letter back home references giving his daughter and wife the enslaved children Harriet, Sue and Sarah. Students of history must fully consider how slaves

were victimized. But equally important, we should look at their assertive agency exemplified through their craft and creativity, religion and family, demonstrating both express and subtle resistance and affirmation of self-worth. Tom, along with, at various times, Hall Walkup and Stephen Walkup, worked as Walkup's "camp servants." As such these slaves provided a vital link between the front lines and home, traveling back and forth communicating and implementing Walkup's instructions. Within the severe constraints of a malignant institution, camp servants earned privileges and a leadership role in the enslaved community. See Peter Carmichael, *"We are the men": The Ambiguous Place of Confederate Slaves in Southern Armies.* While the plenary degradation of enslavement and actual or potential violence experienced by the enslaved were always present in the American South, real paternalism by some slaveholders was also possible and actual. See Peter Kolchin, *American Slavery,* New York: Hall and Wang, 2003. No independent accounts made by those enslaved by Walkup have been located. When considering slavery, forced labor was only one aspect of the malevolent institution. At least equally pernicious was the narrative of White superiority with its legacy extending to today. A compelling argument can be made that slavery did not end with the Thirteenth Amendment, but instead evolved after the Civil War from a de jure to a de facto Southern institution. See Henry Louis Gates, Jr., *Stoney the Road: Reconstruction, White Supremacy and the Rise of Jim Crow,* Penguin Press, New York, 2019, citing Bryan Stevenson, 1.

25. Unlike during the world wars, Civil War correspondence was not subject to review by military censors, so the writers could frankly discuss their superiors, troop movements, tactics and strategy, and express unguarded attitudes about the conflict, camp and field. Walkup's letters to Minnie reflect the common motivation of Southern soldiers fighting for home, property and family, honor and manhood, and fellow comrades in arms, with secondary commitments to their respective states and Confederate nationalism. The perceived duty to home included both white and black dependents. See Nina Silber, *Gender and the Sectional Conflict,* 3–17.

26. Matilda Walkup, sometimes called Tilly, was an enslaved nursemaid caring for Samuel's daughter Lelia Eugene, born July 21, 1861. She was that one female, 11 years old in the "Samuel H. Walkup listing," *1860 Union County Slave Census.* She died July 5, 1862. See "Samuel Walkup Papers," July 15–16, 1862 entry. Periodicals of the era advised that the enslaved nurse be healthy, honest, good tempered, fond of children and free of detriments such as drinking, snuff taking and superstition. See Guion G. Johnson, *Antebellum North Carolina: A Social History,* 236. White women managers of the household like Minnie often developed close relationships of mutual dependency with female domestic enslaved. See Drew Cilpin Faust, *Mothers of Invention: Women of the Slaveholding South in the American Civil War,* 60–62.

27. William Wilshire Walkup, Samuel's planter brother born Sept. 14, 1820, whose mother was Robert's first wife, Elizabeth Hoey (b. Sept. 12, 1786, d. Sept. 1, 1826). On Jan. 25, 1853 William married Jane Elizabeth Miller (b. March 10, 1830, d. Jan. 20, 1893). He was noted in *The Monroe Enquirer* as having been a colonel in the Home Guard, although the title originated from his county militia service during the Mexican War. See *Charlotte Journal,* July 17, 1846; Herman Starnes, "Samuel H. Walkup" article, The Heritage Room, Historic Union County Courthouse, Monroe, North Carolina. Samuel's entry for March 30-April 1, 1865 stated William was elected a Home Guard captain. With William's local service commencing so near the end of hostilities, entry was not made in official military records. Jordan's *Roster* does not list William as having any official Civil War military affiliation. As a planter engaged in cotton and food production, William was exempt from military service. His plantation house still exists and is located on

the west side of Walkup Road, State road 1106 in Jackson Township, Union County. The Greek Revival frame house has a two-story covered front porch topped with a pediment. The property was willed by father Robert to William who got the plantation since Samuel had instead opted for tuition at the University of North Carolina. In antebellum times ten to thirteen slaves cultivated corn and cotton and operated the plantation mill. See *The Monroe Enquirer*, April 4, 1863 reprinting a July 21, 1836 letter to his brother Samuel and April 11, 1963 reprinting of Sept. 21, 1844 letter by Samuel Hoey Walkup to his uncle Sam. The Colonel William Walkup house is described in Suzanne Pickens, *Sweet Union: An Architectural and Historical Survry of Union County*, 231–232. William and Jane had no children, but helped raise Samuel's daughters after his death. See John McDonald, *The McDonalds, Erwins, Irwins and Connections*, C. H. Johnson Publishers, Memphis, Tennessee, 1918, 84.

28. Andre Dunn's property (1822–1893), also known as Bell's Hill, three miles east of Petersburg. Major Dunn was Longstreet's aide de camp. In 1864 Major Dunn constructed a residence on the property that was burned by Federals shortly after completion. During the 1864–65 siege, the Confederate entrenchments were immediately behind the house. See Eloise D. Hauly, *Title Survey Report, Dunn House Site*. The 48th Regiment was a component of Brigadier General Robert Ransom's brigade along with the 24th NC, 25th NC, 26th NC, 35th NC and 49th NC. *Roster*, v. XI, 364.

29. General Joseph Johnson, despite training as a civil engineer and pre-war experience as a railroad surveyor, has been critiqued for failure to fully utilize rail technology as a tool of war, and for mismanagement and destruction of southern track and rolling stock. See Jeffrey Lash, *Destroyer of the Iron Horse*, Kent State University Press, 1991.

30. Daniel Harvey Hill, lieutenant general, was an 1842 West Point graduate with distinguished Mexican War experience. Like brother-in-law Stonewall Jackson, he was religious, strict and highly competent. Unfortunately, his argumentative, outspoken criticism of superiors like Robert E. Lee and later Braxton Bragg brought Hill into disfavor with Jefferson Davis. Lee did not appoint Hill to corps command after Jackson's death and he was left without command after the 1863 reorganization of the Army of Tennessee. Post-war Hill was editor of *Southern Home* and renewed his work in education and college administration. At that time he became one of Walkup's "best friends," with mutual admiration. Hill described Walkup as "one of the purest and noblest and "fearless." See John Hugh McDowell, *History of the McDowells*, C. B. Johnston and Co., Memphis, Tennessee, 1918 and Hal Bridges, *Lee's Maverick General*, University of Nebraska Press, Lincoln, 1991.

31. Peter R. Thomas Jr., *Camp, Combat, and Campaign: North Carolina's Confederate Experience*, 2015, University of North Florida thesis and dissertations, http://digitalcommons.unf/etd/586, comprehensively addresses how "militarized landscapes" modified the nature of camp life. Organized entertainments, religious services, parade drill, simulated engagements, target practice, concerts, political and inspirational speeches were all shared experiences that enhanced morale.

32. Minnie Walkup and other wives, mothers and daughters back home were charged with the complex and demanding management of residences, farms, plantations and shops in the absence of male relations in the army. In households owning enslaved, these farm mistresses were tasked with providing food, clothing, shelter and medical care for the workforce. Like the Walkup situation, most families had no overseer, so the mistress also had to perform or manage household vegetable cultivation, livestock and poultry production, knitting, spinning, sewing, cooking, food preservation, bookkeeping, procurement and bill payment. See Catherine Clinton, *Tara Revisited: Women, War and the Plantation Legend*, 40–41.

33. Private Alfred N. Johnson, Co. D, observed: "... the laides come out from

town very day to se us some times about too hundred of them...but tha don't faver yous much with eating stuf..." See Johnson's June 18, 1862 letter back home to Iredell County girlfriend Adeline White, a relation of Private Alfred M. White of the 48th North Carolina Regiment. Johnson was killed in action at the Battle of Seven Pines about one week after this correspondence. Iredell County Public Library Local History Room, genealogy file photocopy and University of North Carolina Wilson Library, "Alfred M. White Papers," 4976.

34. Battery C, 1st North Carolina Artillery, also called the Charlotte Artillery or Brem's Battery following the usual practice of naming the battery after its current captain, Thomas H. Brem. Designated Graham's Battery after Brem's resignation in June 1862. Charlotte church bells were donated to cast bronze cannons at the Richmond Tredegar works. Like most Confederate batteries, the cannon were an assortment of iron and bronze rifled pieces, smooth bore, and howitzers of varying calibers. Inferior powder and fuses and the difficulty of supplying different caliber cannon within a battery created significant operational and logistical challenges throughout the Southern artillery service. Brem's Battery was engaged at Hanover Court House, May 27, 1862 and at Malvern Hill, July 1, 1862. The battery served though out the war, and was in the thick of fighting at Gettysburg, Bristoe Station, Wilderness, Petersburg, and Appomattox campaign. See *Roster, Artillery*, v. I, 61–62.

35. The U.S.S. *Galena*, launched Feb. 14, 1862, was one of the first three Union ironclads. It was a wooden hulled vessel with relatively thin iron sheathing. During the Peninsula Campaign, it operated out of Fort Monroe, attacking the James River batteries and shelling infantry along the banks. Armament was two 100 pound Parrott riled cannon and four 9 inch Dahlgren smoothbores. Ship logs for June 16, 1862 show operations in conjunction with the U.S.S. *Port Royal*. Around 5:00 p.m. enemy infantry were observed on the banks near the U.S S.

*Mahasha*, which fired upon them, driving them away. On June 17, the Galena proceeded down the James and engaged in heavy firing in the direction of City Point for about an hour, with the *Mahasha* anchored below. "[Enemy] Pickets observed on left bank from before noon until 4:00 p.m." See *Galena Ship Logs*, www.marinersmuseum.org.

36. John H. Anderson. Previously corporal 1st North Carolina Infantry, elected 3rd lieutenant, Co. D, 48th North Carolina Infantry, Feb. 24, 1862, promoted 2nd Lieutenant April 8, 1862. Wounded leg King's School House, Va. June 25, 1862. Promoted 1st lieutenant June 28, 1862. Resigned Nov. 14, 1862 due to disability from wound. Later recruitment officer in North Carolina. *Roster*, v. XI, 409.

37. William A. Collins, private, Co. C., observed the shells "began to burst thick around us." Collins correspondence with Reverend M. Smith, June 21, 1862, Petersburg, in *William A. Collins Papers*, Southern History Collection, Wilson Library, University of North Carolina, Chapel Hill. An Iredell County farmer, Collins enlisted in 1862 at age 20. He was wounded in the left leg or foot and captured at Antietam, Sept. 17, 1862. Hospitalized at Frederick, Maryland, he was paroled Fort McHenry, Oct. 13, 1862. Collins died of gangrene at Chimborazo Hospital, Richmond Dec. 14, 1862. His correspondence reflected the articulate insights of a prospective seminarian. *Roster*, v. XI, 398.

38. Captain W. H. Lawhon, Co. D, described "seeing the elephant": "We went back to our camp having, as we thought, tasted a little of war and seen a little of its dangers. And we all knew we had smelt gunpowder. Not a few of the men told of narrow escapes. Some of them were certain they felt the wind of shells, while others felt the heat of them as they passed, and still others were jarred by the explosions." Lawhon, "Forty-Eight Regimental," v. 3, 115.

39. The battle, variously called Oak Grove, French's Hill and King's School House, was Walkup's first fierce engagement and the start of Lee's command of the Army of Northern Virginia that pre-

ceded his Seven Days offensive. McClellan achieved his very limited tactical objective of straightening and advancing his picket line beyond swampy obstructions but incurred considerable casualties with a gain of about only 600 yards. The Union forces hoped to bring up their heavy siege guns to breach the Richmond defenses before the arrival of Jackson from the Valley of Virginia. Lee saw that a Confederate pre-emptive offensive could drive McClellan back to his river bases, and shortly commenced the Seven Days battles. Lee instructed Benjamin Huger, commanding Ransom's Brigade, to continue to hold his positions "at all Hazards." See Stephen W. Sears, *To the Gates of Richmond: The Peninsula Campaign*, Mariner Books, 2001, 183–186. Walkup was led by Robert Ransom, a professional West Pointer whose by-the-book formal martinet leadership grated upon and antagonized the flexible Walkup. See Clifford Dowdey, *The Seven Days: The Emergence of Lee*, University of Nebraska Press, 1992, 160.

40. John E. Moore. Previously sergeant major, 26th North Carolina Infantry. Elected captain, Co. I, 48th North Carolina Infantry, June 14, 1862. Wounded Fredericksburg, Dec. 13, 1862. Assigned Invalid Corps, March 6, 1865. *Roster*, v. XI, 471.

41. John Henry Michael. Davidson County farmer enlisted aged 40. Elected captain, Co. H, March 13, 1862. Wounded right arm, King's School House, June 25, 1863. Resigned due to disability from wound effective Feb. 10, 1863, *Roster*, v. XI, 457.

42. A Virginia regiment failed to support the right flank, and for some time the 48th in the open field engaged an entire brigade sheltered in woods behind a fence. See Lawhon, Forty-Eight Regimental," v. 3, 114.

43. Christian Correll. Union County mechanic enlisted aged 37, Feb. 28, 1862 as sergeant, Co. E. Wounded finger, Fredericksburg, Dec. 13, 1862. Wounded breast, Bristoe Station Oct. 14, 1863. Reduced to ranks as private. Captured Hatcher's Run, April 1, 1865 and confined Point Lookout

until June 26, 1865 upon taking oath. *Roster*, v. XI, 421.

44. James M. Nesbit. Union County farmer enlisted aged 21, March 23, 1862 as sergeant, Co. F. Wounded both thighs, King's School House, June 23, 1862. Died Richmond, June 26, 1862 of wounds. *Roster*, v. XI, 439.

45. Walkup lamented the regiment "got badly cut-up." See *Fayetteville Observer*, Feb. 22, 1864, 2.

46. Lawhon reported "some unpleasantness" between General Ransom and Col. Hill resulted in the regiment being detached from Ransom's brigade and assigned to Gen. Walker's brigade consisting of the 27th NC, 46th NC, 3rd Arkansas, 30th VA, and 2nd GA. See Lawhon, "Forty-Eight. Regimental," 115.

47. Walkup observed "the battle was over before we reached here and the enemy in flight." See *Fayetteville Observer*, Feb. 22, 1864, 2.

48. Rather remarkably Walkup quoted well-known abolitionist poet William Cowper (1731–1800), one of the earliest British literary figures to denounce slave trafficking. Cowper stated that it was "impossible also to allege an argument in behalf of Man-merchandising...." See James King and Charles Ryskamp, *The Letters and Prose Writings of William Cowper*, v. l. III, 103. A friend of minister and repentant slave trader John Newton renowned for the hymn "Amazing Grace," Cowper maintained that poetry and song could more readily than preaching change the heart and awaken social consciousness and Christian accountability. Walkup apparently recalled from memory Cowper's most famous anti-slavery verse, "The Task," wherein the slave owner is denounced:

"The natural bond of brotherhood is severed...He finds his fellow guilty of a skin not coloured like his own, and having power to enforce the wrong...dooms and devotes him as his lawful prey. Chains him, and tasks him, and exacts his sweat with strips...And what man, seeing him, and having human feelings, does not blanch and hang his head, to think himself a man. I would not have a slave to till

**183**

my ground...I had much rather be myself the slave and wear the bonds, than fasten them on him..." See William Cowper, *The Task*, book II. Walkup clearly epitomized the moral dilemma and ambivalence faced by the well-meaning, devoutly Christian slave owner. Paradoxically he demonstrated deep familiarity with Cowper's poetry and cited that work with apparent endorsement and no disclaimer or criticism of its abolitionist message. That "good masters" like Walkup were able to reconcile owning persons as legal property, expropriating the fruits of their labor and depriving them of liberty, is the most profound indictment of the Antebellum South.

49. Walkup observed, "We got under a terrific fire of gunboats and continued in line of battle under severe shelling..." See *Fayetteville Observer*, Feb. 22, 1864, 2. The regiment arrived too late July 1 to play a significant role in the battle of Malvern Hill, and did not engage infantry but did take heavy cannon fire. Lee's rash effort to strike McClellan at the conclusion of the Peninsula Campaign was an ill-advised, poorly planned and inadequately coordinated frontal assault against an enemy holding open high ground supported by much superior artillery. See Kevin Dougherty, *The Peninsula Campaign of 1862*, University Press of Mississippi, Jackson, 2010.

50. William Alexander Jenkins. Appointed lieutenant colonel, 46th North Carolina Infantry, April 4, 1862. Resigned Jan. 3, 1863 upon death of his father-in-law. He then became responsible for family relations and four plantations worked by three hundred slaves. John Wheeler Moore, *Roster of North Carolina Troops in the War Between the States*, Raleigh, 1882, v. 3, 292, 300.

51. William A, Collins, private, Co. C, declared, "...I am thankful to God that we are blessed with the opportunity of having preaching in our regiment every Sunday and we also have prayer in our company of a night..." Collins to his mother, Camp Lee, Petersburg, July 21, 1862, "Williams A. Collins Papers," Southern History Collection, Wilson Library, University of

North Carolina, Chapel Hill, North Carolina. Chaplains were obligated to conduct services, but army mobilizations, inclement weather, Sunday morning drills or training sometimes prevented worship. See Gardiner Shattuck, Jr., *A Shield and Hiding Place: The Religious Life of the Civil War Armies*, Mercer university Press, 1987, 60.

52. Culpeper Austin was the Union County Sheriff. See Robert McNeely, "Union County and the Old Waxhaw Settlement," *North Carolina Booklet*, 19. The Walkups initially leased their residence from him, then purchased the property in 1863. The house built by John Durham Stewart was situated in the town of Monroe in the block bound by LaFayette (now Main), Franklin, Alley (Stewart) and Alley (Morgan), as shown on a map drawn by Walkup, possibly for his attorney real estate work. The residence was proximate to lots acquired by Walkup in 1846 through father Robert Walkup's will. During the war the house had a neoclassical appearance with a one story front porch with square columns. After the Walkup occupancy the house was altered with some Queen Anne ornamentation, a wrap-around porch and a central pediment above the porch. The lot was later utilized by his Belk relatives as the site of their first "built" retail location in that department store chain, with the residence relocated behind the commercial structure known as the Lee Building. Walkup's law office, a small one or two room structure typical of antebellum practitioners, was moved in 1907 to make room for the Belk store operation. Already re-utilized in the late nineteenth century by an African American barber, it continued as such near the train depot, but was demolished in the latter twentieth century. Patricia M. Poland, Union County Library, has researched the property known as the Stewart-Walkup-Simpson house, utilizing Walkup wills, conveyance deeds, Gray and Sanborn insurance maps, and *The Monroe Journal*. Her work is available at the Union County Library Local History Room, Monroe, North Carolina and online at *Random

*Historical Notes for the City of Monroe and Union County,* http://monroeunion countynchistorystuff.blogspot.com.

53. Samuel Henry Walkup. Cousin of Samuel, Henry was a Union County farmer, born 1839, who enlisted with Henry Clay Walkup on June 5, 1861 as corporal, Co. B, 26th North Carolina Infantry. Wounded with gunshot to left leg and hospitalized Richmond, June 18, 1862. Promoted 1st sergeant, Jan. 1, 1863. Wounded left thigh prior to July 1, 1864. Discharged due to wounds, Feb. 17, 1865. *Roster*, v. VII, 492.

54. William Collins, private, Co. C, found the "bacon so strong and fat and molding at that and you know how that does when but a year old. The beef is not very good…, the corn meal as rough as it could be…" Collins to his father, Camp Lee, Petersburg, August 4, 1862 in "William A. Collins Papers." When supplies were short the corn meal contained a large portion of ground cob. Soldiers sometimes described themselves as "Cornfederates" serving under General Starvation.

55. William Collins, private, Co. C, noted a "right smart sickness now in camp, some fever and jaundice and other complaints…" Collins to his father, Aug. 15, 1862, "William A. Collins Papers."

56. Edwin L. Tysor. Previously captain, 50th North Carolina Militia. Chatham County farmer enlisted aged 31, Co. G, 48th North Carolina Infantry. Appointed 3rd lieutenant, Co. G on March 11, 1862. Promoted 2nd lieutenant Aug. 7, 1862. Wounded wrist Fredericksburg, Dec. 13, 1862. Captured Hatcher's Run, March 31, 1865, confined Old Capital Prison, April 2, 1865, then transferred Johnson Island, Ohio, April 9, 1865. Released June 17, 1865 upon taking oath. *Roster*, v. XI, 444.

57. James C. Dowd. Moore County resident. Elected 2nd lieutenant Feb. 24, 1862. Promoted 1st lieutenant April 9, 1862. Promoted captain, Co. D, 1862. Wounded left foot Fredericksburg, Dec. 13, 1862 and resigned due to wound anchylosis, effective Sept. 7, 1863. *Roster*, v. XI, 408.

58. Walnut Lodge was a masonry two story octagon constructed for J. W. Randolph in 1855 on Nine Mile Road east of Richmond. The house served as headquarters for Robert E. Lee and a Confederate field hospital. Ellen L. Puerzer, *The Octagon House Inventory Book*, Milwaukee, Eight-Square Publishing, 2011.

59. Southerners and Northerners described the horrific "work of death" entailing not only the immediate fighting, killing and dying, but also the battle's ensuing consequences of slaughter, suffering and devastation, impacting both army and home front. See Drew Gilpin Faust, *This Republic of Suffering: Death and the American Civil War*, xiv.

60. After a brief skirmish the regiment captured the canal aqueduct but failed in efforts to destroy the facility. Jordan, *North Carolina Troops*, 364.

61. James Taylor Davis. Previously captain, Co. F, Mecklenburg Guard. Appointed lieutenant, 49th North Carolina Infantry, Nov. 1, 1862. Shot through head and instantly killed, Battle of the Crater, July 30, 1864. *Roster*, v. XII, 26.

62. Dixon Stansbury Miles, a career officer with Seminole and Mexican-American War experience, pursuant to orders defended Harpers Ferry to the last extremity. Jackson's flanking movement resulted in Mile's entrapment and capitulation, during which surrender Miles was mortally wounded by an artillery shell fragment. Attorney Paul R. Teetor asserts that Miles was at best an incompetent and likely a traitor who betrayed his garrison. See Paul Teetor, *A Matter of Hours: Treason at Harpers Ferry*, Rutherford, Dickinson University Press, 1982.

63. Walkup described this engagement as "one of our bloodiest fights." See *Fayetteville Observer*, Feb. 22, 1864, 2.

64. General John G. Walker reported the brigade: "…advanced in splendid style, firing and cheering as they went, and in a few minutes cleared the woods, strewing it with the enemy's dead and wounded. Colonel Manning, with the Forty-sixth and Forty-eight North Carolina and Thirteenth Virginia, and not content with the possession of the woods, dashed forward in gallant style, crossed the open fields

beyond, driving the enemy before him like sheep, until, arriving at a long line of strong post and rail fences, behind which heavy masses of the enemy's infantry were lying, their advance was checked, and it being impossible to climb over these fences under such fire, were compelled to fall back..." See Jordan, *North Carolina Troops*, 365. Had Walker's Division with the 48th not arrived the moment it did at the Dunkard Church to support Stonewall Jackson's broken line, the Army of Northern Virginia might have been destroyed. Lawhon, "Forty-Eight Regimental, 116.

65. Brinkley Franklin Richardson. Union County farmer enlisted aged 25. Elected 1st lieutenant, March 14, 1862. Promoted captain, July 9, 1862. Wounded groin and thigh, Bristoe Station, Oct. 14, 1863 and hospitalized Richmond. Surrendered Appomattox, April 9, 1865. *Roster*, v. XI, 432.

66. Leslie A. W. Turner. Union County clerk enlisted aged 26. Appointed lieutenant, Co. A, Feb. 17, 1862. Promoted captain, July 15, 1862. Wounded foot and/or leg, Wilderness, May 5–6, 1864. Hospitalized Charlotte, June 6, 1864. Returned to duty Oct. 19, 1864. Paroled Greensboro, May 1, 1865. *Roster*, v. XI, 371.

67. Thomas J. Witherspoon. Previously sergeant, 7th North Carolina Infantry. Elected 1st lieutenant, Co. C, 48th North Carolina Infantry, May 31, 1862. Killed Antietam, Sept. 17, 1862. *Roster*, v. XI, 395.

68. John W. Walden. Union County farmer enlisted aged 40. Elected captain, Co. E, Feb. 25, 1862. Resigned Oct. 3, 1862 due to feeble health and a condition greatly impaired by hard service. *Roster*, v. XI, 420.

69. The regiment regrouped and was sent with two artillery batteries to the far left of Jackson's line in support of Jeb Stuart's cavalry. *Roster*, v. XI, 365.

70. Walkup was in the thick of the fighting around the Dunker Church and nearby fields and woods. The thin grey line of the 48th North Carolina and other regiments of John G. Walker's Division of Longstreet's Corps prevented a Federal breakthrough until Lee could adeptly move troops where immediately needed awaiting A. P. Hill's Light Division on the field. Commentators like D. H. Hill questioned why Lee, after successfully seizing Harper's Ferry, fought at Antietam, outnumbered more than three to one, with the Potomac River to his back and not entrenched. Perhaps the battle was one of those occasions where Lee's blood was up and he wanted to strike the enemy a blow. See Stephen W. Sears, *Landscape Turned Red*, 230. Privates Bazil H. Wright and Benoni C. Wright, Co. I, described the Maryland campaign, stating "if we hadn't to a got away in a hurry we would a got to a stead New York." Antietam was "a mighty hard fight." See Wright brother's correspondence to parents Benjamin and Elizabeth, Sept. 20, 1862. See "Wright Papers, 1853–1882," Rubenstein Rare Book and Manuscript Room, Perkins Library, Duke University, Durham, N.C. The brothers were Cleveland County, N.C., residents who enlisted Aug. 16, 1862 for the war's duration. Bazil died in late Sept. 1862 of pneumonia and Benoni died of measles in camp, Milwood, Va., Oct. 23, 1862. *Roster*, v. XI, 484.

71. Marion A. Helms. Union County farmer enlisted aged 27, March 19, 1862 as sergeant, Co. A. Shot Antietam, Sept. 17, 1862 and died from wounds, Bunker Hill, West Virginia, Sept. 20, 1862. *Roster*, v. XI, 376.

72. William Wilson. Previously 1st lieutenant, 26th North Carolina infantry. Defeated for reelection, he enlisted 48th North Carolina, Co. F, private, July 16, 1862. Promoted sergeant, 1862. Hospitalized Richmond, Nov. 22, 1862 with dyspepsia. Transferred and appointed captain, Co. B, 26th North Carolina, June 9, 1863. *Roster*, v. VII, 443.

73. William D. Howard. Union County farmer enlisted aged 22, March 14, 1862 as 1st sergeant, Co. F. Promoted 2nd lieutenant, March 20, 1864. Killed Turkey Bend, Va., May 31, 1864. *Roster*, v. XI, 432.

74. James M. Stitt. Union County farmer enlisted aged 25, March 19, 1862 as sergeant, Co. A. Wounded King's School House, June 25, 1862. Elected 2nd lieuten-

ant, Oct. 10, 1862, promoted 1st lieutenant, Sept. 22, 1863. Hospitalized Richmond, June 25, 1864 with acute diarrhea.
Reported absent without leave, Sept.-Oct.
1864, but subsequently returned to duty.
Surrendered Appomattox, April 9, 1865.
*Roster*, v. XI, 372.

75. The regiment was in Winchester
about a month, undertaking expeditions
to damage the Baltimore and Ohio Railroad, and succeeded in tearing up some
track. *Roster*, v. XI, 365.

76. By General Assembly Act of Sept.
20, 1861, the state agreed to accept Confederate government funding to assume
the obligation to clothe North Carolina
troops in the national service. Any surplus clothing was available for purchase
through the Richmond authorities, and
Confederate agents allowed state officials
to do procurement and disbursement.
North Carolina was the only state to make
such an agreement. See Frontis W. Johnston, *Papers of Zebulon Baird Vance*, 259.
Private William Collins, private, Co. C,
wrote his father back home in Statesville,
N.C., that he still had no shoes which he
anticipated needing soon as the regiment
would be leaving the Petersburg camp.
Collins' June 12, 1862 letter. "William A.
Collins Papers." By 1863 the regiment was
adequately clothed as evidenced by a rep-
resentative photograph showing Private
George Leonard, Co. H, attired in a high
quality British spun wool shell jacket.
Thousands of these uniforms ran the
blockade into Wilmington, N.C. See *Roster*, v. XI, rear cover.

77. With the preliminary announcement of the Emancipation Proclamation
on Sept. 22, 1862, Lincoln notified rebel-
lious owners that their slaves would be
free effective Jan. 1, 1863 unless insurrection ceased. The proclamation established
the new Union objective to curtail slavery
with probable eventual abolition and to
make such African Americans eligible for
military service. The Republican platform
of 1864 called for abolition, subsequently
enacted in the 1865 Thirteenth Amendment. Walkup was concerned that non-
slave owning North Carolinians might be
disinclined to fight a perceived planters'

war. W. E. B. Du Bois articulated a similar
analysis, stating that as the war burdens
became increasingly onerous and the
probability of Rebel success more remote,
the Southern poor and laboring class were
recalcitrant and even actively opposed to
ongoing hostilities, with ensuing desertion a primary cause for ultimate Confederate defeat. See W. E. B. Du Bois, *Black
Reconstruction in America*, Harcourt
Brace, New York, 1935, 71.

78. *The Papers of Zebulon Vance*,
North Carolina Department of Cultural
Resources, University of North Carolina
Press, Chapel Hill, North Carolina, v.3.
Vance later became proactive in devis-
ing means to clothe and feed North Carolina troops in the Confederate service and
Home Guard. He requested and received
General Assembly authorization in Nov.
1862 to employ European agents and purchase blockage runners like the "Advance"
to trade cotton for cloth, spinning mate-
rials, machinery, surgical instruments,
medicines, uniforms, shoes, leather, blankets, overcoats and armaments. After
adequately supplying North Carolina
needs, large quantities of cloth and ap-
parel were made available to the Confederate national government for use by
troops of other states. See Clement Dowd,
*Life of Zebulon B. Vance*, Observer Publishing, Charlotte, 1897, 69–71.

79. Murchison McNeely. Union
County farmer enlisted aged 22 as private,
Co. F, March 25, 1862. Died of disease,
Winchester, Va., Oct. 11, 1862. *Roster*, v.
XI, 438.

80. Alexander C. Godfrey, Union
County farmer enlisted as private, Co. F,
March 14, 1862, aged 24. Died of typhoid,
Winchester, Va. around Oct. 6–9, 1862.
*Roster*, v. XI, 435.

81. Robert R. King. Union County resident enlisted aged 33, March 14, 1862 as
sergeant, Co. I. Appointed acting commissary sergeant and transferred to field
staff, Nov. 1, 1862. Transferred to 1st
North Carolina Cavalry, April 27, 1864 as
private. *Roster*, v. XI, 478.

82. Professor Drew Faust has studied
Civil War correspondence between husbands on the front lines and wives back

home. Faust identified letter writing as an act of discovery and self-exploration, with such communications fostering intimacy, frankness and enhanced personal awareness. See Faust, *Mothers of Invention*, 161–168.

83. Nineteenth century medical practice was not infrequently worse than the illness, although under field conditions surgeons did develop sophisticated procedures. Basic medications, often carried in a field case or pocket kit, included anodynes (pain relievers like opium or morphine), purgatives (cleansers for the stomach and intestines like ipecac), depressants (opium and alcohol, also deemed a stimulant), stimulants (goldenrod, coffee, tea, pepper, spirits of turpentine, alcohol), diuretics (scotch broom infusion and pipsisseway decoction), antiperiodics (fever reducers like quinine and arsenic), anesthetics (chloroform and ether), astringents (St. John's wart, sedum, strawberry, witch hazel and sumac bark), escharotics (blistering agents like nitric acid, mercury and mustard), nervine (bee balm ) and tonics (ironweed, narrow-leaved mountain mint, sage, berry teas, hops, persimmon, willow and wild cherry). In modern medical hindsight, clearly some popular treatments were detrimental. See "Medical Herbs" display, Pest Museum, Lynchburg City Cemetery, Lynchburg, Virginia/ interpreting Confederate hospital care. Dover's Powder, named for the eighteenth-century British physician who first formulated the ipecacuanha and opium compound, was employed to induce sweating for colds and fevers. Blue Mass was an often utilized mixture of mercury, liquor, ice and rose petals for treatment of a variety of ailments, including intestinal stoppage, syphilis and gonorrhea, hence the common expression: "One night with Venus and a lifetime with Mercury." Confederates lacked medications readily available in the Federal service and relied more on herbals and the frequently most effective drugs like quinine, morphine and chloroform, often smuggled or run through the blockade. *The Confederate States Medical and Surgical Journal*, July 1864 enumerated indigenous remedies for use both in the field and general hospitals. Arguable such Southern treatments were more efficacious and less detrimental than virulent drugs, like arsenic, strychnine and mercury, utilized by Union physicians. See Susan Beller, *Medical Practices of the Civil War*, Betterway Books, New York, 1992, 76. Dr. John Ross, a practicing physician and medical historian, has stated that the sick of the era were perhaps wise to avoid doctors altogether. Doctors trained in the 1830s persisted in utilizing the ancient practices advocated by Hippocrates and Galen. "They drained lakefuls of blood with lancets and leeches, raised mountainous blisters with mustard poultices and gave mercury pills enough to cause a flood of diarrhea, turning their patients' bodies into topographies of pain." See John Ross, "The Doctor Will See You Now," *Wall Street Journal*, Aug. 30–31, 2014, C-5.

84. Eber A. Griffin. Union County farmer enlisted aged 23, private, Co. E, March 17, 1862. Wounded left arm, Wilderness, May 5–6, 1864. Detailed Sept. 16, 1864 Charlotte for light duty. *Roster*, v. XI, 423.

85. Daniel D. Rogers, Union County resident enlisted aged 32, Aug. 10, 1862 as private, Co. E. Wounded in back and possibly arm, Fredericksburg, Dec. 13, 1862 and hospitalized. Assigned duty as teamster Jan. 31, 1865. Paroled Charlotte, May 20, 1865. *Roster*, v. XI, 429.

86. Walkup permitted Tom's self-hiring of labor within camp without requiring compensation from his enslaved servant. Tom's initiative demonstrated enterprise utilizing entrepreneurial skill within a context where equitable economic participation was unavailable.

87. William Baucom. Union County resident enlisted aged 28, Aug., 1862, as private, Co. F. Died of disease, Winchester, Va., Oct. 18, 1862. *Roster*, v. XI, 433.

88. Britton Belk. Union County farmer enlisted aged 18, Feb. 14, 1862 as private, Co. F. Wounded finger at Bristoe Station, Oct. 14, 1863. Deserted to enemy, March 17, 1865. Confined Washington, D.C.,

March 24, 1865 and released upon taking oath. *Roster*, Vol. XI, 434.

89. John H. Mabry. Davidson County station agent enlisted aged 26, Feb. 22, 1862 as private, Co. B. Appointed 2nd lieutenant, March 21, 1862 and captain, Oct. 20, 1862. Paroled Greensboro May 1, 1865. *Roster*, v. XI, 383.

90. John K. Potts. Iredell County resident enlisted aged 29, May 16, 1862 as private, Co. C. Elected 2nd lieutenant, May 31, 1862. Wounded with 30 holes shot through his clothes, King's School House, June 25, 1862. Wounded Antietam, Sept. 17, 1862 and Fredericksburg, Dec. 13, 1863. Promoted captain July 24, 1863. Hospitalized Richmond with gunshot wound left hand, July 20, 1864. Took oath at Salisbury, N.C., June 6, 1865. *Roster*, v. XI, 395.

91. Peter W. Plyer. Union County farmer enlisted aged 26, March 15, 1862 as sergeant, Co. E. Appointed 3rd lieutenant, Nov. 26, 1862. Killed Fredericksburg, Dec. 13, 1862. *Roster*, v. 420.

92. Irvin Simpson. Union County farmer enlisted aged 34, March 14, 1862 as private, Co. F. Promoted sergeant, May 10, 1862. Killed Fredericksburg, Dec. 13, 1862. *Roster*, v. XI, 441.

93. Erasmus H. Smith. District of Columbia farmer enlisted aged 20 as sergeant, Co. H, March 3, 1862. Wounded face, Fredericksburg, Dec. 13, 1863. Promoted 2nd captain, Feb. 10, 1863. Killed Cold Harbor, June 3, 1864. *Roster*, v. XI, 458.

94. Robert James Howie. Union County farmer enlisted aged 28 and elected 3rd lieutenant, Co. I, March 15, 1862. Promoted 2nd lieutenant, Jan, 6, 1863. Wounded arm, Wilderness, May 5–6, 1864. Captured Hatcher's Run, March 25, 1865 and confined Old Capitol Prison. Transferred Fort Delaware March 30, 1865 and released June 17, 1865 upon taking oath. *Roster*, v. XI, 471.

95. John C. Stafford. Forsyth County student enrolled aged 20 and elected 2nd lieutenant, Co. K, March 12, 1862. Promoted 1st lieutenant, July 3, 1862 and captain Sept. 27, 1862. Wounded leg at Fredericksburg, Dec. 13, 1862 and died

of wounds, Winston, North Carolina, Jan. 21, 1863. Eulogized as "good and brave" in *Greensboro Patriot*, Feb. 12, 1863, *Roster*, v. XI, 484.

96. William F. Beasley. Washington County resident elected 2nd lieutenant, Co. H, Aug. 5, 1862. Wounded left thigh, Fredericksburg, Dec. 13, 1862. Promoted 1st lieutenant, Feb. 10, 1863. Hospitalized Richmond, Oct. 4, 1863 for gunshot left thigh. On detached service from Nov. 3, 1863. Appointed major, 2nd North Carolina Junior Reserves, June 2, 1864. *Roster*, v. XI, 457.

97. John Rogers Cooke was Walkup's brigade commander after Antietam. Cooke, born 1833 Jefferson Barracks, Mo., was the son of Philip St. George Cooke, then a lieutenant of Dragoons. The father remained in U.S. service as a major general during the Civil War and alienated from his son until after the conflict. John Cooke earned an engineering degree at Harvard, then in 1855 was commissioned second lieutenant, Eighth Infantry and assigned to Indian frontier service. He resigned his U.S. commission and in April 1862 was elected colonel of the 27th North Carolina Infantry. After Antietam he was Walkup's brigadier commander. Cooke was wounded seven times during the Antietam, Fredericksburg, Bristoe Station and Wilderness battles. He could be gruff and profane when his integrity or competency was questioned. At Antietam, he told Longstreet's aide, "...by God Almighty, he needn't doubt me! We will stay here, by Jesus Christ, if we must go to hell together!" See Jeffrey D. Wert, *A Glorious Army*, 140. He was known as a strict disciplinarian and courageous. Some accounts stated, "He watched over the comfort and welfare of his men with fatherly care, and secured for them every supply that the commissary and quartermaster department yielded. Officers and privates alike idolized him." See R. A. Brock, *Southern Historical Society Papers*, Vol. 18, 322 et seq. Walkup voiced a critical perspective as to Cooke's solicitousness, having witnessed first-hand ration and clothing inadequacies and Cooke's willingness to incur casualties. "No doubt

Cooke's ambition has thrust his brigade forward, hoping to push himself forward by the blood of his brigade." See July 13, 1863 entry, "Samuel Walkup Papers."

98. John J. Costly. Previously private, 24th North Carolina Infantry. Enlisted Co. F. 48th North Carolina on Aug. 1, 1862. Died diarrhea, Mount Jackson, Va. hospital, Oct. 30, 1862. *Roster*, v. XI, 434.

99. Possibly the property of lawyer Vachel P. Chears, brother of Dr. Benjamin F. Chears. Conversation with Patricia Poland, Union County Library, Monroe, North Carolina, Feb. 4, 2014.

100. William Jasper Shannon. Union County resident enlisted aged 41, April 22, 1863 as private, Co. F. Deserted and confined Richmond March-April 1864. Died typhoid Richmond Hospital, June 5, 1864. *Roster*, v. XI, 441.

101. John B. Shannon. Union County farmer enlisted aged 29, as private, Co. F. Hospitalized Richmond, foot abscess and furloughed Feb. 6, 1864. Absent without leave April 6, 1864. Returned to service and reported absent sick Sept.-Oct. 1864. *Roster*, v. XI, 440.

102. Aware that Ambrose Burnside was concentrating on the Rappahannock River across from Fredericksburg, Lee positioned on high ground overlooking the town. The 48th was still a component of Longstreet's Corps and Col. John R. Cooke of the 27th North Carolina succeeded to command Walker's former brigade. *Roster*, v. XI, 365.

103. Walkup noted the regiment "remained exposed to a most destructive fire from shot, shell and small arms until dark, over four hours." See *Fayetteville Observer*, Feb. 22, 1864, 2.

104. John Walker Bitting. Surry County clerk enlisted aged 18, March 23, 1862 as 1st sergeant, Co. K. Elected 2nd lieutenant, Oct. 10, 1862. Wounded left hip, Fredericksburg, Dec. 13, 1862. Promoted captain, Jan. 24, 1863. Wounded Bristoe Station, Oct. 14, 1863. Hospitalized Richmond with gunshot left hip, May 15, 1864. Resigned Feb. 24, 1865. *Roster*, Vol. XI, 485.

105. Henry Clay Banner. Forsythe County planter enlisted aged 22, Co. K.

Elected 2nd lieutenant, March 25, 1862 and promoted 1st lieutenant, Sept. 27, 1862. Wounded hand, Fredericksburg, Dec. 13, 1862. Died Jarratt's Hotel, Petersburg, Dec. 21, 1862 in route home. "Amiable and accomplished...(he) won the esteem of all..." *Roster*, v. XI, 485.

106. Irvin Simpson. Union County farmer enlisted aged 34, March 14, 1862 as private, Co. F. Promoted sergeant, May 10, 1862. Killed Fredericksburg, Dec. 13, 1862. *Roster*, v. XI, 441.

107. John Franklin Heitman. Davidson County student enlisted aged 22, March 21, 1862 as 1st sergeant, Co. H. Elected 2nd lieutenant, Aug. 6, 1862. Promoted 1st lieutenant, Aug. 13, 1862. Wounded arm fracture, Fredericksburg, Dec. 13, 1862. Promoted captain, Feb. 10, 1863. "Acted gallantly" at Bristoe Station, Oct. 14, 1863. Attempted unsuccessfully to resign, Oct. 21, 1863 to pursue ministry, with denial stating he "can serve his country very materially where he now is..." Captured Sayler's Creek, April 6, 1865. Confined Washington, D.C., then transferred to Johnson's Island, Ohio, April 21, 1865 and released July 1, 1865 upon taking oath. *Roster*, v. XI, 457.

108. John Osborne Thomas. Union County resident enlisted aged 26, April 28, 1862 as private, Co. B. Killed Fredericksburg, Dec. 13, 1862. *Roster*, v. XI, 382.

109. J. P. Presson. Union County resident enlisted aged 26 as private, Co. A. Killed Fredericksburg, Dec. 13, 1862. *Roster*, v. XI, 381.

110. John A. Long. Union County resident enlisted May 12, 1862 as private, Co. I. Promoted sergeant prior to Nov. 1, 1862. Killed Fredericksburg, Dec. 13, 1862 "heroically fighting at the front of his company." *Roster*, v. XI, 479.

111. John E. Moore. Previously sergeant major 26th North Carolina. Elected captain, Co. I, June 14, 1862. Wounded Fredericksburg, Dec. 13, 1862. Returned to duty, Invalid Corps, March 6, 1865. *Roster*, v. XI, 471.

112. Benjamin Franklin Hilliard. Davidson County resident enlisted aged 29, Aug. 8, 1862 as private, Co. B. Promoted 1st sergeant, Jan.1, 1863 for "signal

courage at Fredericksburg," Dec. 13, 1862. Absent due to wound, Sept.-Oct. 1864. Paroled Greensboro, N.C., May 3, 1865. *Roster*, v. XI, 388.

113. John T. Yarmouth. Davidson County resident enlisted aged 23, July 30, 1862. Served as blacksmith and teamster. "Displayed great courage" at Fredericksburg. Paroled Greensboro, May 3, 1865. *Roster*, v. XI, 394.

114. John H. McManus. Union County farmer enlisted aged 38, March 11, 1862 as sergeant, Co I. Wounded, King's School House, June 25, 1862. Reduced to ranks prior to Nov. 1, 1862. Promoted sergeant prior to March 1, 1863. Died typhoid Richmond hospital, June 21, 1863. *Roster*, v. XI, 480.

115. Elias J. Krimminger. Union County carpenter enlisted aged 29, March 15, 1862 as private, Co. A. Promoted 1st sergeant, Nov. 1862. Wounded right shoulder, Wilderness, May 5, 1862 and absent with wounds, Sept.-Oct. 1864. *Roster*, v. XI, 377.

116. Joseph H. McCoy. Union County clerk enlisted aged 16, Feb. 17, 1862 as private, Co. A. *Roster*, v. XI, 378.

117. Ellison Hays. Union County resident, born Philadelphia, enlisted aged 19, May 8, 1862 as private, Co. E. Note discrepancy in Walkup's estimate of age. Wounded arm Fredericksburg, Dec. 13, 1862. Wounded shoulder, Bristoe Station, Oct. 14, 1862. Wounded Cold Harbor, June 3, 1864. Died prior to Jan. 1, 1865. *Roster*, v. XI, 424.

118. Alvin T. Parker. Union County farmer enlisted aged 19, March 15, 1862 as private, Co. E. Captured Hatcher's Run, April 1, 1865 and confined Point Lookout, Maryland until released June 16, 1865 upon taking oath. *Roster*, v. XI, 427.

119. Daniel Harkey. Union County resident enlisted aged 29, May 9, 1862 as private, Co. F. Killed Fredericksburg, Dec. 13, 1862. *Roster*, v. XI, 436.

120. Charles B. McInnis. Union County teacher enlisted aged 25, March 14, 1862 as private, C. F. Promoted sergeant prior to Nov. 1862. Killed Fredericksburg with Minie ball passing through head. "He was a good soldier and bore the hardships of the service without complaint." *Roster*, v. XI, 438.

121. Hugh A. Grey. Union County teacher enlisted aged 26, Co. F. Elected 3rd lieutenant, April 5, 1862. Promoted 2nd lieutenant, July 9, 1862. Wounded face and/or left shoulder by sharpshooters, Fredericksburg, Dec. 13, 1862. Resigned April 4, 1864 due to constant suppuration from Fredericksburg wound. *Roster*, v. XI, 432.

122. William D. Howard. Union County farmer enlisted aged 22, March 14, 1862 as 1st sergeant, Co. F. Elected 3rd lieutenant, Sept. 21, 1862. Note that Walkup still referred to him as sergeant. Promoted 2nd lieutenant, March 20, 1864. Killed Turkey Bend, Va., May 31, 1864. *Roster*, v. XI, 432.

123. James W. Vickory. Union County farmer enlisted aged 24, March 25, 1862 as private, Co. F. Killed Fredericksburg, Dec. 13, 1862. *Roster*, v. XI, 442.

124. Walkup showed an early appreciation for field entrenchments and the tactical defensive, a perception not always shared by West Pointers trained in antiquated Napoleonic warfare. Throughout the war he made special requisitions for shovels, picks, axes and hatchets, and on occasion lamented absence of these tools. See Perry Jamieson, *Crossing the Deadly Ground*, 1–6. Earl Hess, in his innovative analysis of infantry tactics on the regimental and company level, maintains that historians have over emphasized the long range effectiveness of the rifle, and that most Civil War casualties were incurred within the same 100 yard effectiveness of the Napoleonic smoothbore musket. See Hess, *Civil War Infantry Tactics*, xv–xx. Walkup acknowledged the devastating anti-personnel impact of rifles and artillery grape/canister shot at ranges of 500 yards and less, while also recognizing the necessity for concentrating troop strength and firepower close to the enemy line for successful assault.

125. Lewis Clark Hanes. Davidson County notary public enlisted aged 34, as private, Co. B. Appointed 1st lieutenant, March 21, 1862. Appointed captain, assistant quartermaster, July 8, 1862.

Hospitalized Dec. 3, 1863 with diarrhea and later typhoid. Relieved from regimental duty and reassigned Salisbury Quartermaster Department. Paroled Greensboro, May 3, 1865. *Roster*, v. XI, 369.

126. James M. Stitt. Union County farmer enlisted aged 25, March 19, 1862 as sergeant. Wounded King's School House, June 25, 1862. Elected 2nd.lieutenant, Oct. 10, 1862 and promoted 1st lieutenant, Sept. 27, 1863. Hospitalized diarrhea Richmond, June 25, 1864. Surrendered Appomattox, April 9, 1865. *Roster*, v. XI, 371.

127. Hall Walkup. One of the Walkup's enslaved laborers, born 1836, originally owned by Minnie and brought into the household in 1860. Around Jan. 1865 Hall married Mary, born 1835, and they legally solemnized their marriage as recorded in the 1866 Union County Cohabitation Registry, entered June 1, 1866 by J. E. Irby, clerk. Both husband and wife were illiterate. Walkup family tradition related that Hall assisted in the apprehension of three of Sherman's foragers in Union County. A search of wartime court records and post-war Confederate pension applications and awards has not corroborated the claim. Moreover, Hall's name is not listed in the Union County memorial to "Confederate Pensioners of Color." See Commemorative Landscapes," http://docsouth.uncedu/commland/monument/353/. Another Union County slave, Aaron Perry, born 1838, did capture some Federals. The Union County Court of Peas and Quarter Sessions Oct. 1864 term directed "Ten Dollars to be paid over to a slave of Capt. Wm. Perry by the name of Aaron for meritorious conduct in arresting some Yankees." See *Union County Court of Pleas and Quarter Sessions Minutes*, Vol. D (1852–1867), 375: Frances R. Small, *Union County North Carolina Marriages*, 391. Perhaps the confusion arose out of Walkup's July 16, 1863 diary reference to "Hall's coming with the prisoners." Historian Kevin Levin maintains that in the post-war South, the narrative describing the "loyal slave" evolved into the "loyal and faithful

camp servant" and ultimately, in some instances, what he deems the "mythical" black Confederate soldier. In contrast, a very few historians continue to assert that some enslaved workers supported and volitionally served the Confederacy. Earl Ijames, Curator, North Carolina Museum of History, purports that some African Americans, both free and enslaved, served the Confederacy with some degree of free will. See http://www.abbevilleinstitute.org/blog/black-soldier-north-and-south-1861–1865/. A consensus of historians share the perspective set forth by Levin, *Searching for Black Confederates: The Civil War's Most Persistent Myth*, University of North Carolina Press, 2019, that whatever the motivation and volition of the enslaved "camp servant," "Confederate slave" or "body servant" at any given instance, his legal status as property subject to an owner's authority remained unchanged.

128. When home on leave in Feb. 1863, Walkup did purchase the home he and Minnie had been renting from C. Austin. See deed recorded 18 Feb. 1863, Book 7, Page 50, Union County Registry of Deeds, conveying parts lots 13 and 14, Town of Monroe.

129. John Wesley Irby. Union County resident enlisted aged 31, July 29, 1862, as private, Co. A. Wounded head Fredericksburg, Dec. 13, 1862. Wounded left hand, Bristoe Station, Oct. 14, 1863 and two fingers amputated. Discharged April 9, 1864 due to missing fingers. *Roster*, v. XI, 376.

130. Dr. Josephus W. Hall. A Salisbury resident, he served as chief surgeon at the Salisbury Military Prison and other facilities such as the 2nd North Carolina Hospital in Petersburg. See *North Carolina Standard*, Raleigh, July 29, 1863.

131. This facility was located in Petersburg proximate to the railroad. It featured heated wards, hot and cold water, kitchens, bathing rooms, laundry and apothecary. Staffing included surgeons, assistant surgeons, dressers, steward and matrons. The hospital was available for use by troops from other states when excess capacity remained after addressing North Carolina patients. See "General Medical

Hospital for the North Carolina Troops," UNC Southern History Collection, *Confederate Hospital Records, 2nd North Carolina Hospital*, UNC Southern History Collection.

132. On leave, Walkup did not accompany the regiment to Pocataligo, South Carolina. The 48th remained there through July, Commencing in 1862, Federals made several attempts to destroy the Pocotaligo bridge and other Charleston and Savannah Railroad infrastructure to isolate those essential logistic Confederate port cities. The regiment camped about a half mile from the Pocotaligo Station and constructed earthworks but was not actively engaged. Lawhon, "Forty-Eight Regiment," 117.

133. Walkup references a livestock transaction. Hyper-inflation had not reached its zenith. See Gene Armistead, *Horses and Mules in the Civil War: A Complete History*, McFarland and Co., Jefferson, North Carolina, 2013. By mid-month he was "at home very sick." *Fayetteville Observer*, April 16, 1863, 1.

134. Leslie A. W. Turner. Union City clerk appointed 1st lieutenant, Feb. 17, 1862. Appointed captain, Co. A, July 15, 1862.Wounded foot and/or left leg, Wilderness, May 5–6, 1864. Hospitalized Charlotte, June 6, 1864. Paroled Greensboro, May 1, 1865. *Roster*, v. XI , 371.

135. Henry Middleton Rutledge. Henderson County resident enlisted aged 22 in 25th North Carolina Infantry. Appointed lieutenant colonel, April 29, 1862 and promoted colonel, May 1, 1862. Wounded Malvern Hill, July 1, 1862. Hospitalized gunshot left arm Richmond, July 4, 1864. Paroled Appomattox, April 12, 1865. *Roster*, v. VII, 355.

136. Paul Fletcher Faison. Previously major, 14th North Carolina Infantry, Appointed colonel, 56th North Carolina Infantry, July 31, 1862. Surrendered, Appomattox, April 9, 1865. *Roster*, v. XIII, 592.

137. Edward Dudley Hall. Previously major, 7th North Carolina State Troops. Transferred and promoted colonel, 46th North Carolina Infantry, April 4, 1862. Resigned Dec. 27, 1863 upon election as

Sheriff of New Hanover County. "A brave man, a good disciplinarian, a most valuable and efficient officer." *Roster*, v. XI, 134.

138. Stephen M. Timmons. Union County resident, enlisted aged 17, Aug. 21, 1862 as private, Co. A. As one of the younger soldiers, Walkup took a fatherly interest in Stephen and often had him preparing their mess, eating and visiting together as a non-official aide. In Walkup's letter Dec. 18. 1863 letter to Minnie, he is solicitous and protective of Stephen who would feel disgraced by his sister Lou Alsobrook's incestuous affair. See *Roster*, v. XI, 381.

139. Henry Franklin Schenk. A merchant enlisted aged 26, 56th North Carolina Infantry and appointed captain, Co. 7. Promoted major, July 1862. At the Battle of First Gum Swamp, April 28, 1863, Major Schenk commanded companies A, B, D and F of the 56th North Carolina, detaining a vastly superior Federal infantry on his front, then being cut-off by the enemy to his flank and rear, led his companies through devastating fire and the swamp to safety. Resigned, Aug. 1863 due to illness. *Roster*, v. XIII, 592, 647. For an account of the battle see Robert D. Graham, "56th Regiment Narrative," *History of the Several Regiments*, 320–324.

140. William MacRae, born 1834, was the son of an affluent Wilmington, North Carolina commission merchant/railroad engineer. He studied and learned civil and locomotive engineering through internship, then around 1860 he moved to Monroe, N.C. as a civil and railroad engineer and surveyor. There MacRae in his capacity with the Carolina Central Railroad had professional dealings with Walkup and formed a friendship. MacRae enlisted in the Monroe Light Infantry in April 1861, and in May was mustered in as captain, Co. B, 15th North Carolina Infantry. After William W. Kirkland's wounding at Cold Harbor in 1864, MacRae assumed command as a temporary brigadier general. Though of small stature with a high-pitched voice, and lacking formal military training, he was noted for bravery and innate tactical prowess in an army where

such qualities were both expected and appreciated. Although he incurred only a jaw wound during the war, his uniform was riddled and his saber cut in half by shot. MacRae enforced the highest degree of unbending discipline, such that the commonsensical and pragmatic Walkup on several occasions deemed him "Napoleonic" and too quick to find fault with the 48th North Carolina. See "Samuel Walkup Papers," March 15, 1864. This stern regimen was demonstrated when MacRae first assumed brigade command, and reversed his predecessor's practice of letting troops ride in empty wagons and instead demanded a brisk march. See Earl J. Hess, *Lee's Tar Heels*, 235.

141. Arthur M. Walker. Iredell County hotelkeeper appointed captain, Co. C, Feb. 21, 1862. Wounded abdomen, King's School House, Va., June 25, 1862. Resigned July 9, 1863 due to disabling wounds. *Roster*, v. XI, 395.

142. William Bynum Small. Union County farmer enlisted aged 41, March 11, 1862, Co. I. Nov. 1863 released from Richmond Castle Thunder Prison having been confined for two desertion incidents. Wounded head, Wilderness, May 5–6, 1864. Captured Hatcher's Run, April 2, 1863, confined Hart's Island, New York Harbor and released June 17, 1865 after taking oath. *Roster*, v. XI, 482.

143. Stephen H. Ashcraft. Union County resident enlisted aged 41, Aug. 23, 1862. Deserted June 5, 1863, but returned to duty. Wounded Bristoe Station, Oct. 14, 1863. Captured Spotsylvania, May 12, 1864 and confined Point Lookout, Md. and Elmira, N.Y. Died diarrhea, Elmira, Sept. 9, 1864. *Roster*, v. XI, 372.

144. Private John Medlin, Jr., of the 28th North Carolina Infantry had previously escaped after being apprehended in Monroe for desertion from the Camp of Instruction, Camp Lee, Richmond and the murder of arresting officer Lt. Hosea Little of the 82nd Regiment, North Carolina Militia. While in custody, Medlin jumped train at the North Carolina Railroad Company Shops, even though tightly handcuffed. See "Reward Notice," *Weekly Standard*, Raleigh, N.C., Dec. 31, 1862;

*North Carolina Argus*, Wadesborough, Jan. 15, 1863.

145. Henry Ringstaff was a Monroe mechanic who enlisted in the "Union (County) Farmers," Co. B, 43rd North Carolina Infantry, and was appointed a 1st lieutenant of that regiment on Feb. 12, 1862. He led a party of five soldiers ordered to arrest Private John Medlin, who had deserted to the Medlin family home in Union County. Lt. Ringstaff demanded entrance into the residence, at which time Medlin shouted, "damn you" and discharged a shot into that officer's face. Medlin and three accomplishes then fired upon their pursuers, killing Lt. Hosea Little, and made good their escape until apprehended in or around Raleigh. See Janet B. Hewett, *North Carolina Confederate Soldiers, 1861–1865*, v. III; Joseph Glatthaar, *General Lee's Army: From Victory to Collapse*, 416.

146. Chief Justice Richmond Munford Pearson of the North Carolina Supreme Court viewed the Confederate conscription law as questionable under the national and state constitutions. The Chief Justice ruled that under state law the North Carolina Militia and Home Guard could not arrest deserters for violation of Confederate national law. In that no Confederate Supreme Court was appointed, the North Carolina decision was deemed controlling precedent within the state. These Pearson habeas corpus rulings were viewed by Confederate civil and military authority as most disruptive to enforcing conscription and minimizing desertion. Governor Vance, as the chief executive of his state, was placed in the difficult position of working with Richmond to promote army efficiency while also upholding his state's judicial decisions and sovereignty. Walkup, a pre-war Unionist Whig lawyer like both Pearson and Vance, as a colonel commanding in the field saw a necessity for application of Confederate national law to maintain a functional army. By acts of January 5, 1864 and Feb. 17, 1864, the Confederate Congress enacted legislation revoking the writ of habeas corpus so as to preclude state courts from interfering with

conscription and apprehension of deserters. In the 1864 North Carolina Supreme Court case *Gatlin v. Walton*, the full Court overruled the Chief Justice and held the Confederate law suspending habeas to be constitutional. Although known as "cantankerous," Pearson remained as Chief Justice during Reconstruction, and was instrumental in promoting the 1868 North Carolina Constitution requiring election of judges. See J. G. Hamilton, "The North Carolina Courts and the Confederacy," 366–408, *N.C. Historical Journal* 4 (Oct. 1927); Joe Mobley, *The Papers of Zebulon Baird Vance*, v. 2, xv–xx.

147. William Henry Harris Lawhon. Moore County student, enlisted aged 20, Feb. 25, 1862 as sergeant, Co. D. Elected 3rd lieutenant, April 16, 1862, promoted 2nd lieutenant, July 9, 1862, and promoted 1st lieutenant, Feb. 10, 1863. Promoted captain, Sept. 7, 1863. Captured a Federal battle flag at Reams' Station, Va., Aug. 25, 1864. Paroled Appomattox, April 12, 1865. Authored a detailed regimental history, April 9, 1901. *Roster*, v. XI, 408.

148. John H. Mabry. Davidson County station agent enlisted Feb. 22, 1862. *Roster*, Vol. XI, 382.

149. Duncan McRae. Cumberland County resident appointed colonel to rank from May 16, 1861 and assigned to 5th North Carolina Infantry. Wounded South Mountain, Maryland, Sept. 14, 1862. Resigned Nov. 13, 1862 when passed over for promotion. *Roster*, v. IV, 127.

150. William V. Bonner. Previously assistant surgeon, 15th North Carolina Infantry. Appointed surgeon, 48th North Carolina, May 26, 1863. *Roster*, v. XI, 370.

151. John Minor. Davie County farmer enlisted aged 24 in Co. B, March 24, 1862. Hospitalized Winchester, Va., Sept.-Oct. 1862 and Danville, Va., Dec. 28, 1862 with remittent fever, returning to duty 1863. *Roster*, v. XI, 389.

152. John A. Thompson. Chatham County clerk enlisted aged 24, Co. G. as 2nd lieutenant. Promoted 1st lieutenant, Aug. 7, 1862. Wounded left leg Bristoe Station, Oct. 14, 1863 and hospitalized Richmond. Captured Hatcher's Run, April

2, 1865 and confined Johnson's Island, Ohio. *Roster*, v. XI, 444.

153. George W. Pope. Davidson County carpenter enlisted aged 31, March 7, 1862 as private, Co. B. Promoted sergeant, Jan. 1, 1863. Died gunshot Staunton hospital, May 20, 1864. *Roster*, v. XI, 390.

154. James M. Walker. Union County farmer enlisted aged 19, March 14, 1862 as corporal, Co. G. Reduced to ranks but subsequently promoted sergeant, prior Nov. 1, 1862. Wounded Bristoe Station, Oct. 14, 1863, with left leg amputated. Died tetanus Richmond hospital following amputation. *Roster*, v. XI, 442.

155. Elam Crawford Stewart. Union County farmer enlisted aged 38, March 7, 1862 as sergeant, Co. I. Promoted sergeant major, Dec. 1, 1862 and transferred to regimental filed and staff for gallantry at Richmond, Harpers Ferry and Sharpsburg. Died Raleigh hospital Feb. 16, 1863 from erysipelas, typhoid and pneumonia. *Roster*, v. XI, 370, 483.

156. Walkup noted the brigade was ordered to join Heth's division for the Pennsylvania campaign, but the enemy was reported advancing under General Dix, in force from the White House upon Richmond, and Cooke's Brigade was ordered back to Richmond. See *Fayetteville Observer*, Feb. 22, 1864, 2.

157. Robert James Howie. Union County farmer enlisted aged 28, Co. I. Elected 3rd lieutenant, March 15, 1863. Appointed 2nd lieutenant, Co. H. Wounded arm Wilderness, May 5–6, 1864. Captured Hatcher's Run, March 25, 1865 and confined Old Capital Prison and Fort Delaware. Released June 1865 upon taking oath. *Roster*, v. XI, 471.

158. William Hogan Jones. Chatham County farmer enlisted aged 36, Co. G. Appointed captain, March 11, 1862. Appointed major, Dec. 4, 1863 and transferred to regiment field and staff. *Roster*, v. XI, 443.

159. Walkup learned that Minnie was pregnant with daughter Ester Alice Jane, born Oct. 20, 1863. See John Hugh McDowell, *The McDowells, Erwins, Irvins and Connections*, 85.

160. Prior to the Vicksburg capitula-

tion, the holiday was popularly celebrated in the South consistent with Thomas Jefferson's encouragement. Even during the war, the day was observed, with Confederates comparing their own states' rights fight against a purportedly overbearing Union government with patriot efforts almost a century earlier. In the North the commemorations emphasized the Declaration of Independence with its messages of equality and egalitarianism. See *Mapping the Fourth of July in the Civil War Era*, Virginia Center for Civil War Studies, civilwar.vt.edu.

161. Christian Moretz. Mecklenburg County Lutheran pastor. Appointed chaplain, May 2, 1863. *Roster*, Vol. XI, 370. In contrast to Walkup, Private Rufus White, Co. C, held Moretz in high esteem: "... we have regular preaching in camp by Rev. Mr. Moretz. I think well of him: he is none of your hifalutin fools; he don't strut around and look down on others because they are not preachers. I think he is very well thought of in the Regiment." White correspondence, June 18, 1863, Camp near Richmond, "Albert M. White Papers," #4976-Z, Southern History Collection, Wilson Library, University of North Carolina–Chapel Hill.

162. Various denominations sponsored institutions publishing religious sheets, tracts, hymnals and Bibles, such as The Evangelical Tract Society of Petersburg, The General Tract Agency of Raleigh, The South Carolina Tract Society of Charleston and The Sunday School and Publication Board of Virginia. The sheets were typically free, whereas tracts sold for one or two cents, and hymnals and Bibles generally at cost. See Troy D. Harman, *The Great Revival of 1863: The Effects Upon Lee's Army of Northern Virginia*, 107.

163. William Wilson, Union County resident enlisted aged 20, 26th North Carolina Infantry. Elected 1st lieutenant, July 5, 1861, but defeated for reelection April 21, 1862, He then enlisted Co. F, 48th North Carolina as private, July 16, 1862 and promoted sergeant. Subsequently appointed captain, Co. B, 26th North Carolina Infantry. Killed Gettysburg, July 1, 1863 while "gallantly leading his men up

the hill through McPherson's woods." *Roster*, v. VII, 481.

164. William W. Richardson. Union County resident enlisted aged 26, June 5, 1861 as private. Promoted sergeant, after Jan. 1862. Elected 2nd lieutenant, 1863. Killed Gettysburg, July 1, 1863. *Roster*, v. VII, 482.

165. John McWhorter. Union County resident enlisted aged 18, June 5, 1861, 26th North Carolina Infantry. Killed, Gettysburg, July 1, 1863. *Roster*, v. VII, 488.

166. Walkup quotes Thomas Gray, "Elegy Written in a County Churchyard," R. Dodsley, London, 1751.

167. The reference to Hall and prisoners may be the basis for the family belief that he apprehended Federals.

168. "God being our guide, nothing is to be despaired." A comparable motto was adopted for the official Confederate Great Seal, *Deo Vindice*, meaning "With God, our defender." See *Southern Historical Society Papers*, Vol. XVI, 1888.

169. Confederates keenly noted the rioting of July 13–16 against conscription that caused over 100 deaths. African American longshoremen along the Manhattan waterfront were the primary casualties, with numerous public and private structures destroyed. The Peace Movement by disaffected Northern Democrats and anti-war Copperheads led some Southerners to believe a negotiated peace recognizing Confederate independence was feasible. The civil unrest did temporarily divert some Union troops that might otherwise have pressed the Army of Northern Virginia following its Gettysburg retreat. See Adrian Cook, *The Armies of the Street: The New York City Draft riots of 1863*, University Press of Kentucky, 1974.

170. Walkup was able to buy the specified quantity of rations and cloth at the cost of government procurement plus freight. For a subsequent legislative authorization of this existing practice, see *Chapter XLV, An Act to Allow Commissioned Officers of the Army Rations and the Privilege of Purchasing Clothing from the Quartermaster's Department, Statutes at Large of the Confederate States of*

*America*, James Matthews, editor, Richmond, Va., 1864.

171. The University of Virginia was founded by the General Assembly in 1819, with Thomas Jefferson designing the buildings, establishing curriculum and hiring faculty. The "Academic Village" housed faculty, staff and students in classical, symmetrical colonnaded rows of brick pavilions for quarters and classrooms. A central commons, or "lawn," provided a green expanse, headed by a rotunda facsimile of the Pantheon. Jefferson was the guiding light of the endeavor, assisted by James Madison and James Monroe. See Erwin Jordan, Jr., *Charlottesville and the University of Virginia in the Civil War*, 1–42. Even in the later twentieth century founder Jefferson was virtually venerated by students and faculty, who frequently begin lectures with "What would Jefferson do?" To the other extreme, some now vilify the slave owner, asking "What *wouldn't* Jefferson do?" Conversation June 1, 2020 with George O. Burpeau III, graduate of the University School of Arts (1977) and School of Law (1980). Revisionist history now offers a diametrically opposed portrait of this Founding Father. On a copy of the Declaration of Independence displayed at the New Hanover County, North Carolina Government Center in 2016, posted notes described Jefferson as "racist, rapist, hypocrite and forced labor camp commandant." A response posted, "All true, but the good words of Declaration are greater than the bad man," while another commented: "Patriot, Philosopher, Educator and Statesman."

172. University operations were severely disrupted during the war by enlistment and conscription of many students and faculty. The Charlottesville General Hospital, founded July 15, 1861, Midway Hospital and Delevan Hospital were situated in town. Charlottesville was deemed an excellent site for military medical facilities because of good rail service, proximity to Richmond and availability of university facilities and School of Medicine staff, particularly Dr. James Lawrence Cabell, chief surgeon. Jordan, *Charlottesville*, 45–60.

173. Entries are lacking for several months hereafter. Late September the regiment was assigned to Major General Henry Heths's division, A. P. Hill's corps. At the Oct. 14, 1863 Battle of Bristoe Station, A. P. Hill imprudently, without reconnaissance so unaware of Federal strength, sent only Cooke's and Kirkland's brigades unsupported on their flanks against the Army of the Potomac rear guard. Cooke and Kirkland attacked over open field three divisions entrenched along a railroad embankment supported by artillery. General Cooke was wounded and Col. Edward Hall of the 46th NC assumed brigade command. Confederate losses were three times those of Federal. Robert E. Lee replied to Hill's explanations, "Well, well, general, bury these poor men and let us say no more about it." Douglas S. Freeman, *Lee's Lieutenants*, Scribner, New York, 1946, v.3, 326–327. Bristoe may well have been the basis for Walkup's subsequent diary entries critiquing A. P. Hill's competency.

174. Private Felix Miller, Co. H, stated, "...it is a hard matter for us to get shoes here and probably I may need a pair after a while and if you make jean cloth to save it for I shall need some clothing after a while." See correspondence to wife, Nov. 19. 1863, "Felix Miller Papers," Manuscript Collection 256, Joyner Library, East Carolina University, Greenville, N.C. Miller noted he needed to wear all his clothes "to keep from freezing." See correspondence to wife, Dec. 7, 1863, "Felix Miller Papers." Miller was a Davidson County resident who enlisted Oct. 13, 1863 for the duration of the war. He died in Gordonsville, Virginia hospital May 29, 1863 of chronic diarrhea. See *Roster*, v. XI, 466.

175. Walkup characteristically avoided self-aggrandizement by declining conscript additions to his regiment, recognizing the men were best utilized elsewhere in the brigade.

176. General Orders No. 93 sought to implement an Act of the Confederate Congress approved Oct. 13, 1862 authorizing the President to grant medals and badges for conspicuous courage on the

field of battle. For non-commissioned officers and privates, the rank-and-file were to select the soldier of their company whose name would be forwarded to the President for confirmation and conferral of the distinction. Due to difficulties in procuring actual metals and badges, General Orders No. 131 authorized compilation of a Roll of Honor memorializing those eligible conferees. See *General Orders*, Adjutant and Inspector General's Office, Richmond, Va., Nov. 22, 1862 (General Orders No. 93) and Oct. 3, 1863 (General Orders No. 131).

177. Zebulon Vance made a marginal note on the correspondence, directing Capt. L. Dowd to facilitate Walkup's request, with the accolade, "he is the best fellow in the world." "Zebulon Vance Papers," North Carolina Archives and History, Raleigh, North Carolina, 9135.

178. Felix Miller, Co. H, indicated opossums sold for five dollars and chickens twenty. See correspondence to wife, Oct. 20, 1863, "Felix Miller Papers." He lamented, "I can inform you that times are hard here and those that are back home can guess at it but those that are here knows all about it." See correspondence to wife, Oct. 24, 1863, "Felix Miller Papers." "Rashens were so short now that we can hardly make out on them...our mess has not got meal anuf..." See correspondence to wife, Jan. 26, 1864, "Felix Miller Papers."

179. Walkup had pre-war investments in such Union County cotton plantations, usually with his brother, and recognized the speculative value of cotton marketed for shipment through the Union blockade. He does not reflect on the immorality of the planter's fixation with the vicious cycle of raising cotton to buy more slaves. See Gene Dattel, *Cotton and Race in the Making of America*, 48.

180. Stephen Walkup. One of Walkup's enslaved farm laborers, most likely the reported 45 years old referenced in the 1860 Union County Slave Census, Schedule 2, line 38, page 17, although the 1880 Census, 439 showed him born 1825 rather than 1815. Wife Luvina Walkup was born 1825, and was a housekeeper post-war. Robert Walkup devised Stephen to son

Samuel in provision 12 of his will, described as "a negro boy Stephen he now has in pofsefsion." See Robert Walkup will, Union County Court of Pleas and Quarter sessions, Oct. term 1846 and Will Book 1, Page 33, Monroe County Registry; Frances Small, *Union County Marriages*, 392. Family history relates that Stephen was literate, having been permitted by the Walkups to circumvent legal constraints and take lessons. Conversation with Walkup's great-great granddaughter Virginia Adams of Galveston, Texas, Jan. 9, 2011.

181. The monetary value of the enslaved depended upon their age, sex, health, strength and skill, and market factors of supply and demand. Such human commodification reflects both the economic nature and intrinsic evil of slavery. See Daina Ramsey Berry, *The Price for Their Pound of Flesh: The Value of the Enslaved, from Womb to Grave, in the Building of a Nation*, 41.

182. Margaret Walkup was a domestic slave owned by Walkup along with her children Eliza, Harriet, Fanny, Sarah, Wilson and Jenny. See "Walkup Will," 16 Oct. 1864, Loose Wills Collection, North Carolina Archives and History.

183. Working on Union County cotton plantations, Hall and Stephen would plow and seed corn and cotton in the spring, repair fencing, cart compost to the fields, make cotton harvest baskets, and pick crops in late summer. In Monroe they worked the house vegetable garden at Minnie's direction. As a Southern housewife, she managed the enslaved engaged in domestic work. See G. Johnson, *Antebellum North Carolina*, 236, 479–480 and Stephanie Jones-Rogers, *They Were Her Property: White Women as Slave Owners in the American South*, xi–xvii. While Minnie owned slaves herself either before or after marriage and was a "mistress in the making" as described by Jones-Rogers. As a young woman Minnie's parents imbibed in her the roles of instructor and disciplinarian in the management of the enslaved household.

184. William Calvin Plyler. Iredell County Methodist-Episcopal minister,

enlisted aged 33. Appointed chaplain, Sept. 21, 1863. *Roster*, v. XI, 370.

185. Promotion to colonel was based on seniority within the regiment, so a lieutenant colonel like Walkup was eligible to succeed to the colonelcy. After 1862, to prevent incompetent junior officers from being promoted as a matter of course, a merit examination board composed of generals and colonels tested prospective colonels on knowledge of tactics and regulations, and took relevant testimony and recommendations of other officers. If the examining board rejected the candidate, a more junior officer could be considered and examined. Some colonelcy candidates resigned in favor of junior officers rather than stand examination. See Bruce Allardice, *Confederate Colonels*. Walkup's examination board was comprised of Brigadier General James Henry Lane, Colonel George Henry Faribault and Col. John Marshall Stone, all A. P. Hill's Third Corps.

186. John W. Reed. Previously served as private, Co. B, 27th North Carolina Infantry. Mustered in as sergeant, Dec. 4, 1862. Wounded Fredericksburg, Dec. 13, 1862. Elected 3rd lieutenant, March 3, 1863. Captured Hatcher's Run, April 2, 1865 and confined Old Capitol Prison and Johnson's Island, Ohio. Paroled upon taking oath June 19, 1865. *Roster*, v. XI, 485.

187. James M. Hix. Previously private, 4th Tennessee Infantry. Transferred to Co. B, 48th North Carolina, Aug. 13, 1862 as private. Elected 2nd lieutenant, Jan. 1, 1863. Paroled Salisbury, May 29, 1865. *Roster*, v. XI, 383.

188. A university professor and graduate of Virginia Military institute and the University of Virginia, Lane was commissioned major, 1st North Carolina Infantry, then by Sept. 15, 1861 promoted colonel, 28th North Carolina Infantry. He was twice wounded in the Seven Days battles. Promoted brigadier general, Nov. 1, 1862. Wounded during Pickett's charge when his horse shot from under him. In Feb.-March, 1865 commanded Cadmus M. Wilcox's division and surrendered Appomattox, April 9, 1865. See Ezra Warner, *Generals in Grey*, 173.

189. George H. Faribault. Previously captain, 14th North Carolina Infantry. Appointed lieutenant colonel, 47th North Carolina infantry, April 9, 1862 and promoted colonel, Jan. 5, 1863. Wounded shoulder and foot, Gettysburg, July 3, 1863. Resigned Nov. 22, 1864. *Roster*, v. XI, 244.

190. Robert L. Stewart. Union County farmer enlisted aged 25, Co. F. Promoted 2nd lieutenant, July 9, 1862. Captured South Mountain, Maryland, Sept. 13, 1862 and confined Fort Delaware. Paroled Oct. 2, 1862 and exchanged Aiken's Landing, James River, Nov. 10, 1862. Hospitalized Charlotte, April 7, 1865 with typhoid. *Roster*, v. XI, 433.

191. William B. Hamner. Davidson County saddler enlisted, aged 29. March 6, 1862, Co. B. Elected 1st lieutenant, Aug. 7, 1862. Promoted 2nd lieutenant, Oct. 20, 1862. Paroled Greensboro, May 1, 1865. *Roster*, v. XI, 383.

192. Colonels were expected to master the intricacies of grouping and maneuvering companies for march and battle, and aligning and guiding those combinations for maximum effectiveness. As regimental commander, Walkup needed to personally direct and control his ranks, maintaining discipline and cohesion while readily adjusting for the fluid situation in the field. To learn his craft Walkup consulted such tactical manuals such as the Winfield Scott and William Hardee texts that constituted standardized instruction for American military training. His experience as a pre-war militia general would have only helped with parade ground formation and was more a political than military accomplishment. See Earl Hess, *Civil War Infantry Tactics: Training, Combat and Small-unit Effectiveness*, 34–60.

193. Consistent with regulations of the Army of the Confederate States, the War Department issued the colonelcy commission to date and rank from the date of vacancy. See *Regulations*, 3rd edition, 1863.

194. Henry Brown Howie. Previously 1st sergeant, 35th North Carolina Infantry. Appointed 2nd lieutenant, Co. A, Jan. 26, 1863. Paroled Greensboro, May 1, 1865. *Roster*, v. XI, 371.

195. Stephen M. Simmons. Union County resident, enlisted aged 17, Feb. 21, 1862 as private, Co. A. *Roster*, v. XI, 381.

196. Augustin Crouch. Davidson County planter enlisted aged 23, March 20, 1862 as private, Co. K. Wounded Antietam, Sept. 17, 1862. Returned to duty prior to March 1, 1863. Deserted on or about May 5, 1863. Roster incorrectly states he was home on sick furlough Jan.-April 1864. *Roster*, v. XI, 487. Private Theophilus Frank, Co. B, wrote wife Elizabeth he "Had to help shoot a man in Co. K, 48th Regiment last Monday for deserting." See Frank letter, Jan. 27, 1864, "Frank Family Papers."

197. Private Felix Miller, Co. H, described the public execution of Crouch, a soldier in his same company: "I marched out with the regiment but I did not look to see him shot." See correspondence to wife, Jan. 26, 1864, "Felix Miller Papers."

198. Pinkney A. White. Iredell County farmer enlisted aged 34, March 3, 1862 as 1st sergeant, Co. C. Wounded leg fracture King's School House, Va., June 25, 1862. Reduced to sergeant May–June 1863. Transferred 2nd North Carolina Cavalry, Nov. 12, 1864. Roster, v. XI, 407.

199. William Delaney. Union County resident enlisted aged 16, April 22, 1863 as private, Co. F. Paroled Appomattox, April 12, 1865. *Roster*, v. XI, 435.

200. At Bristoe Station Walkup's regiment, and Cooke's entire brigade were new to Heth's Division. A. P. Hill impetuously and negligently determined to assault the enemy waiting to cross Broad Run above the rail station. Hill failed to undertake an appropriate reconnoiter, and thought he faced only a modest rearguard, where in actuality three Union divisions were entrenched and two Union corps proximate. He ordered Heth to cross the expansive field, intending to commit three brigades with one in reserve. On the right Cooke's troops rushed into position. Hill directed Heth to immediately engage with only the two brigades that were up to prevent the Federals from escaping. As the enemy advanced on Heth's right, a courier was dispatched to warn Cooke who was encountering brisk fire from the railroad cut. Cooke advanced skirmishers who ascertained the presence of Federals in large numbers. Nevertheless, Hill stated that supporting artillery was in place and additional brigades were coming up, and ordered Cooke to proceed. More perceptive than Hill, Cooke stated, "Well, I will advance, and if they flank me, I will face my men about and cut my way out." Kirkland's and Cooke's brigades proceeded over the open space for about 800 yards against a Federal division protected by the rail cut and artillery on a considerable elevation sweeping the Confederates with canister and grape shot. The 48th North Carolina and companion regiments suffered a murderous fire. Cooke was shot. The Cooke and Kirkland brigades then had to retreat as best they could amidst withering shot and shell. Within forty minutes the battle ended and night fell. Cooke's brigade lost over 700 men. After the slaughter, Lee told Hill, "It is your fault. You committed a great blunder yesterday; your line of battle was too short, too thin, and your reserves were too far behind." Philip Katcher, *The Army of Robert E. Lee*, 37. Probably only Lee's forbearance prevented Hill from being relieved of command. Walkup formed an initial and lasting impression of Hill as a glory seeking incompetent unfitted for corps command. See Walkup's further critique of Hill in the May 29, 1864 entry, "Samuel Walkup Papers,"; James I. Robinson, Jr., *General A. P. Hill*, 226–240.

201. George W. Howie. Union County farmer enlisted aged 22, March 14, 1862 as sergeant, Co. F. Promoted 1st sergeant, Nov. 1862. Wounded both cheeks, Bristoe Station, Oct. 14, 1863, hospitalized Charlottesville. Wounded, Reams' Station, Aug. 25, 1864 and hospitalized Richmond. Appointed ensign (1st lieutenant), April 28 for "gallantry and merit" and transferred to field and staff. *Roster*, v. XI, 370, 437.

202. Private Levi Miller, Co. H, bemoaned, "We haft to go on picket every day and we go about three miles and stand in the rain and snow and ice...I feel very much like it would ware me out [and] we don't get much to eat..." See undated

correspondence to mother, Winter 1863/1864, letter no. 10, "Felix Miller Papers." Miller joined the same company where his father and uncles served, enlisting at Orange Court House, Va., at aged 18 on January 28, 1864. He was wounded in both arms at Petersburg in the summer of 1864. His left arm was amputated, and he was furloughed to hospital in Richmond on Aug. 22, 1864. He survived the war. *Roster*, v. XI, 467.

203. William O. Stearns. Union County farmer enlisted aged 27, March 15, 1862 as 1st sergeant, Co. E. Elected 1st lieutenant, Nov. 26, 1862. Wounded hand, Fredericksburg, Dec. 13, 1862 and shoulder, Wilderness, May 5–6, 1864. Promoted captain, Oct. 14, 1864. Captured Hatcher's Run, April 2, 1865. Confined Old Capital Prison and Johnson's Island, Ohio. Released June 20, 1865 upon taking oath. *Roster*, v. XI, 420.

204. Drew Gilpin Faust, *This Republic of Suffering: Death and the American Civil War*, maintains that the horrendous carnage of the war led to profound changes in society, particularly giving rise to an expectation that government, through an increasing bureaucracy, was responsible for assisting its citizens devastated by conflict. See also Megan Kate Nelson, *Ruin Nation: Destruction and the American Civil War*, University of Georgia Press, Athens, 2012, demonstrating the profound impact the war had on both battlefield and home front, creating a defining traumatic experience shared by civilians and soldiers.

205. Walkup envisioned the ideal plenty of home in contrast to Private Felix Miller's unvarnished account of field conditions where "rashen is so short that we can hardly make out on them." Correspondence to wife, January 26, 1864, "Felix Miller Papers."

206. Court-martial proceedings as transcribed with final determination were to be transmitted to the Inspector-General of the Army/Judge Advocate, as specified in *Army Regulations*, Article XXXVIII, Courts-Martial, section 877. See Aldo S. Perry, *Civil War Courts-Martial of North Carolina Troops*. Pursuant to

A.P. Hill's directive, the trial on the gross neglect of duty charge was duly conducted Feb. 2, 1864. Walkup's probable defense was that no Army regulation or other order required that the regimental colonel notify a deserter that a death sentence had been imposed. Walkup was released from arrest and in charge of his regiment Feb. 11, 1864. Apparently no official sanction or public reprimand was ordered. Thomas Power Lowery, a leading authority in Civil War courts-martial and author of *Confederate Death Sentences: A Reference Guide*, has thoroughly examined archives and located no record of this proceeding.

207. Walkup was not alone in thinking purchase of Confederate bonds might be a wise financial investment as well as a patriotic endeavor. The bonds, available at a very steep discount to par on secondary markets, had appreciation potential as well as a high interest rate return. See Barney, *The Making of a Confederate*, 66.

208. Perhaps due to campaigning constraints imposed by his active combat in Virginia and strong opposition from the Peace Party, Walkup did not win election. "Announcement," *The Charlotte Democrat*, Charlotte, North Carolina, Aug. 2, 1864, 1.

209. Effective 1864 officers were allotted one ration in the same "quality and quantity" as allowed privates without the usual obligation that officers pay for their provisions. See *Rations to Officers*, Section 1, Chapter 45, *Confederate States of America: A Digest of the Military and Naval Laws*, Columbia, S.C., 1864.

210. Private Levi Miller, Co. H, described "a bully snow balling." Correspondence to mother, March 24, 1864, "Felix Miller Papers."

211. Thomas W. Dial. Forsythe County resident enlisted aged 21, March 18, 1862, as private Co. K. Deserted Sept. 2, 1862. *Roster*, v. XI, 488.

212. Private Levi Miller, Co. H, told his mother "I saw another man shot a few minutes ago for desertion. This was the fourth man I have seen shot since I left home." Correspondence, March 24, 1864, "Felix Miller Papers."

213. Mid-nineteenth century America viewed dying as a skill or attribute to master, the *ars moriendi*. The "good death" was an end of life exhibiting moral good and dedication to duty, with contemplative recognition of earthly finitude and heavenly transcendence. In stark contrast, the "bad death" was best exemplified by public execution for such dereliction of duty as desertion, with the shamed soldier accompanying his coffin to face a firing squad in front of his assembled regiment. See Drew Gilpin Faust, *This Republic of Suffering*, 3–31.

214. Although Walkup and Vance were both Unionist Whigs, fellow bar members and friends before and after the war, their personalities were quite different, with Vance folksy and flamboyant, while Walkup was more sedate and analytical, with an appreciation for appropriate solemnity. A Vance biographer described the Governor's speaking style as "easy, plain and for the most part colloquical." He was said to be good natured and to enjoy a jest, to use merry illustrations and occasional ridicule and that "his diction was never very ornate when speaking extemporaneously." During his gubernatorial campaign against the "peace and reconstruction" candidate William Holden, Vance visited the Army of Northern Virginia frontline, and spoke for two hours at a general review in his honor hosted by Lee. A fellow U.S. Congressman in a post-war account related "a more appropriate, effective and eloquent address was never uttered by human lips" and that the audience was "stirred, enthused and carried away as if by the spell of a magician." See Clement Dowd, *Life of Zebulon B. Vance*, 105–107, 124–125. Vance was reelected, gaining votes of most North Carolina servicemen: 13,209 to Holden's 1,826. Some company level officers were not receptive to Holden supporters casting ballots, in which instance the dissident soldier could only decline to vote. See Earl J. Hess, *Lee's Tar Heels*, 240 and Glenn Tucker, *Zeb Vance*, 366; Adelphos Burns, Co. G, 48th North Carolina Infantry, stated that if he were to vote, he would do so for Holden and that talk in the brigade speculated

that Holden might win statewide. See July 17, 1864 letter, "Adelphos J. Burns Papers," 1708.1, North Carolina State Archives.

215. Clearly the Confederate opinions failed to appreciate Grant's tenacity, a willingness to sustain necessary losses and his ultimate commitment to destroy Lee's ability to wage war.

216. Private Felix Miller, Co. H, stated: "Governor Vants made a speech to the soldiers the other day. He told them they could stand it he could. I think it was poor encouragement for him to do anything for us." Correspondence to wife, April 6, 1864, "Felix Miller Papers."

217. Benjamin F. Fincher. Union County resident enlisted aged 33, March 19, 1862 as corporal, Co. A. Transferred to Navy, April 15, 1864. *Roster*, v. XI, 378.

218. Jesse L. Parker. Union County farmer enlisted aged 27, March 14, 1862 as corporal, Co. F. Promoted sergeant, around Nov. 1862-Feb. 1863. Wounded left foot, Bristoe Station, Oct. 14, 1863 and hospitalized Richmond. Reduced to ranks prior Jan. 1, 1864. Transferred to Navy, April 1, 1864. *Roster*, v. XI, 439.

219. Spencer Murray. Chatham County laborer enlisted aged 23, Feb. 25, 1862 as private, Co. G. *Roster*, v. XI, 453.

220. John H. Nading. Forsythe County painter enlisted aged 21, May 1, 1862 as private, Co. K. Promoted sergeant, Nov. 62–Feb. 1863, and 1st sergeant, March-April, 1863. Transferred to Navy, April 1, 1864. *Roster*, v. XI, 493.

221. Christian Correll. Union County mechanic enlisted aged 37, Feb. 28, 1862 as sergeant, Co. G. Wounded finger, Fredericksburg, Dec. 13, 1862 and breast, Bristoe Station, Oct. 14, 1863. Reduced to ranks. Captured Hatcher's Run, April 1, 1865. Confined Point Lookout, Maryland and released June 26, 1865 upon taking oath. *Roster*, v. XI, 421.

222. Nathaniel Hendrix. Forsythe County resident enlisted aged 21, May 1, 1862 as private, Co. K. Promoted sergeant, July 1863. Reduced to ranks and apparently allowed to resign non-commission officer status. Captured Burgess' Mill, Va., Oct. 27, 1864. Confined Point Lookout, Maryland, Nov. 24, 1864

and died there in hospital, May 6, 1865 of chronic diarrhea. *Roster*, v. XI, 490.

223. Milton H. Fulp. Forsythe County planter enlisted aged 27, March 19, 1862 as sergeant, Co. K. Elected 2nd lieutenant, Jan. 24, 1863. Wounded left arm Reams' Station, Aug. 25, 1864 and hospitalized Richmond. Paroled Appomattox, April 12, 1865. *Roster*, v. XI, 485.

224. Lee directed observation of the Day of Fasting, Humiliation and Prayer in compliance with resolutions of the Confederate Congress and President. All military duties except those deemed absolutely necessary were suspended. Chaplains were desired to hold services in the regiments and troops were requested to attend "...beseeching the aid of the God of our forefathers in the defense of our homes and our liberties..." See John William Jones, *Personal Reminiscences, Anecdotes and Letters of General Robert E. Lee*, 424.

225. Joseph Medlin. Union County farmer enlisted aged 21, March 12, 1862 as private, Co. A. Captured as deserter, April 7, 1864 and confined Castle Thunder Prison, Richmond, through Jan. 1865. Released to regiment, then captured by Federals, Amelia Court House, April 3, 1865. Confined Point Lookout, Maryland and released June 4, 1865 upon taking oath. *Roster*, v. XI, 378.

226. James I. Richardson. Union County farmer enlisted aged 24, March 15, 1862 as private, Co. E. Wounded back, Cold Harbor, June 3, 1864. Captured Hatcher's Run, April 2, 1865. Confined Hart's Island, N.Y. Harbor and released June 17, 1865 upon taking oath. *Roster*, v. XI, 428.

227. Robert T. Watson. Union County farmer enlisted aged 20, March 25, 1862 as private, Co. F. Wounded left knee fracture, Petersburg, Feb. 15, 1864 and hospitalized. *Roster*, v. XI, 443.

228. Joseph J. McNeeley. Union County farmer enlisted April 1862 as private, Co. F. Deserted to enemy, Nov. 5, 1864 and confined Camp Hamilton, Va. Released Nov. 12, 1864 upon taking oath. *Roster*, v. XI, 438.

229. Nathan E. Baker. Union County farmer enlisted aged 18, Feb. 14, 1862 as private, Co. F. Returned from desertion, Sept. 23, 1863. Deserted to enemy around Nov. 5, 1864. Confined, Camp Hamilton, Va. Released Nov. 12, 1864 upon taking oath. *Roster*, v. XI, 433.

230. Evan Watson. Union County farmer enlisted aged 22, March 14, 1862 as private, Co. G. Paroled Appomattox, April 12, 1865. *Roster*, v. XI, 442.

231. Allen M. Gordon. Union County farmer enlisted aged 19, March 25, 1862 as private, Co. F. Wounded arm Wilderness, May 5–6, 1864. Deserted to enemy around March 3, 1865 and confined Washington, D.C., March 7, 1865. Released upon taking oath. *Roster*, v. XI, 436.

232. William Vickory. Union County farmer enlisted aged 26, March 25, 1862 as private, Co. F. Wounded Fredericksburg, Dec. 13, 1862. Paroled Appomattox, April 9, 1865. *Roster*, v. XI, 442.

233. Adam A. C. Phillips. Union County Farmer enlisted aged 16, March 14, 1862 as private, Co. F. Paroled Charlotte, May 17, 1865. *Roster*, v. XI, 439.

234. Samuel Thomas Adams. Union County farmer enlisted aged 19, March 14, 1862 as private, Co. F. Deserted Aug. 2, 1863, but returned Sept. 21, 1863. Captured, Petersburg, Oct. 11, 1864. Confined Point Lookout, Maryland and released Oct. 18, 1864 upon taking oath and joining Federal army. Assigned 4th Regiment. U.S. Volunteer Infantry, Co. D. *Roster*, v. XI, 433.

235. John I. Richardson. Union County farmer enlisted aged 24, March 15, 1862 as private, Co. E. Wounded, Cold Harbor, June 3, 1864. Captured, Hatcher's Run, April 2, 1865. Confined Hart's Island, New York harbor and released June 17, 1865 upon taking oath. *Roster*, v. XI, 428.

236. Private Levi Miller, Co. H, stated his "Captain is a going to engage a Sabbath School which is to read Testament or a Bible every Sunday..." Correspondence to father, Feb. 15, 1864, "Felix Miller Papers."

237. A wave of piety swept the Army of Northern Virginia, particularly 1862–1864. The fervor was fostered by religious literature and daily camp-style open air services of several hours' duration led

by popular revivalists. Evangelism was manifested throughout the organization, from General Lee and the top leadership through the rank and file enlisted men. Zealous colonels like Walkup were instrumental in appointing and encouraging dedicated and competent chaplains. See Troy D. Harman, *The Great Revival of 1863: The Effects Upon Lee's Army of Northern Virginia*. Private William Collins, Co. C, was "Thankful to God that we are blessed with the opportunity of having preaching in our Regiment very Sunday and we also have prayer in our company..." Collins letter to his father, Camp Lee, Petersburg, July 21, 1862, "William A. Collins Papers."

238. Montpelier was primarily influenced by the designs of Thomas Jefferson, who assisted his friend Madison with renovations, rather than Washington's Mount Vernon style. See Edward A. Chapel, *The Restoration of James Madison's Montpelier*, http://colonialwilliamsburg.org.

239. In contrast to Walkup's reticence to inform relatives back home regarding the scarcity of provisions, Private Felix Miller, Co. H, declared: "our rashins here is very short. We draw corn meal and last year's bacon. We haven't drawed flower but only one day since I came home the last time." Correspondence to wife, April 18, 1864, "Felix Miller Papers."

240. William T. Montgomery. Maryland physician, appointed surgeon, April 10, 1863. Paroled Appomattox, April 12, 1865. *Roster*, v. XI, 370.

241. John C. Grandberry. Bishop of the Methodist-Episcopal Church and Chaplain, 11th Virginia Infantry. He wrote to the *Richmond Christian Advocate*, "I have never before witnessed such a widespread and powerful religious interest among the soldiers...It would delight your hearts to watch the seriousness, order, and deep feelings..." See Harman, *The Great Revival*, 108, 112.

242. John Randolph Lane. Previously captain, Co. G. 26th North Carolina Infantry, the "Chatham Boys." Appointed lieutenant colonel, Aug. 19, 1862. Wounded neck, jaw and mouth, Gettysburg, July 1,

1863. Appointed colonel to rank from July 1, 1863. Wounded, Wilderness, May 4, 1864. Wounded right leg, Yellow Tavern, Summer 1864, but refused to leave the field. Wounded left breast, Rheam's Station, Aug. 25, 1864. Paroled Greensboro, May 2, 1865. *Roster*, v. VII, 463.

243. Howie later accepted appointment as ensign and transferred to staff and field. The ensign was the color-bearer of the regiment. Given the dangers of that privilege, the ensign held commissioned officer status but not command authority. *Roster*, v. XI, 370.

244. On May 4, 1864 Lee discerned that Grant was not moving east toward Fredericksburg nor west toward Mine Run, but rather had crossed the Rapidan to the Wilderness. Lee expressed pleasure that Grant had not profited by Hooker's disastrous experience there, and that the Federals would forfeit to a significant extent their numerical and artillery advantages best employed in open terrain. Hill's Corps was directed to engage by the Orange Plank Road. Hill attacked at Parker's Store and occupied the crossroads. Heth deployed across the Plank Road with Walkup in the center. Hancock's II Corps struck and desperate fighting ensued. During that night Cooke's battered brigade was placed in reserve. By this time Hill finally acknowledged Heth's advice to try to get Longstreet up as soon as possible. Longstreet did not move until after 1:00 a.m. despite a headquarters aide directive to press onward. Around 5:00 a.m. the next day thirteen Federal brigades assaulted Hill. Cooke's Brigade with Walkup's regiment, assisted by Kirkland's Brigade, stood fast for a considerable duration but eventually yielded. Hill himself manned an artillery piece. Lee and staff went forward hoping to spot and direct the First Corps forward as soon as it appeared. Upon the appearance of Longstreet's Texans, Lee waved his hat, hurrahed, and seemed ready to ride forward with those troops. The men demanded Lee to the rear before they would go into the fray. See Noah Trudeau, *Bloody Roads South*, 41–116.

245. Lee's performance of duties ordi-

narily undertaken by a competent commander of a corps, division or even brigade indicates the lack of expertise, inadequate staff support and insufficient depth of leadership in the 1864–1865 Army of Northern Virginia. Earlier in the war Lee was in a position to allow his subordinates considerable discretion without the scrutiny of looking over their shoulder. See Dowdey, *Lee's Last Campaign.*

246. Longstreet's corps arrived just in time to support Hill and prevent collapse of the Confederate right wing. Dense vegetation inhibited use of artillery, but the thicket was cut down by the intensity of rifle fire. Robert E. Lee remarked that the brigades of General Cooke and General Kirkland held in check 25,000 Federals for more than two hours. As Lee rode the lines, he was acclaimed with cheers and the greatest rebel yell of the war. See Lawhon, *48th Regimental History*, 118–119.

247. He survived his wound and was paroled Greensboro, May 3, 1865. *Roster,* v. XI, 388.

248. Federals set fire to the woods and used artillery to impede Confederate advance. Lawhon, "Forty-Eight Regiment," 119.

249. The regiment did not fight at the vulnerable Mule Shoe in the Confederate center, but did occupy and reinforce lines of units rushed to that salient. See *Roster,* v. XI, 367.

250. The Early attack Walkup criticized apparently was a probing action expressly ordered by Lee. See *Official Records*, 36, part 1, 1029. A. P. Hill's corps was under the temporary command of Early. While Civil War accounts related Early was impetuous, opinionated, critical and profane, such that Lee called him "my bad old man," no incidents of wartime drunkenness have been located. In fact, his command during the Wilderness and Spotsylvania, including his temporary leadership of the Third Corps during one of A. P. Hill's frequent illnesses, was deemed favorable, excepting the criticisms of Walkup and some other officers of Cooke's and Kirkland's Brigades. Early's drunkenness was commented on post-war. Members of the Rocky Mount

and Lynchburg bar recalled him attired in a grey suit resembling a Confederate uniform, staggering down the street, with a whiskey bottle in one hand and a cane posed menacingly in the other, mumbling "damn your eyes." See conversation with Roy R. Young, Jr., attorney-at-law, Martinsville, Va., July 1, 1994; Bushong, *Old Jube,* 304–306.

251. Edward Crotts, Cleveland County resident enlisted aged 29, Aug. 16, 1862 as private, Co. I. Wounded Spotsylvania Court House, then hospitalized Richmond, May 16, 1864. *Roster,* v. XI, 474.

252. Walkup transcribed the communications. Hall's childhood education is unknown. North Carolina law after 1830 prohibited teaching slaves to read or write. Nevertheless, some owners disregarded the law and taught their slaves for purposes of Christian education and Bible study. Although profoundly religious with an appreciation for moral education and Bible reading, as an attorney Walkup was cognizant of the expectations that officers of the court, most of all, were to be fully compliant with the law. See "An Act To Prevent All Persons from Teaching Slaves to Read or Write, the Use of Figures Excepted," Session 1830–31, *General Statutes of North Carolina*, Raleigh, 1831. 1870 Census shows the Walkup Freedmen as unable to read or write.

253. Willie Pegram was a University of Virginia law student who enlisted as a private in the Richmond Purcell Artillery. He rose to colonel under A. P. Hill, commanding sixty cannon in the Third Corps. Serving with distinction in all the major engagements of the Army of Northern Virginia, Pegram was noted for fearlessness. The courage of this 23-year-old was exemplified by his death in April 1865 at the Battle of Five Forks, where he was mortally wounded beside one of his guns. General Henry Heth praised him as "one of the few men who, I believe, was supremely happy when in battle." See Peter Carmichael, *Lee's Young Artillerist: William R. J. Pegram*, University of Virginia Press, 1995.

254. Far from venerating Lee, Walkup was critical. He had noted Lee's costly

frontal charges and piecemeal assaults against high ground protected by concentrated artillery at Malvern Hill. In the Overland campaign and Petersburg siege, Grant may not have initially planned a war of attrition, but his objective was the Army of Northern Virginia, not Richmond. He tenaciously forced an ongoing series of battles then eventually put Lee into the trenches, even if he failed to maneuver around Lee's right flank and to get the Southerners out in the open where superior Union artillery could take its toll. Grant recognized that he would prevail even if he did not win each battle because Lee's losing three men to Grant's every five would ultimately destroy Lee's ability to wage war. Lee accepted the risks of defending Richmond rather than preserving his army and moving south to consolidate with Joseph Johnson while that opportunity was still viable. Lee's tactical aggressive defense did inflict great losses on the Federals in the Wilderness, Cold Harbor and Spotsylvania, but the Confederates themselves suffered irreparable damage throughout May and June 1864, particularly at Spotsylvania. Against Grant's predecessors Lee had garnered tactical victories that initially disheartened the Army of the Potomac and dampened Northern home-front support for the war. However, as attrition intensified, Lee had to rule out offensive maneuvers because neither the strength of his forces nor the availability of horses and mules allowed prolonged, rapid movement. See J. F. C. Fuller, *Grant and Lee: A Study in Personality and Generalship;* Edward Hagerman, *The American Civil War and the Origins of Modern Warfare,* 252.

255. Thomas J. Cureton. Union County farmer enlisted as sergeant, Co. B. 26th North Carolina, the "Waxhaw Jackson Guards." Elected 3rd lieutenant, Oct. 15, 1862. Promoted 2nd lieutenant, Nov. 26, 1862. Promoted 1st lieutenant, Jan. 5, 1863. Promoted captain, July 2, 1863. Wounded shoulder, Gettysburg, July 3, 1863 and wounded left leg, Hanover Junction, May 23, 1864 while commanding skirmishers. Paroled Appomattox, April 12, 1865. *Roster,* v. VII, 481.

256. The regiment was ordered to track the enemy with stealth. Under guard were Federal prisoners who asked why rebels wore such dirty, ragged clothing. An Irishman in Co. D replied, "Faith and be jabbers, we Southerners always put on our sorriest clothes when we kill hogs, and it is hog killing day with us now." Despite the order to make no noise, raucous laughing gave rise to a rebel yell along the line. Lawhon, 'Forty-Eight Regiment,' 120.

257. Major General Henry Heth was a friend, cousin and Academy classmate of his superior corps commander, A. P. Hill. Although Heth earned criticism for his precipitating the Battle of Gettysburg with his less than stellar handling of his division on July 1, 1863 and his mismanagement in the Bristoe Station debacle, he was quite effective during the 1864 Overland Campaign. Consistent with Walkup's impressions, most commentators found Heth personally attractive and socially adept with the manners of an old Virginia family gentleman. Although strongly opinionated, Heth was willing to acknowledge his shortcomings. This editor's ancestors, the Youngs, are related to Heth through marriage. In our family tradition, the General was usually called by his nickname "Billy Goat Harry," in that he was the "goat" or the bottom cadet in his West Point Class of 1847. See E.S. Rafuse, *John Henry Heth, Encyclopedia Virginia,* Virginia Foundation for the Humanities, 25 March 2014.

258. K. Potts. Iredell County resident enlisted aged 29, May 16, 1862 as private, Co. C. Elected 2nd lieutenant, May 31, 1862. Wounded hip, thigh and shoulder, King's School House, June 25, 1862 with 30 different holes shot through his clothes. Wounded Antietam. Promoted 1st lieutenant, Sept. 17, 1862. Wounded Fredericksburg, Dec. 13, 1862. Promoted captain, July 24, 1863. Hospitalized gunshot Richmond, July 20, 1864. Took oath, Salisbury, June 6, 1865. *Roster,* v. XI, 395.

259. James W. Hancock. Discrepancy as to enlistment date and location. Alternate is at Orange Court House, Feb. 13, 1864 for duration of war. *Roster,* v. XI, 424.

260. Pinkney A. White. Iredell County farmer enlisted aged 34, May 3, 1862 as 1st sergeant, Co. C. Wounded King's School House, June 25, 1862. Reduced to rank of sergeant, May-June 1863. Transferred to Co. B, 2nd North Carolina Cavalry, Nov. 12, 1864. *Roster*, v. XI, 407.

261. Leander R. Ferguson. Union County farmer enlisted aged 18, Feb. 17, 1862, Co. F. Wounded Antietam, Sept. 17, 1862 and hospitalized, Richmond. Wounded in hand, Cold Harbor, June 3, 1864 and died of wounds, Richmond hospital. *Roster*, v. XI, 435.

262. John H. Mabry. Davidson County station agent enlisted aged 26, Feb. 22, 1862 as private, Co. B. Appointed 2nd lieutenant, March 21, 1862. Promoted 1st lieutenant, May 1, 1862. Promoted captain, Oct. 20, 1862. Paroled Greensboro, May 1, 1865. *Roster*, v. XI, 383.

263. The Federals made repeated futile charges. A line would advance and fall down for cover, then step over another, fire and fall down, progressing incrementally to within sixty or seventy feet of the regiment's position. The Federals ultimately having to fall back, the 48th rose in unison with a rebel yell and fired into the retreating enemy, cutting them down until the front was covered with their dead. Captain Lawhon observed that at no time in the war did the regiment do better fighting. See Lawhon, "Forty-Eight Regiment," 120.

264. Shelby H. Polk. Union County farmer enlisted aged 28, March 17, 1862 as private, Co. A. Promoted to sergeant, Nov.-Dec. 1862. Wounded arm and leg, Fredericksburg, Dec. 13, 1862. Deserted 1863 and reduced to ranks, Aug. 1, 1863. Stunned by a shell, Bristoe Station, Oct. 14, 1863. Killed Cold Harbor, June 3, 1864. *Roster*, v. XI, 380.

265. John T. Laney. Union County farmer enlisted aged 24, March 15, 1862. Wounded Fredericksburg, Dec. 13, 1862 and hospitalized Richmond. Wounded head, Wilderness, May 5–6, 1864. Wounded leg fracture, Cold Harbor and died Richmond hospital, June 19, 1864. *Roster*, v. XI, 377.

266. Archibald Clarke. Union County

resident enlisted aged 18, Co. A for war duration. Wounded both sides and captured, Cold Harbor, June 2, 1864. Hospitalized Washington and confined Old Capitol Prison. Transferred Elmira, New York where he died of pneumonia, Sept. 12, 1864., v. XI, 374.

267. Isaac Simms. Enlisted Orange Court House, Va., April 1, 1864, as private, Co. E. Wounded hand, Wilderness, May 5–6, 1864 and hospitalized, Charlottesville. Killed Cold Harbor, June 3, 1864. *Roster*, v. XI, 429.

268. Churchwell J. Horton. Union County farmer enlisted aged 38, March 15, 1862 as private, Co. E. Promoted sergeant, July 1863-April 1864. Killed Cold Harbor, June 3, 1864. *Roster*, v. XI, 425.

269. Absalom B. Hays. Union County resident enlisted aged 24, May 8, 1862 as private, Co. E. Hospitalized, Farmville, Va., Dec. 21, 1862 with gunshot of right arm. Wounded, Cold Harbor, June 3, 1864 and died, Richmond hospital, June 8, 1864. *Roster*, v. XI, 424.

270. John M. Fincher. Union County farmer enlisted aged 21, March 14, 1862 as private, Co. F. Blinded, Cold Harbor, June 3, 1864. Assigned Invalid Corps, Dec. 29, 1864. *Roster*, v. XI, 435.

271. John A. McCall. Previously private, 1st North Carolina Cavalry. Transferred to Co. I, 48th North Carolina Infantry, April 27, 1864. Wounded right leg fracture, Cold Harbor, June 2, 1864 and hospitalized Richmond. *Roster*, v. XI, 480.

272. Theophilus Frank, private, Co. B, related "...on the first line the Yanks were about one hundred yards from us and the sharpshooters were pecking at us but did not hit any of our company. The balls are flying right smart... The boys are all tired and worn out; we had to stand guard half the time, stand two hours and rest two hours and three days and nights will tire them out..." Frank to wife Elizabeth, June 1864, "Frank Family Papers," Southern History Collection, Wilson Library, University of North Carolina-Chapel Hill.

273. On June 5, 1864, two days after the initial attack, Grant belatedly opened communications with Lee regarding retrieval

of the wounded and dead lying between the respective trenches. Grant implied that the opportunity would be mutually beneficial. Under the accepted rules of war, the losing side was to send a flag of truce requesting the cease-fire. Lee responded that he had no casualties beyond the breastworks, and that Grant had not complied with the military conventions. Grant then conceded and asked for a truce, and on June 7 both sides retrieved any wounded and dead. Grant was castigated by some officers in the Army of the Potomac who felt his delay and refusal to acknowledge that the June 3 attack was a major failure resulted in the death of brave wounded troops lying in front of the Confederate works. See *Official Records of the Civil War*, series I, v. XXXVI. Part 3, 599–604, 638–639, 666–667.

274. Comparable to those formal and informal truces of World War One, Civil War soldiers often were reluctant to fire on the enemy during meal time, special holidays and inclement weather. Sometimes the belligerents would leave their respective trenches to engage in amiable conversation and exchange tobacco, coffee and newspapers. On some occasions Federals and Confederates participated in a camaraderie grounded in shared needs and experiences. Robert M. Sapolsky discusses the World War experience in "When the Guns Went Silent," *Wall Street Journal*, Dec. 20, 2014, C1.

275. In spring 1864 Lee's army organized sharpshooter units as skirmishers and special shock troops. Brigadier General Joseph Davis's Brigade of Heth's Division organized such a battalion commanded by Captain Alfred Moore O'Neal. See W. S. Dunlop, *Lee's Sharpshooters*.

276. Developed by Sir Joseph Whitworth, British engineer, steel manufacturer and scientist, at the request of Lord Hardinger, United Kingdom Commander-in-Chief. Whitworth experimented with a unique hexagonically rifled barrel and a special matching bullet of hard lead. The long heavy bullet reduced air resistance to carry accurately over greater distance. At short range the regular Enfield rifle and Whitworth were

approximately equal. At ranges beyond 500 yards the Whitworth was superior, and was accurate at 1800 yards, over a mile. A long scope protruded beyond the rear of the hammer. Snipers generally reclined and shot from a back position with the gun resting on the thigh or between the feet. Even if fired at a high trajectory and under most favorable conditions, the 10,000 foot distance estimate given by Walkup would be unlikely. See William B. Edwards, *Civil War Guns*, 219–222.

277. Although perhaps unfairly deemed "Butcher" Grant for his predilection for frontal assault, here he demonstrated his tactical skill in maneuvering, stealthily crossing the James stealing a march on Lee and threatening Petersburg. See Joel Achenbach, "Ulysses S. Grant: Hero or Butcher? Great Man or Doofus?," *The Washington Post*, April 25, 2014.

278. Henry N. Hill. Appointed regimental assistant commissary of subsistence (captain), June 8, 1862. Dropped from rolls July 31, 1863 after the office was abolished. *Roster*, v. XI, 369.

279. Unlike many West Pointers and professional military officers, Walkup was perceptive in recognizing the superior firepower afforded by repeating arms, and the superiority of breech loaders in facilitating rapid fire and minimizing the shooter's exposure as a target. The "back-loading" rifles and carbines, like the Burnside, and particularly lever actions with magazines like the Spencer and Henry, afforded fire response many times faster than conventional muzzle loaders, without significantly compromising accuracy and effective range. See Edwards, *Civil War Guns*.

280. Thomas S. Galloway, Jr. Rockingham County resident enlisted aged 21 in 22nd North Carolina Infantry. Elected major, June 1, 1861, but defeated for re-election, June 13, 1862. Appointed captain, Co. H, 45th North Carolina Infantry to rank from Feb. 27, 1863. Elected colonel of 45th and transferred back to that regiment, Sept. 17, 1863. Paroled, Appomattox, April 12, 1865. *Roster*, v. VII, 10.

281. *The Military Handbook*, 83–84

advised, "Do not sit, and especially do not sleep upon the ground, even in hot weather. If you sleep during the day, have some *extra cover* on you." "Never go to sleep, especially after a great effort, even in hot weather, without some covering on you." See *Handbook*, 85.

282. Walkup appears dismissive of the African American soldiers. After enactment of the Second Confiscation and Militia Act of July 17, 1862, over 179,000 such United States Colored Troops enlisted to dramatically alter the momentum of the war in favor of Union victory. In light of such participation, the conflict can be seen as a blue, black and grey fight, where Union and African American interests coincided although certain of their respective social and political objectives remained distinct. The 48th was positioned on the Confederate extreme right to protect the essential Petersburg and Weldon Railroad, which together with the Wilmington and Weldon, formed the logistical lifeline for Richmond and the Army of Northern Virginia. See *Roster*, v. XI, 367.

283. Confederate Fort Clinton was a earthworks on the Appomattox River comprising a component of the Richmond-Petersburg defenses. Situated on a high bluff at the junction of the Appomattox and Swift Creek, the fort effectively controlled river navigation north of Petersburg. The strong bastion was never forcibly taken by Federals until the April 3, 1865, abandonment of Petersburg. See picture of Fort Clinton, *Harper's Weekly*, Aug. 20, 1864.

284. Confederates dealt out particularly cruel treatment toward captured U.S. Colored Troops, often murdering them outright, trying them on capital charges as enslaved insurrectionists or placing them in bondage. In reprisal for such violations of the Lieber Code compelling equal treatment of captured Union combatants regardless of race, the Federals halted prisoners-of-war exchanges for much of the latter part of the war. See "Instructions for the Governance of the Armies of the United States in the Field," *The War of the Rebellion: A Compilation*,

Government Printing Office, Washington, 1899, series III, 3, 148–164.

285. Wool, although retaining more heat, does dry faster than cotton. *The Military Handbook*, 83, advised, "wear flannel all over in all weather."

286. Walkup received the furlough to facilitate recovery from his Wilderness wound and chronic stomach/intestinal bleeding. He noted, "My journal was continued, other papers which will be inserted." He was present for duty with his regiment in September and October 1864, and served through Appomattox. Some additional diary pages and correspondence never in the custody of the Southern History Collection, University of North Carolina were lost over time, commencing in the 1870s when a diary section was loaned to a fellow veteran, and most recently when Hurricane Ike struck Galveston destroying documents in possession of the Lelia Walkup Davis descendants. Conversation with Virginia Adams of Galveston, Texas, Jan. 9, 2011.

287. Joe Mobley, *The Papers of Zebulon Baird Vance*, v. 2.

288. Private John J. Mendenhall, Co. K, reported during the Petersburg campaign that he would have been "half clothed unless I cloth myself and nothing to eat but bread and meat and not a bit more than half enough of that unless I buy it...." See Mendenhall's Oct. 11, 1864 letter to brother and sister from line of battle, two miles south of Petersburg, "Mendenhall Papers," The American Civil War Museum, Richmond, Va.

289. Sir Walter Scott, the nineteenth-century Scottish romantic novelist, was particularly popular in the antebellum American South. His themes of the Scottish underdog striving valiantly but often forlornly against English domination and his tales of chivalrous gentry leading small farmers and peasants stuck a chord with Southern readers. Mark Twain denounced the antiquarian pretentions engendered by Scott:

"It was Sir Walter that made every gentleman in the South a Major or Colonel, or a General or a Judge, before the war; and it was he, also, that made these gentlemen value these bogus decorations. For it was he that created rank and caste down there... Sir Walter had such a large hand in making Southern character, as it existed before the war, that he is in great measure responsible for the war."

See Scott Horton, "How Walter Scott Started the American Civil War," *Harper's Magazine*, July 29, 2007.

290. The Hampton Roads Peace Conference, held Feb. 3, 1865, was the result, in large part, of efforts by Francis P. Blair, a mutual friend of Abraham Lincoln and Jefferson Davis, to mediate settlement of the conflict. President Lincoln and Secretary of State William H. Seward met with Confederate Commissioners Vice President Alexander H. Stephens, Senator Robert Hunter, and Assistant Secretary of War John A. Campbell. Lincoln insisted on restoration of national authority, no recession on slavery, and no cessation of hostilities short of a total end to fighting. Davis was not inclined to concede anything short of Confederate sovereignty. Both presidents were criticized by their respective peace advocates. The expectation of foreign recognition referenced by Walkup demonstrated the prevalence of outlandish rumors and the desperate need for good news during the final months of the Petersburg trench warfare. See Mann, *The Political and Constitutional Thought of John Archibald Campbell*, 215.

291. Rewards and expenses paid for apprehending deserters were set off against the deserter's pay when adjudged by a court-martial or when the deserter was restored to duty where no trial occurred. See *Confederate Army Regulations*, Article XVIII, Deserters, 153.

292. While William Sherman did not invent what Napoleonic tactics called "le systeme de maurade," his army did engage in extremely aggressive foraging coupled with unofficial vandalism and theft to frustrate the will to resist on the Confederate home front. See Matthew Carr, *Sherman's Ghosts*, New Press, 2014.

293. Rufus White, private, Co. C, lamented, "I know more about war now then I want to know for I think war is more expense than profit..." White to his cousin, Camp, 48th North Carolina, Jan. 18, 1865. "Albert M. White Papers," Southern History Collection, Wilson Library, University of North Carolina-Chapel Hill. White was a 23-year-old Iredell County resident who enlisted Aug. 1, 1862. He was reported absent sick, Sept.-Oct. 1862. Captured at Hatcher's Run, Va., March 31, 1865, and confined Point Lookout, Md., and released June 22, 1865 upon taking oath of allegiance. *Roster*, v. XI, 407–408. Private John Mendenhall, Co. K, commenting on desertion in the Petersburg campaign, noted, "if they keep on going to the Yankees like they have for the past few months the army is bound to breakup. The soldiers generally both officers and privates are the most out of heart I have seen them. There has been many killed and disabled for life and those that are still alive thinks they cannot escape always and besides that they have about given up the ideal of ever getting a southern confederacy...." See Oct. 11, 1864 letter, "Mendenhall Papers." Sherman's march through Georgia and the Carolinas had a devastating and irreversible impact on the Southern will to fight. The Federals lived off the land, created panic and fear on the Confederate home front and decimated the ability of the heartland to support the war effort. See Joseph T. Glatthaar, *General Lee's Army*, 449.

294. Historians have studied why some Confederates stayed and others went home or over to the enemy, when both groups knew defeat was inevitable. The consensus is that men had to make difficult choices between conflicting interests of survival, duty and loyalty. Those soldiers who stayed in the field generally did so because they fought with and for their friends, neighbors and community and would not abandon those comrades. See J. Tracy Power, *Lee's Miserables*. 314–315.

295. In August 1864, Lee communicated with the Secretary of War: "Unless some measure can be devised to replace our losses, the consequences may be disastrous. Our numbers are daily decreasing...If we had a few thousand more men to hold the stronger parts of our lines

where an attack is least likely to be made, it would enable us to employ with good effort our veteran troops. Without some increase of our strength, I cannot see how we are to escape the natural military consequences of the enemy's numerical strength." See Philip Katcher, *The Army of Robert E. Lee*, 71.

296. Walkup asserts a modern notion of an uncompromising fight to the death against all odds, come what may, in lieu of surrender. Such perspective contrasts with the then existing concept that surrender following a brave fight was humane and honorable. See David Silkenat, *Raising the White Flag: How Surrender Defined the American Civil War*, University of North Carolina Press, 2019.

297. Like Robert E. Lee, Walkup embraced the credo "duty is ours, results are God's." See Douglas Southall Freeman, *R.E. Lee: A Biography*, New York, 1934, 194. Interestingly, the same maxim was also used by the antislavery movement. See Thomas Price, *Slavery in America: With Notices of the Present State of Slavery and the Slave Trade Throughout the World*, London, 1837, 64. A devout Walkup saw God's providence evidenced in both victory and loss. God's inscrutable will might direct Confederate defeat to redeem through suffering,

298. The motivation for the Federal desertion is uncertain, particularly given the dire straits of the Confederacy. The individual may have simply found the ongoing hardships of military service unbearable or have sought to escape some serious military discipline to risk capital sanction for desertion. See Ella Lonn, *Desertion in the Civil War,* University of Nebraska Press, Lincoln, Nebraska, 1998.

299. Arguably to an even greater extent than World War One, trench warfare physically and mentally exhausted the besieged dealing with close quarter combat, insufficient rations for men, horses and mules and contaminated water and unsanitary living conditions. Particularly at the company level, by late 1864 and 1865 attrition had taken its toll and available officers were not adequately experienced to maintain discipline and

implement tactics. See Glatthaar, *General Lee's Army*, 385–386.

300. While there is no indication that Minnie encouraged Walkup to resign his commission and return to Monroe, many women on the home front became less supportive of the war with each Confederate setback. Rampart rank and file desertion is attributed to letters from wives and parents imploring soldiers to return home. See Silber, *Gender and the Sectional Conflict*, 45.

301. Historians disagree regarding the "gulf of experience" that existed between soldiers on the front and civilians back home. Contrasting perspectives emphasize either the dichotomy of conflict in the war zone or instead the continuity and shared values of the front and home. See Gerald Linderman, *Embattled Courage: The Experience of Combat in the American Civil War*, Simon and Schuster, New York, 1987, contrasted with Jonathan White, *Midnight in America: Darkness, Sleep and Dreams during the Civil War*, University of North Carolina Press, Chapel Hill, 2017.

302. Abel Nelson Washington Belk was generally believed to have been killed by Sherman's bummers. Belk was unable to serve in the Confederate army because of weak lungs. Upon learning that Sherman's troops could be in the vicinity of his Lancaster County, South Carolina, farm situated on the south side of Twelve Mile Creek, Belk fled. He apparently feared he would be hung and his livestock and household goods stolen. He proceeded to his father's place on Giles Creek approximately seven miles east of Lancaster, where a small gold mine was in production. The Federals interrogated a resident who informed about the gold mine, then these troops encountered Abel and demanded he reveal the secreted barrels of mined gold. He replied he knew nothing of such a stash. He was said to have been taken to the creek and repeatedly submerged to force an admission, until he eventually collapsed and was drowned. The body was found on March 8, 1865 buried in nearby Graham's field. Although decomposed, Abel was identified by the

proximity of his slaughtered mule near the site where the body was recovered. With Sherman having taken most of the horses in the locality, it was with difficulty that a team was found to transport the corpse for re-internment at Shiloh Church. Widow Sarah Narcissus Walkup Belk (b. 1836, d. March 9, 1932), Samuel's sister, was a graduate of Carolina Female Academy. She home schooled her children, and son William Henry Belk later opened a department store in Monroe, North Carolina that became Belk Brothers, still in operation in the Southeast as Belk. See Paul Wychef, "William Henry Belk," *Dictionary of North Carolina Biography*, 129; LeCette Blythe, William Henry Belk, *Merchant of the South*.

303. With Lee's approval Lieutenant General John Gordon, Second Corps, planned a midnight, March 25, 1865 assault on Fort Stedman, situated about a mile south of the Appomattox River. Select shock troops, marked with identifying strips of white cloth, were to silently advance from Colquitt's Salient, remove Federal abatis and take out the defending picket line without raising an alarm. Lee was prepared to commit about one-half of his available troops to capitalize on any break-through. A successful assault might buy time for Lee's orderly evacuation, or even cut Grant's army in two and force his withdrawal. The initial attack achieved the objective of capturing Fort Stedman and supporting batteries X and XI. Unfortunately, the guides became separated from Gordon's main forces and much time was lost wandering around the trenches, while some soldiers engaged in looting the Union camps for foodstuffs. Federal reserves and batteries came up quickly and Gordon's forces had to retreat, with many men taken prisoner or killed. Figuring that the Confederate entrenchments had been stripped of defenders for the Fort Stedman attack, Grant ordered an assault that captured significant sections of picket line. Fort Stedman, Lee's last offensive, was an unmitigated disaster, losing over 4,000 irreplaceable men and ground. See John Horn, *The Petersburg Campaign*, 209–216. As succinctly stated by the insightful and ana-

lytical historian Clifford Dowdy, Lee tried to assume a counteroffensive even after his depleted army revealed even in very limited action that the physical weakness of the men and the loss of capable leaders had destroyed forever the potential of attack. See Clifford Dowdey, *Lee's Last Campaign*, 386. Cooke's brigade was held in reserve and did not participate in the Fort Stedman attack. See *Roster*, v. II, 368.

304. John W. Reed. Previous private, 27th North Carolina Infantry. Transferred to regiment, Co. K, Dec. 4, 1862 as sergeant. Wounded arm, Fredericksburg, Dec. 13, 1862. Elected 3rd lieutenant, March 3, 1863. Captured, Hatcher's Run and confined Old Capitol Prison, D.C., April 5, 1865. Confined Johnson's Island, Ohio and released June 19, 1865 upon taking oath. *Roster*, v. XI, 485.

305. James E. Austin. Previously corporal, Co. I, before election 3rd lieutenant, Co. E, March 17, 1863. Promoted 1st lieutenant, Oct. 14, 1864. Killed Fort Stedman, March 25, 1865. *Roster*, v. XI, 420.

306. James Taylor Davis. A Mecklenburg County lawyer, he graduated Emory and Henry College, Va., at the age of 17, then studied law and licensed 1857.He initially enlisted aged 24, June 24, 1861 in the Hornet's Nest Rifles, Co. B, 1st North Carolina as private. He then joined Co. F, 49th North Carolina Infantry, the "Mecklenburg Guards" as captain. Appointed major, Sept. 16, 1863 and transferred to field and staff. Promoted lieutenant colonel, July 30, 1864. Wounded bowels, Fort Stedman, March 25, 1865. For gallantry in that attack he was promoted brigadier general but died before receiving that commission. Hospitalized Petersburg where he died speaking of peace, home and God. His last words to Walkup were "I owe my country nothing." See McDowell, *The McDowells*, 61; *Charlotte Western Democrat*, Aug. 15, 1865; *Roster*, v. XII, 26.

307. Walkup's regiment was one of those dependable remnant units that Lee used as shock forces during 1864 and 1865. With forces stretched beyond the breaking point, Lee had to ask the virtually impossible—that brigades like Cooke's

face entire Union divisions or corps. That dedicated officers like Walkup were able to maintain such a high level of combat efficiency, given curtailed food rations, desertions and casualties, was a testament to their leadership. The last ditch defense prolonged the life of the Confederacy by at least several months. See Hess, *Lee's Tar Heels*, 351. John Cooke, a Confederate whose post-war histories narrated experiences with the Army of Northern Virginia and whose works Walkup owned, read and noted with handwritten margin comments, stated Lee constantly beseeched the Davis Administration for more men. The army had nearly fifty linear miles of earthworks to man while outnumbered three or four to one, such that unless heavily reinforced retreat or surrender was inevitable. See John Esten Cooke, *Personal Portraits*, 586. (Virginia Adams of Galveston, Texas, Walkup's great-great granddaughter, has the referenced Cooke book owned by the colonel in her possession.) Even the rank and file soldier recognized the dire situation, with Private John Mendenhall, Co. K, remarking, "...our line of battle is about 20 or 25 miles long and we have to keep marching and countermarching along the line as the Yankees moves and fighting more or less every few days...." See Oct. 11, 1864 letter, "Mendenhall Papers."

308. Following Phil Sheridan's routing of George Pickett at Five Forks on April 1, 1865, Heth was assaulted by Major General Andrew Humphrey's II Army Corps at Hatcher's Run and the Confederates abandoned their lines from Burgess Mill westward to Clairborne Road. Union forces engaged Heth's remnant brigades, at that time commanded by Cooke, at Sutherland Station. Behind hastily erected breastworks, initially Cooke was able to repulse the onslaught, but with the arrival of more Federals the works were swept. Cooke's troops fled disorganized across the Appomattox or were killed or captured. See Horn, *Petersburg*, 243–245. Recognizing that Richmond must be evacuated, Lee ordered a general evacuation, retreating toward Amelia Court House only to learn expected provisions

had not arrived. Under constant cavalry attack, the 48th regiment in the rear guard was further scattered at Sayler's Creek. Captain Lawhon related that the regiment was ordered to protect the wagon trains, but upon arrival the enemy had fired the wagons and Federal infantry was arriving in force. Cut off in the rear by Federal cavalry, many of the regiment surrendered or scattered and "every man was left to take care of himself." Captain Lawhon lost his hat while fleeing from cavalry pursuit, and would have been captured had he not reached protection in a deep gully. See Lawhon, "Forty-Eight Regiment," 121.

309. At the Appomattox Court House surrender, the regiment was so decimated that only enough men were present to constitute a company. Co. D only had Captain Lawhon and one other soldier present. See Lawhon, "Forty-Eight Regiment," 121.

310. At Appomattox Court House, April 12, 1865, Walkup was listed as a prisoner of war and issued a parole pass. He was permitted to retain his side arms (revolver and sword), valise, clothing and two horses. See *Combined Service Records*, roll 191, 48th North Carolina Infantry, Walkup entry. His standard Boyle and Gamble foot officer's sword with a guard inscribed "Walkup," manufactured in Richmond by the Confederacy's most prolific maker of edged weapons, passed out of family possession after the Centennial commemoration, and was recently marketed. See Dave Taylor's Civil War Antiques Catalog, Oct. 2012. The route followed by Walkup can be discerned on the 1808 Price-Strother map. See William Cummings, *North Carolina in Maps*. Walkup chose to travel in a small group that was less intimidating to civilians when soliciting food and accommodations. See Bradley Foley and A. Whicker, *The Civil War Ends*, 27–29.

311. Confederates burned the wooden structure over the Stanton River on the Stage Road from Lynchburg to Danville. See National Park Service, *Historic American Engineering Record*, HAER VA-106.

312. Walkup's decision not to travel more due south into Confederate held

Greensboro is interesting, particularly since he was aware that some soldiers of the 48th North Carolina Infantry had been detached there from the Army of Northern Virginia in Feb. 1865 to assist Joseph Johnston and to apprehend deserters and to conduct requisitions. Elements of these detached companies protected Confederate Quartermaster and Subsistence supplies in Greensboro from pillaging by Southern civilians, paroled soldiers from Lee's army, and foragers from other Confederate units. Thousands of Army of Northern Virginia parolees, often undisciplined and plundering food, valuables and alcohol, followed the railroad tracks south to Greensboro hoping to secure food from the Confederate and North Carolina warehouses. Perhaps Walkup anticipated that Confederate commissaries would not make provisions available to parolees. See Robert Dunkerly, *The Confederate Surrender at Greensboro*, 69.

313. Here Walkup and his party reached North Carolina crossing at Cascade Creek in Rockingham County. The area was once part of William Byrd's Land of Eden, being 26,000 acres acquired in 1738 when Byrd led the Virginia survey commissioners. The road taken by Walkup ran generally southwest staying on the north side of the Dan River. The reference to William Aiken and "large tobacconist" referred to "The Meadows" plantation, part of the old Land of Eden tract east of Leaksville. Walkup then crossed the Smith River at Leaksville. A resident, Daniel E. Field, described the town at that time: "But we should speak of the closing scene of the War. On April 9 news reached us that General Lee's surrender was inevitable. Large bodies of soldiers, hungry, poorly clad, tired, were constantly passing day and night, for ten days or more, until it was estimated eight or ten thousand had passed. At their sad plight—hungry, poorly clad, tied—every heart was moved and the liberal spirit seemed to catch from soul to soul until every family in the community was given food or clothing to these needy. Tables were spread in the old Dillard porch and adjacent buildings and supplies of vegetables, meats and nick-nacks, with great quantities of buttermilk, were placed upon these tables; while our noble women, old and young, gave them a hearty welcome from six in the morning until nine at night. Good order prevailed all the while and at least eight thousand hungry soldiers went away with their hunger satisfied and with expressions of gratitude to old Leakesville." See *Webster's Weekly*, August 22, 1901.

314. Leaving Leaksville Walkup continued west across the Mayo River north of the town of Madison to Davis Town or Saura Town that is "Sauratown Hill," the very large Peter Hairston plantation and Davistown or "Red Shoals," the James Davis plantation. These plantations occupied the site of Upper Sauratown of the Saura Native Americans. The road crosses the Dan River at a ford in Stokes County into extensive bottomland crop fields with the Sauratown Mountains in the distance northwest. See Price-Strother map.

315. Walkup traveled along the north side of Town Fork Creek to Germantown that was until 1858 the county seat before the southern half of Stokes County became Forsyth County. See Price-Strother map.

316. Old Town refers to Bethabara, the first town in the Moravian Wachovia Settlement that predated the other colonial developments, Bethania and Salem, hence the Old Town designation. See Price-Strother map.

317. In Davie County along the route Walkup would have seen "Cooleemee," the then recently constructed (circa 1855–58) massive plantation house of Peter Hairston of Sauratown Hill. The Greek cross shaped edifice was designed by New York architect W. H. Ranlett as an Anglo-Grecian villa. See Price-Strother map. The diary concluded at this point without reference to the further journey of approximately sixty-five miles through Rowan, Cabarrus and Union Counties to reach home in Monroe.

# Bibliography

## Manuscripts and Public Records

Belk and Everett Family Papers. J. Murrey Atkins Library Special Collections, University of North Carolina–Charlotte, Charlotte, North Carolina.

Adelphos J. Burns Papers. Union County Superior Court Minute Docket, 1866–1877.North Carolina State Archives, Raleigh, North Carolina.

William A. Collins Papers. Southern History Collection, Wilson Library, University of North Carolina, Chapel Hill, North Carolina.

Confederate Hospital Records, Second North Carolina Hospital. Southern History Collection, Wilson Library, University of North Carolina, Chapel Hill, North Carolina.

John Rogers Cooke Papers, 1860–1894. Virginia Museum of History and Culture, Richmond, Virginia.

Frank Family Papers Southern History Collection, Wilson Library, University of North Carolina, Chapel Hill, North Carolina.

Mendenhall Papers. American Civil War Museum, Richmond, Virginia.

Felix Miller Papers Joyner Library, East Carolina University, Greenville, North Carolina.

North Carolina Field Office Combined Service Records of Confederate Soldiers. Excise Tax of the United States Federal Census National Archives and History, Washington, District of Columbia Bureau of Refugees, Freedman and Abandoned Lands.

Charles Phillips Papers. Southern History Collection, Wilson Library, University of North Carolina, Chapel Hill, North Carolina.

Herman Starnes Papers. Heritage Room, Historic Union County Courthouse, Monroe, North Carolina.

Union County Clerk of Superior Court, Monroe, North Carolina Estate Files.

Union County Library Local History Room, Monroe, North Carolina Random Historical Notes Walkup Family Genealogy.

Union County Registrar of Deeds, Monroe, North Carolina Cohabitation Records Marriage License File.

Samuel Hoey Walkup Papers. Southern History Collection, Wilson Library, University of North Carolina, Chapel Hill, North Carolina.

Samuel Walkup Papers. Special Collection, Eastern Kentucky University, Richmond, Kentucky.

Alfred M. White Papers. Southern History Collection, Wilson Library, University of North Carolina, Chapel Hill, North Carolina.

Wright Papers, 1853–1882. Perkins Library Rubenstein Rare Book and Manuscript Room, Duke University, Durham, North Carolina.

## Newspapers

*Anson Record,* Wadesboro, North Carolina

*Charlotte Democrat,* Charlotte, North Carolina

*Charlotte Journal,* Charlotte, North Carolina

*Daily Carolina Times,* Charlotte, North Carolina

# Bibliography

*Daily Journal,* Wilmington, North Carolina

*Fayetteville Observer,* Fayetteville, North Carolina

*Fayetteville Weekly Observer,* Fayetteville, North Carolina

*Greensboro Patriot,* Greensboro, North Carolina

*Messenger-Intelligencer,* Wadesboro, North Carolina

*Monroe Enquirer,* Monroe, North Carolina

*Monroe Examiner,* Monroe, North Carolina

*Monroe Journal,* Monroe, North Carolina

*North Carolina Argus,* Wadesboro, North Carolina

*Semi-Weekly Standard,* Raleigh, North Carolina

*Southern Home,* Charlotte, North Carolina

*Webster's Weekly,* Reidsville, North Carolina

*Weekly Raleigh Register,* Raleigh, North Carolina

*Western Democrat,* Charlotte, North Carolina

## Books and Articles

Achenbach, Joel. "Ulysses S. Grant: Hero or Butcher? Great Man or Doofus?" *Washington Post* (April 25, 2014).

Ainsworth, Fred and Joseph Kirfley, eds. *The War of the Rebellion: A Compilation of the Official Records of the Union and Confederate Armies.* Washington, DC: Government Printing Office, 1902.

Allardice, Bruce. *Confederate Colonels: A Biographical Registry.* Columbia: University of Missouri Press, 2008.

Armistead, Gene. *Horses and Mules in the Civil War: A Complete History.* Jefferson, NC: McFarland, 2013.

Barney, William L. *The Making of a Confederate: Walter Lenoir's Civil War.* New York: Oxford University Press, 2009.

Battle, Kemp. *History of the University of North Carolina, From its Beginning to the Death of President Swain.* Raleigh: Edwards and Broughton Publishing Company, 1907.

Beaty, Mary D. *A History of Davidson College.* Davidson, NC: Briarpatch Press, 1988.

Beller, Susan Provost. *Medical Practices of the Civil War.* New York: Betterway Books, 1992.

Benet, Stephen V. *Selected Works: Poetry.* New York: Farrar and Rinehart, 1942.

Berry, Daina Ramsey. *The Price for Their Pound of Flesh: The Value of the Enslaved, from Womb to Grave, in the Building of a Nation.* Boston: Beacon Press, 2017.

Blythe, L. *William Henry Belk: Merchant of the South.* Chapel Hill: University of North Carolina Press, 1950.

Blythe, L., and C. Brockman. *The Story of Charlotte and Mecklenburg County.* Charlotte: Library of Charlotte and Mecklenburg County, 1961.

Bridges, Hal. *Lee's Maverick General.* Lincoln: University of Nebraska Press, 1991.

Brock, R.A., ed. *Southern Historical Society Papers.* Richmond: Virginia Historical Society, 1910.

Burke, James Lee. *In the Electric Mist with Confederate Dead.* New York: Hyperion, 1993.

Bushong, Millard. *Old Jube: A Biography of General Jubal A. Early.* Boyce, VA: Carr, 1955.

Carmichael, Peter. *Lee's Young Artillerist: William R. J. Pegram.* Charlottesville: University of Virginia Press, 1995.

Carmichael, Peter. "'We are the men': The Ambiguous Place of Confederate Slaves in Southern Armies." Cwmemory.com, 2008.

Carr, Mathew. *Sherman's Ghosts: Soldiers, Civilians, and the American Way of War.* New York: New Press, 2012.

Clark, Erskine. *A Dwelling Place.* New Haven: Yale University Press, 2005.

Clark, William. *Histories of the Several Regiments and Battalions from North Carolina, in the Great War, 1861–1865.* Goldsboro: Nash Brothers, 1901.

Clinton, Catherine. *Tara Revisited: Women, War, and the Plantation Legend.* New York: Abbeville Press, 1995.

Confederate States of America. *A Digest of the Military and Naval Laws of the*

# Bibliography

*Confederate States.* Columbia: Evans and Cogswell, 1864.

Cook, Adrian. *The Armies of the Street: The New York City.* Lexington: University Press of Kentucky, 2014.

Cooke, John Esten. *Wearing of the Gray: Being Personal Portraits, Scenes and Adventures of War.* New York: E. B. Treat, 1867.

Cooper, William. *The Complete Poetical Works.* London: Oxford University Press, 1913.

Cummings, William. *North Carolina in Maps.* Chapel Hill: University of North Carolina Press, 1966.

Davidson College Alumni Association. *The Semi-centennial Catalogue of Davidson College, 1837–1887.* Raleigh: E. M. Uzzell Printer, 1891.

Dortch, William, ed. *The Code of North Carolina,* New York: Banks and Brothers, 1883.

Dougherty, Kevin. *The Peninsula Campaign of 1862.* Jackson: University of Mississippi Press, 2010.

Dowd, Clement. *Life of Zebulon B. Vance.* Charlotte: Observer Printing, 1897.

Dowdey, Clifford. *The Seven Days: The Emergence of Lee.* Lincoln: University of Nebraska Press, 1993.

Dowdey, Clifford. *Lee's Last Campaign.* Lincoln: University of Nebraska Press, 1993.

Du Bois, W.E.B. *Black Reconstruction in America.* New York: Harcourt Brace, 1935.

Dunkerly, Robert. *The Confederate Surrender at Greensboro.* Jefferson, NC: McFarland, 2013.

Dunlop, W.S. *Lee's Sharpshooters.* Dayton, OH: Morningside Press, 2000.

Edwards, William B. *Civil War Guns.* Lanham, MD: Stackpole Books, 1962.

Elliott, Mike. *Samuel H. Walkup Entry. Heritage of Union County.* Ed. Virginia Kendrick. Monroe, NC: The Carolinas Genealogical Society, 1993.

Ellison, Ralph. *Invisible Man.* New York: Random House, 1952.

Escott, Paul D. *Many Excellent People: Power and Privilege in North Carolina.* Chapel Hill: University of North Carolina Press, 1985.

Farmer, Fannie M. "Legal Education in North Carolina, 1820–1860." *North Carolina Historical Review,* v. XXVII, 3 (July 1951).

Farmer, Fannie M. "Legal Practice and Ethics in North Carolina." *North Carolina Historical Review,* v. 30, 3 (July 1953).

Faust, Drew G. *Mothers of Invention: Women of the Slaveholding South in the American Civil War.* Chapel Hill: University of North Carolina Press, 1966.

Faust, Drew G. *This Republic of Suffering: Death and the American Civil War.* New York: Vintage, 2009.

Foley, Brantley, and A. Wicker. *The Civil War Ends: Greensboro, April 1865.* Greensboro, NC: Guilford County Genealogical Society, 2008.

Frazier, E. Franklin. *The Free Negro Family: A Study of Family Origins Before the Civil War.* Nashville: Fisk University, 1932.

Freeman, Douglas S. *Lee's Lieutenants: A Study in Command.* New York: C. Scribner's Sons, 1944.

Freeman, Douglas S. *R. E. Lee: A Biography.* New York: Charles Scribner's Sons, 1934.

Friedman, Lawrence. *A History of American Law.* New York: Simon & Schuster, 1975.

Fuller, J. F. C. *Grant and Lee: A Study in Personality and Leadership.* Bloomington: Indiana University Press, 1982.

Gallagher, Gary W. *The Wilderness Campaign.* Chapel Hill: University of North Carolina Press, 1999.

Gates, Henry L. *Stoney the Road: Reconstruction, White Supremacy and the Rise of Jim Crow.* New York: Penguin Press, 2019.

Glatthaar, Joseph T. *General Lee's Army from Victory to Collapse.* New York: Free Press, 2009.

Grant, Daniel L. *Alumni History of the University of North Carolina.* Chapel Hill: Christian and King Publishing, 1924.

Grant, Ulysses S. *Personal Memoirs of General U.S. Grant.* New York: C. L. Webster, 1888.

Green, Don. "Constitutional Unionists."

# Bibliography

*The Historian,* 69 (2) (Summer 2007), pp. 231–252.

Griffith, J., and C. Fortenberry. *First Presbyterian Church, Monroe, North Carolina.* Monroe: First Presbyterian Church, 1973.

Hagerman, Edward. *The American Civil War and the Origins of Modern Warfare: Ideas, Organization and Field Command.* Bloomington: Indiana University Press, 1992.

Hamilton, J. G. "The North Carolina Courts and the Confederacy." *North Carolina Historical Review,* v. 4 (Oct. 1927), 366–408.

Harman, Troy D. *The Great Revival of 1863: The Effects upon Lee's Army of Northern Virginia.* Gettysburg: Pennyhill Press/National Parks Service, 2001.

Harris, William. *William Woods Holden: Firebrand of North Carolina Politics.* Baton Rouge: Louisiana State University Press, 1987.

Haywood, Marshall, ed. *The North Carolina Booklet.* Raleigh: North Carolina Daughters of the American Revolution, 1912.

Hess, Earl. *Civil War Infantry Tactics: Training, Combat and Small-Unit Effectiveness.* Baton Rouge: Louisiana State University Press, 2015.

Historic American Engineering Record. *Built in America: Historic American Buildings Survey/Historic American Engineering Record.* Washington: Library of Congress Cataloging Distribution Service, 1995.

Horn, John. *The Petersburg Campaign.* Boston: Da Capo Press, 1993.

Hyman, Harold. *Era of the Oath: Northern Loyalty Test Oaths during the Civil War and Reconstruction.* Philadelphia: University of Pennsylvania Press, 1954.

Jamieson, Perry. *Crossing the Deadly Ground.* Tuscaloosa: University of Alabama Press, 2004.

Johnson, Guion G. *Ante-Bellum North Carolina: A Social History.* Chapel Hill: University of North Carolina Press, 1937.

Johnson, Rossiter. *Campfire and Battlefield.* New York: Knight and Brown, 1896.

Johnston, Frontis W. ed. *Papers of Zebulon Baird Vance.* Chapel Hill: University of North Carolina Press, 1963.

Jones, John W. *Personal Reminiscences, Anecdotes and Letters of General Robert E. Lee.* New York: D. Appleton, 1876.

Jones-Rogers, Stephanie. *They Were Her Property: White Women as Slave Owners in the American South.* New Haven: Yale University Press, 2019.

Jordan, Ervin L. Jr. *Charlottesville and the University of Virginia in the Civil War.* Lynchburg: H. E. Howard, 1988.

Jordan, Weymouth T. *North Carolina Troops, 1861–1865: A Roster.* Raleigh: North Carolina Office of Archives and History, 1987.

Katcher, Philip. *The Army of Robert E. Lee.* London: Arms and Armour Press, 1996.

King, James, and Charles Ryskamp, eds. *The Letters and Prose Writings of William Cowper.* Oxford: Clarendon Press, 1982.

Lawhon, W.H. *Forty-Eight Regiment.* Ed. Walter Clark. *Histories of the Several Regiments and Battalions from North Carolina in the Great War, 1861–1865.* Goldsboro: Nash Brothers, 1901.

Layburn, James G. *The Scotch-Irish: A Social History.* Chapel Hill: University of North Carolina Press, 1962.

Le Grand, Louis. *The Military Hand-Book and Soldier's Manual of Information.* New York: Beadle and Company, 1862.

Levin, Kevin M. *Searching for Black Confederates: The Civil War's Most Persistent Myth.* Chapel Hill: University of North Carolina Press, 2019.

Linderman, Gerald. *Embattled Courage: The Experience of Combat in the American Civil War.* New YorK: Simon & Schuster, 1987.

Lonn, Ella. *Desertion in the Civil War.* Lincoln: University of Nebraska Press, 1998.

Lowery, Thomas Power. *Confederate Death Sentences: A Reference Guide.* Scotts Valley: Createspace Independent Publishing, 2009.

Mann, Justine Stalb. *The Political and Constitutional Thought of John Archibald Campbell.* Ann Arbor, MI: University Microfilms, 1966.

McCarthy, Carlton. *Detailed Minutiae of Soldier Life in the Army of Northern Virginia*. Richmond: B. F. Johnson Publishing, 1899.

McDowell, John Hugh. *The McDowells, Erwins, Irvins and Connections*. Memphis: C. B. Johnston, 1918.

Medley, Mary. *History of Anson County, North Carolina*. Charlotte: Heritage Printers, 1976.

Merritt, Keri. *Masterless Men: Poor Whites and Slavery in the Antebellum South*. Cambridge: Harvard University Press, 2017.

Mobley, Joe, ed. *The Papers of Zebulon Vance, 1864–1865*. Chapel Hill: University of North Carolina Press, 2013.

Moore, Samuel Preston ed. *The Confederate States Medical and Surgical Journal*. Richmond: Ayes and Wade, 1864.

Nelson, Megan Kate. *Ruin Nation: Destruction and the American Civil War*. Athens: University of Georgia Press, 2012.

North Carolina General Assembly. *General Statutes*. Raleigh: State Printer and Binder, 1831.

North Carolina General Assembly. *Journal, 1858–1859 Session*. Raleigh: State Printer and Binder, 1859.

North Carolina General Assembly. *Journal, 1860–1861 Session*. Raleigh: State Printer and Binder, 1861.

North Carolina General Assembly, *Journal of the Convention*. Raleigh: Cannon and Holder Printers, 1865.

North Carolina General Assembly. *Journal, 1866–1867 Session*. Raleigh: North Carolina State Printer and Binder, 1867.

North Carolina General Assembly. *Legislative Documents*. Raleigh: W. Holden Printer, 1854.

North Carolina General Assembly. *Private Laws, 1874–1875*. Raleigh: Josiah Turner, 1875.

Orth, John. *The North Carolina State Constitution with History and Commentary*. Westport, CT: Greenwood Press, 1993.

Perry, Aldo S. *Civil War Courts-Martial of North Carolina Troops*. Jefferson, NC: McFarland, 2012.

Pickens, Suzanne. *Sweet Union: An Architectural and Historical Survey of Union County*. Monroe, NC: Union County Board of Commissioners, 1990.

Pollard, Edward. *The Lost Cause: A New Southern History of the War of the Confederates*. New York: E. B. Treat, 1868.

Powell, William. *Dictionary of North Carolina Biography*. Chapel Hill: University of North Carolina Press, 1996.

Power, J. Tracy. *Lee's Miserables: Life in the Army of Northern Virginia from the Wilderness to Appomattox*. Chapel Hill: University of North Carolina Press, 2015.

Price, Jonathan, and John Strother. *This First Actual Survey of the State of North Carolina*. London: Prime Meridian, 1808.

Price, Thomas. *Slavery in America with Notices of the Present State of Slavery and the Slave Trade*. London: G. Wightman, 1837.

Rafuse, E. S. John Henry Heth Entry. *Encyclopedia Virginia*. Charlottesville: Virginia Foundation for the Humanities, 2014.

Raper, Charles L. *The Church and Private Schools of North Carolina*. Greensboro: Jos. J. Stone Printers, 1898.

Robinson, James. *General A. P. Hill: The Story of a Confederate Warrior*. New York: Vintage Publishing, 1992.

Ross, John. "The Doctor Will See You Now." *Wall Street Journal* (Aug. 30–31, 2014) C-5.

Sears, Stephen W. *Landscape Turned Red: The Battle of Antietam*. New York: Houghton Mifflin Harcourt, 2003.

Shepard, E. Lee. "Breaking into the Profession." *The Journal of Southern History*, V. XLVIII, 3 (Aug. 1982).

Silber, Nina. *Gender and Sectional Conflict*. Chapel Hill: University of North Carolina Press, 2008.

Silkenat, David. *Raising the White Flag: How Surrender Defined the American Civil War*. Chapel Hill: University of North Carolina Press, 2019.

Sitterson, J.C. *The Secessionist Movement in North Carolina*. Chapel Hill: University of North Carolina Press, 1939.

Steiner, Mark S. *An Honest Calling*. DeKalb: Northern Illinois University Press, 2009.

# Bibliography

Stowe, Gene. *Inherit the Land: Jim Crow Meets Miss Maggie's Will.* Jackson: University Press of Mississippi, 2006.

Teetor, Paul. *A Matter of Hours: Treason at Harpers Ferry.* Rutherford, NJ: Fairleigh Dickinson University Press, 1982.

Thomas, Peter R., Jr. "Camp, Combat, and Campaign: North Carolina's Confederate Experience." Jacksonville: University of North Florida thesis, 2015.

Trelease, Alan W. *White Terror: The Ku Klux Klan Conspiracy and Southern Reconstruction.* New York: Harper & Row, 1971.

Trudeau, Noah. *Bloody Roads South: The Wilderness to Cold Harbor, May-June 1864.* Boston: Little, Brown and Company, 1989.

United States War Department. *Army Regulations of 1861.* Washington, DC: Government Printing Office, 1863.

University of Alabama Press. *Statutes at Large of the Confederate States of America.* ed. Richmond: R. M. Smith Printer, 1864.

Walkup, Samuel H. "An Address Delivered at the Annual Commencement of the Carolina Female College". Waxhaw: Pee Dee Star Publisher, 1854.

Walkup, Samuel H. "An Address on the Bible, Its Influences, and the Duty of the Christian World to Extend Its Influence." Waxhaw: Waxhaw Bible Society, The Ledger Office Printer, 1857.

Walkup, Samuel H. "The Birth-Place of Andrew Jackson." *North Carolina University Magazine,* New Series V.X (1891).

Warner, Ezra Jr. *Generals in Gray: Lives of the Confederate Commanders.* Baton Rouge: Louisiana State University Press, 2006.

Wert, Jeffrey. *A Glorious Army: Robert E. Lee's Triumph, 1862–1863.* New York: Simon & Schuster, 2012.

White, Jonathan. *Midnight in America: Darkness, Sleep and Dreams during the Civil War.* Chapel Hill: University of North Carolina Press, 2017.

Williams, Max, ed. *The Papers of William Alexander Graham.* Raleigh: North Carolina Department of Cultural Resources, 1976.

Zuber, Richard L. *Jonathan Worth: A Biography of a Southern Unionist.* Chapel Hill: University of North Carolina Press, 1965.

# Index

# Index

# Index

Washington, D.C. 13, 103, 131, 116
Washington Peace Conference 150
Waxhaw 33, 34, 39–40, 154
Whig Party 8, 10, 12, 107, 127
Wilderness, battle of 132–133, 145, 209n286

Winchester, John R. 41, 46, 70, 82, 97, 102, 115, 117, 119, 122, 129, 136, 137–138, 140, 147
woman in South 13–14
Worth, Jonathan 30